G000269409

'A comprehensive survey of the role o[...]
its neglect in economics, as well as a [...]
this essential requirement for life has b[...] [...]
majority of young Britons, thanks to the march of finance and the
compliance of Parliament.'

Steve Keen, author of *Debunking Economics*

'Land policy is the missing issue in any discussion on planning,
development and the property market. This book is therefore long
overdue. It returns land to its central role in both economic theory
and in built environment discourses.'

**Duncan Bowie, author of *Radical
Solutions to the Housing Supply Crisis***

Dr Josh Ryan-Collins is senior economist at the New Economics Foundation, where he has been based since 2006. He leads a research programme at NEF focusing on monetary and financial reform and the economics of land and housing and has published widely across these areas. Josh is the lead author of *Where Does Money Come From?*, a comprehensive guide to the workings of the modern monetary system, which is used as a textbook to teach banking and finance courses at universities in the UK and United States. He has a PhD in economics from the University of Southampton and is visiting research fellow at Southampton Business School and City University's Political Economy Research Centre in London.

Toby Lloyd is head of housing development at Shelter, the UK's largest housing charity, where he was previously head of policy. He has worked on housing issues across the public, private and voluntary sectors for over twelve years, advising ministers, mayors, businesses and communities. His proposal for a new Garden City won the runner-up award in the Wolfson Economics Prize 2014.

Laurie Macfarlane is an economist at the New Economics Foundation, working on land and financial reform issues. He was previously head of economic analysis at the Water Industry Commission for Scotland and also spent one year working in the markets and economics division at Ofwat. Laurie has written on land and housing reform for the progressive Scottish think tank Common Weal. He has a first class degree in economics from the University of Strathclyde.

The New Economics Foundation is the only people-powered think tank. It works to build a new economy where people really take control.

RETHINKING THE ECONOMICS OF LAND AND HOUSING

Josh Ryan-Collins, Toby Lloyd
and Laurie Macfarlane

Foreword by John Muellbauer

ZED

Rethinking the Economics of Land and Housing was first published in 2017 by Zed Books Ltd, The Foundry, 17 Oval Way, London SE11 5RR, UK.

www.zedbooks.net

Typeset in Sabon by seagulls.net
Index by Rohan Bolton
Cover design and illustration by David A. Gee

A catalogue record for this book is available from the British Library.

ISBN 978-1-78699-119-5 hb
ISBN 978-1-78699-118-8 pb
ISBN 978-1-78699-120-1 pdf
ISBN 978-1-78699-121-8 epub
ISBN 978-1-78699-122-5 mobi

CONTENTS

· · · · · · · · · · · · · · · · · · · ·

FIGURES, TABLES AND BOXES

Figures

Tables

Boxes

ACKNOWLEDGEMENTS

The authors are most grateful to the following individuals for reviewing initial drafts and chapters of the book and providing invaluable suggestions: John Muellbauer, Kate Barker, Alison Wallace, Howard Reed, James Bruges, Allana Yurko, Steve Keen, Michael Kumhof, Nicholas Tideman, Ken Gibb, Bob Colenutt, Duncan Bowie, Paul Gilbert and Giorgos Galanis.

Thanks to Duncan McCann, Alice Martin and Beth Stratford for intellectual and practical support in getting the book written. The book has also benefited from the insights of participants at a roundtable on the financialisation of housing held at the Bank of England in July 2016.

Josh and Toby would like to thank their respective families for their considerable patience in the writing up process. Thanks also to Ken Barlow and colleagues at Zed for their support in bringing the book to publication.

Finally, thanks to the RH Southern Trust and James and the late Marion Bruges for their financial support for this project. Sadly Marion passed away before this book was completed – we dedicate it to her memory.

ABBREVIATIONS

· ·

ARLA	Association of Residential Letting Agents
BSA	Building Societies Association
BTL	buy-to-let
CAP	Common Agricultural Policy
CLT	community land trust
CMU	Capital Markets Union
CPI	consumer price inflation
CRE	commercial real estate
FPC	Financial Policy Committee
GDP	gross domestic product
HEW	home equity withdrawal
IHT	inheritance tax
IMF	International Monetary Fund
ISA	Individual Savings Account
LBTT	land and buildings transaction tax
LTI	loan-to-income (ratio)
LTV	loan-to-value (ratio)
LVT	land value tax
MBS	mortgage-backed security
MIRAS	mortgage interest relief at source
NIMBY	not-in-my-back-yard
OECD	Organisation for Economic Co-operation and Development
OPEC	Organization of the Petroleum Exporting Countries
QE	quantitative easing
RMBS	residential mortgage-backed security
SDLT	stamp duty land tax
SMEs	small and medium sized enterprises
SPV	special purpose vehicle

GLOSSARY

· ·

Bank capital – Bank capital can be considered as a bank's 'own funds'. For banks, capital mainly consists of common shares (also known as common equity) and retained earnings which can easily absorb losses and therefore protect them from insolvency. Taken together, these 'own funds' are equivalent to the difference between the value of total assets and liabilities.

Buy-to-let – When a property is purchased with the specific intention of being let out to tenants. A buy-to-let mortgage is a mortgage taken out by a landlord specifically designed for this purpose.

Capital gains tax – A charge on gains realised due to the disposal of assets, calculated as the difference between the cost of acquiring the asset and the income acquired due to the disposal of that asset.

Collateral – Something pledged as security for repayment of a loan. If the borrower fails, the bank covers its losses by repossessing the underlying asset the loan was raised against.

Credit creation – Lending by deposit-taking banks, involving the creation of both an asset (the loan) and a simultaneous liability (the deposit), the latter adding to the money supply.

Economic rent – Economic rent refers to any return deriving from the possession of a scarce or exclusive factor of production, in excess of the cost of bringing it into production. Since land has no cost of production, any payment given for its use can be considered economic rent.

Feudal system – The economy and political power structure prevalent in the medieval era, under which the nobility held land in return for loyalty, and providing services such as serving or fighting for their lord.

Financialisation – A term used to describe the transformation of work, services, land or other forms exchange into financial instruments, for example debt instruments like bonds, that can traded on financial markets.

Foreign exchange controls – Various forms of controls imposed by a government on the purchase/sale of foreign currencies by residents or on the purchase/sale of local currency by non-residents.

Gini coefficient – A measure of statistical dispersion intended to represent the income distribution of a nation's residents. It is represented as a number between 0 and 1, where 0 corresponds with perfect equality (where everyone has the same income) and 1 corresponds with perfect inequality (where one person has all the income and everyone else has zero income).

Gross domestic product (GDP) – The monetary value of all the finished goods and services produced within a country's borders in a specific time period.

Home equity withdrawal (or equity release) – Home equity withdrawal is a way of getting cash from the value of a home without having to move out. It occurs whenever households increase their secured borrowing without spending the proceeds on improving or enlarging the housing stock

Housing tenure – Tenure refers to the legal forms under which land and landed property are owned, occupied and used. Most housing tenures are forms of tenancy, in which rent is paid to a landlord, or owner-occupancy. Mixed forms of tenure are also possible.

Imputed rent – The 'in kind' income that homeowners receive from their property, which is calculated as the rent that would be paid for a similar property in the private rented sector.

Keynesian economics – A school of economic thought associated with British economist John Maynard Keynes (1883–1946) which maintains that free markets have no self-balancing mechanisms and government intervention is required to stabilise the economy.

Land value tax (LVT) – A levy of the unimproved value of land.

Loan-to-value (LTV) ratio – A financial term used by lenders to express the ratio of a loan to the value of an asset purchased.

Marginal productivity theory – A theory that states that incomes are determined according to contribution to production (the 'marginal productivity theory'). Under this theory, wages reflect the amount of additional output an extra worker would produce – the 'marginal product' of labour.

Monetarism – A school of economic thought mainly associated with Nobel Prize-winning economist Milton Friedman which maintains that, in the absence of major unexpected fluctuations in the money supply, markets are inherently stable and will adjust to disruptions quickly.

Mortgage – A loan secured against landed property. A legal agreement by which a bank or building society lends money at interest in exchange for taking title of the debtor's property, with the condition that the conveyance of title becomes void upon the payment of the debt.

National accounts – The national accounts provide an integrated description of all economic activity within a country, including activity involving both domestic units and external units (those resident in other countries). The accounts deal with the transactions between the various sectors of the economy (corporations, households, government, rest of the world) and cover production, consumption, generation, distribution, redistribution of income, capital investment and financing.

Neoclassical economics – A school of economics with its origins in the late nineteenth century which views the economy as a self-equilibrating system driven by the voluntary exchange of goods and services by individuals and firms in seeking to maximise their utility and profits.

Net wealth – The balance of a household's assets subtracted from its liabilities. For example, if a household has savings of £50,000, owns a home worth £250,000 and has mortgage and credit card debts of £100,000, its net wealth will be £200,000.

Property – In this book, property will be understood to refer to a spatially defined area of land and the structures on top of it that is legally owned by an individual or firm.

Quantitative easing – An unconventional form of monetary policy where a central bank creates new money electronically to buy financial assets like government bonds from commercial banks and other financial institutions.

Real estate – Property consisting of land or buildings.

Residential mortgage-backed security (RMBS) – A type of asset-backed security that is secured by a collection of domestic mortgages.

Section 106 – A section of the Town and Country Planning Act 1990 which allowed local planning authorities to enter into legally binding agreements with developers, with the latter having to provide certain public benefits as part of the development.

Securitisation – A financial innovation undertaken by banks involving the pooling together and repackaging a number of illiquid loans – loans that cannot easily be sold or exchanged for cash – and issuing tradable debt securities against these loans that are sold to investors. These securities are repaid as the underlying loans are repaid.

Special purpose vehicle (SPV) – An entity set up, usually by a financial institution, for the specific purpose of purchasing the assets and realising their off-balance-sheet treatment for legal and accounting purposes.

Tenure – The legal form under which land is owned, occupied and used. Private ownership of land has risen to become the dominant form of land tenure around the world but many alternatives exist that support collective as well as individual ownership of land and resources.

Wholesale money markets – Refers to the lending and borrowing of large quantities of liquid assets in a range of currencies, generally between financial institutions such as banks, as well as non-financial companies and the government.

FOREWORD

· ·

John Muellbauer

Rethinking the Economics of Land and Housing is an important book. It combines history of thought, economic history, political economy and the findings of recent research to address probably the most fundamental problems faced by British society and some other advanced economies. Deepening inequality and social exclusion, poor prospects for sustainable growth, intergenerational conflict and risks of financial instability have at their root poor policy choices concerning land and housing over many decades. These concern the legal and institutional framework governing land use, property contracts, taxation and subsidies and financial regulation. The book also has a wider significance in rebalancing the economics literature to treat land more seriously as a factor of production, along with labour and reproducible capital.

Among all the OECD countries, the UK has experienced the largest rise since 1970 in house prices relative to average household disposable income and also greater volatility in house prices. While in the US, average house prices relative to median income in 2015 were roughly at the levels of 1980, in the UK they were far higher, and in London and the South East the deterioration in housing affordability was even more extreme.

One consequence has been a huge intergenerational redistribution in the UK: those born after Margaret Thatcher came to power in 1979 are a 'lost generation', missing out on huge capital gain windfalls driven by rising land and property prices. Since 1995, owner-occupation in the 25-to-44-year age group has fallen by around 20 percentage points and, since 2002, rising housing costs have contributed to wiping out real income gains for the lower half of the income distribution of working households, as described in Chapter 7 of the book. Moreover, house prices reflect access to good schools, transport and clean environment, creating privileged opportunities for children of the wealthy.

Behind the rise in house prices relative to income is the fact that demand for housing in the UK, particularly since the mid-1990s, has grown far faster than supply. The main demand factors are higher average income per head and higher population, an ageing population, the deregulation of mortgage finance, lower mortgage interest rates, reductions in effective property taxes and demand by foreign investors. Housing economists emphasise the role of expected capital gains and the evidence is that many investors tend to form expectations based on recent price rises, intensifying house-price booms. The 'financialisation' of housing and land is the subject of Chapter 5. There were waves of liberalisation of mortgage credit conditions in the 1980s and in the late 1990s and 2000s. Moreover, banks increasingly switched lending away from relationship banking to collateral-based lending, with property the preferred form of collateral.

On the supply side, in the post-war period there was heavy public intervention with social housing construction, a good deal of it under the aegis of the New Town programme, accounting for a large part of house building in the run up to the early 1980s. With the election of Thatcher, this came to an end. The right-to-buy at large discounts, extended to social tenants, reduced the stock of social housing. Planning constraints on the private sector became increasingly onerous and, if anything, intensified when New Labour came to power in 1997. Subsidies, which had been more focused on the supply side, increasingly switched to the demand side, partly through housing benefit and partly through special measures designed to help selected groups into owner-occupation. Chapter 4 provides an excellent account of the history of UK housing policy. For the public purse, the rise in the housing benefit bill, to £24 billion in 2014–15, has been one obvious cost.

Economic growth in the UK has suffered from restrictions on supply and the failure to limit demand growth for housing as a high-return asset. An important mechanism emphasised in the book concerns the diversion of finance into higher land prices, effectively increasing the share of land relative to capital and labour. This almost certainly diverted investment from more productive areas, damaging productivity growth. It also shows up in the low quality and small size of new-build housing in the UK compared to the past and to other countries, also discussed in Chapter 4.

The accumulation of household debt relative to income is a major constraint on future demand growth. Mortgage credit liberalisation boosts consumption in the short term by lowering required down-payments, at given house prices. But it also raises house prices. In many countries this soon reduces or even cancels the boost to consumption by once more raising down-payments relative to income. However, in the UK and the US, the home-equity withdrawal channel boosts consumption as existing homeowners are able to finance higher consumption on the back of higher collateral values. In the long run, this makes highly indebted households vulnerable to downturns in house prices. As argued in Chapter 5, this and the power of vested interests explains the reluctance of policy makers to address the fundamental problems.

The policy suggestions made in the concluding chapter include property tax reforms that I have long espoused, and the discussion of land value taxation is excellent. The examples of Singapore, Hong Kong and South Korea show how planning gain and the spillover effects of income and population growth on land values can be partly socialised to benefit the nation, rather than a relatively concentrated class of landowners. In Germany, for example, the planning law freezes the value of the land when the local municipality decides to specify an area for residential construction.[1] The uplift in land values then finances infrastructure. A national public land bank, as in Korea, or public or community-owned land banks able to acquire land at existing use values can achieve the same objective. In many respects the UK's New Town building programme from 1946 to 1970 was also able to do this.

Though addressing the UK's pressing problems is important, the book also examines the neglect of land in economic theory more generally. Chapter 3 argues that the literature on income distri-

---

1 T. Aubrey, 'Bridging the infrastructure gap: financing infrastructure investment to unlock housing', 2016, http://progressive-capitalism.net/wp-content/uploads/2016/06/Bridging-the-infrastructure-gap-June-2016.pdf

bution focusing on factor shares has neglected the role of land. Because land is largely fixed and irreproducible, local monopoly power allows landowners to charge high rents, while benefitting from the spillover effects of investment by others and of population and income growth on rental values. Restraints on city expansion, whether because of restrictions on land use or because of physical barriers such as the sea or mountains, increase this monopoly power.

For macroeconomics too, the significance of property prices, which largely reflect underlying land values, and their interaction with financial markets and banking, had long been neglected in models popular with central banks. Proponents of these so-called 'dynamic stochastic general equilibrium' models argued that, unlike an older generation of models, they were properly 'micro-founded' on optimising behaviour at the level of individual households and firms. To the book's diagnosis of how this came about, I would add a failure to use correct micro-foundations that took into account the asymmetric information revolution initiated by George Akerlof, Michael Spence and Joseph Stiglitz, and the research of Angus Deaton and Christopher Carroll on how households behave when facing uncertainty and liquidity constraints.[2] The global financial crisis has highlighted the mistake made by most of the macroeconomics profession and central banks in not incorporating asset prices, including property prices, credit and household balance sheets more generally in their models and their understanding.

The broad range of the book, including its historical depth and use of evidence-based research, and a very extensive set of references make it eminently suitable as a learning source for undergraduate and postgraduate students of economics and related disciplines, as well as the more general interested reader. Economics teaching needs to be more relevant to the real world, where markets do not always work perfectly and where externalities, monopoly, information problems, finance and economic inequality matter. All these issues are well addressed in this book.

---

2 J. Muellbauer, 'Macroeconomics and consumption: Why central bank models failed and how to repair them', VOXEU, 2016, http://voxeu.org/article/why-central-bank-models-failed-and-how-repair-them

CHAPTER 1

· ·

Introduction

Buy land – they're not making it anymore.
MARK TWAIN (ATTRIBUTED)

Attention salesmen, sales managers:
location, location, location, close to Rogers Park.
1926 REAL ESTATE CLASSIFIED AD IN THE *CHICAGO TRIBUNE,*
IN SAFIRE (2009)

This is a book about land and its role in the economy. By land we don't mean physical earth and rock, we mean locational space. Land plays a central role in the economy but one that is often overlooked and poorly understood. This lack of understanding is a major weakness in much orthodox economic thinking, and helps to explain many of the policy failures and problems that bedevil modern societies. These include the crisis in the affordability of housing (the main use for land in modern economies), rising inequality, financial instability, excessive household debt and falling investment and productivity levels, despite increasing paper wealth.

This book should help the reader understand how these problems came about and provide some clues as to how they might be addressed in the future. The book has two sets of audiences and objectives. Firstly, it is aimed at the interested reader who wishes to better understand some of the challenges facing modern economies and societies. These questions include:

- Why are house prices in advanced economies rising faster than incomes and the growth of the economy? Is it simply a case of building more homes or having fewer people? Why don't politicians or policy makers want or allow house prices to fall?

- Why is landownership so concentrated and wealth inequality growing so fast?
- Is it desirable for society to aspire to home- and landownership as the best route to wealth?
- What is the relationship between the financial system and land? Why have banks begun to lend more for the purchase of existing property and land than to businesses for investment? Why are household debt levels historically so high?
- What is the cause of the large boom and bust cycles in house prices experienced in the UK and other countries over the last forty-five years?
- How does the value of land relate to the technologies of production, the distribution of wealth and economic inequality over time?
- Why isn't land and location taught or seen as important in modern economics or integrated into national accounting?

Secondly, this book is aimed at students and academics in the social sciences, including politics, political economy, law, sociology, geography, urban studies and, perhaps most of all, economics, where the topic of land has almost completely disappeared from most textbooks. To understand land properly, we must take a cross-disciplinary approach – we need a bit of history, a bit of economics and a bit about power and the law.

This book is focused on the macroeconomics and political economy of land – in other words, how it impacts on aggregate or national economic phenomena, such as the distribution of wealth and income, changes in asset prices, flows of credit and stocks of debt, and, for the most part, the national rather than international or local/regional policy and political sphere. A particular goal is to help develop a more coherent analysis of the role of 'economic rent' in modern economies: that is, the excess returns derived from the ownership of a natural (usually scarce) resource. Land, we believe, is the most important source of such rents in advanced economies and also the most neglected. The book is motivated by the failure of mainstream macroeconomics to develop theories adequate to explaining these dynamics. This has been a long-term problem and we are not the first to tackle it,[1] but it is one that has been brought into particularly sharp definition in the post-financial crisis period since 2007–8.

This book does not examine the economics of cities or urban space more generally, or the role of land in agricultural or development economics settings. These are fields which we felt were already well covered in the existing literatures.[2] The focus of the book is also primarily on the use of land as housing rather than commercial real estate, although the latter is discussed in a number of places. Similar dynamics apply to both, but there are important differences that space has not allowed us to examine.

The economic story of land is global, and much of the evidence and arguments presented in this book are relevant to advanced economies generally. But the way in which land's role in the economy has played out in different places depends largely on the laws, institutions and political history of particular nations, and so varies widely. Rather than attempt to comprehensively cover the world – an endeavour that would have required a book six times the length of this one – we mainly focus on the United Kingdom as our case study. The UK is a large and mature economy, and many aspects of its land economy, legal institutions and financial system have been exported around the world (particularly to Anglo-Saxon, common law countries), making it a useful reference point for more generalised discussion of the issues. But throughout the book we also incorporate examples of the role of land in other advanced countries.

1.1 What is land?

In classical political economy (the predecessor to modern economics), land was understood to be one of the three factors of production, along with capital and labour. Any economic activity requires the combination of all three: a farm obviously requires land to produce food, but so too does a factory to produce goods, or a lawyer's office

---

1 See for example the writings of US economists Nicolas Tideman, Michael Hudson and Mason Gaffney and British economist Fred Harrison.

2 See, inter alia, the following academic journals: *The Journal of Urban Economics, Urban Studies* and *Real Estate Economics*.

to provide legal services. Looked at like this, it is clear that land is not simply soil, and its economic uses are not simply agricultural. In fact, land is better understood as *space* and the occupation of that space over time.[3]

Throughout most of economic history the primary function of land was for agricultural production. But since the birth of modern, capitalist economies other uses have become predominant: first as the site of industrial production, and later as the site of service provision and domestic housing. Today, it is in the housing market that the economic function of land is most visible, as the value of residential property has overtaken the value of land used for other purposes, as the economist Thomas Piketty (2014) makes clear in his recent book *Capital in the Twenty-First Century*. For this reason, much of the book focuses on housing as the main economic use of land.

Land has several unique features that differentiate it from the other 'factors of production' that form the central focus of the economics discipline: capital and labour. Most obviously land is *immobile*: you can't move land from one place to another, because land *is* the place itself. The supply of land is highly inelastic, if not fixed, because you cannot make any more of it (with the small exception of reclamation from the sea).[4] To all intents and purposes, land is *eternal* (with the small exception of coastal erosion), although climate change looks set to lead to a reduction in its habitable surface. Most importantly, land is essential for all economic activity to take place – and indeed for life itself.

These unique features determine much of the special economic functions of land. Notably, they are features that do not fit well into mainstream (neoclassical) economic models where the supply of commodities, labour and capital can easily adjust according to the demand for them and find an equilibrium price and quantity (see Box 1.1). But rather than adjust their models for this reality, economics has neglected land or conflated it with other factors

---

3 Economists often refer to other natural resources such as oil, water, air, or light as 'land', but these too can be best understood as the products of certain locations.

4 The supply of land in aggregate is certainly fixed (at least until we are able to colonise other planets) but the supply for a particular uses is fixed artificially, for instance by planning rules.

of production, most notably 'capital'. This failure to distinguish between land and 'capital' as factors in the production process, in notions of 'wealth' and in national accounting is a major conceptual error in the evolution of economic theory that we explore in this book (Chapters 3 and 5 in particular).

Throughout this book we treat land as the physical space within which economic activity takes place.

Box 1.1 Neoclassical economics

Neoclassical economics is a school of economics with its origins in the late nineteenth century which views the economy as a self-equilibrating system driven by the voluntary exchange of goods and services by individuals and firms in seeking to maximise their utility and profits. Neoclassical economics assumes people and firms are able to make rational preferences between identifiable outcomes and attach value to those outcomes. It also assumes people are able to act independently on the basis of full and relevant information. The interaction between market supply and market demand, which are aggregated across firms and individuals, determines equilibrium output and price.

Within the broad school of neoclassical economics there are a range of different approaches; however they mainly share the above core assumptions and a general requirement that economic theory should be grounded in the actions of individuals – that economics needs 'micro-foundations'. Neoclassical economics became the dominant school in teaching, research and economic policy making in the 1970s and remains so today, but in recent times it has come under considerable criticism for its failure to help predict and explain the financial crisis of 2007–8 and the slow recovery that has followed it.

Policies influenced by neoclassical economics focus upon removing barriers to the free and independent exchange of goods and services that may temporarily prevent markets achieving equilibrium conditions. The emphasis is on 'supply-side' solutions, such as tariffs, labour market regulations and certain taxes.

In this book we will use the terms 'mainstream', 'orthodox' and 'neoclassical' economics interchangeably.

1.2 What is the value of land?

The economic value of any piece of land initially stems from the uses it can be put to – as a field, a factory, an office, a shop or a home. The economic value of these uses will vary not only with the natural features of the land, but with their geographic relationship to the rest of the economy. A fertile field is obviously more valuable than a desert, all else being equal, but fertile ground miles from people to farm, roads to carry or markets to consume its produce is less valuable than one near a city with good transport connections. Estate agents like to say that 'location, location, location' is the most important factor in selling a home, because everything else can be changed. What they are referring to is the fundamental locational value of the land itself. This can be seen in the often huge discrepancy between the 'replacement cost' of a home calculated for insurance purposes and the actual market price it commands: the difference between the two is essentially the value of the land in that particular place.

Land values in any particular location reflect the level of wider economic activity in that area.[5] The price of a home in a thriving city can be many times that of an identical home in a remote, depressed region, because of the access to economic opportunities that living in the city brings. Most obviously, investment in infrastructure increases the value of land, by increasing the range and quality of uses it can be put to, and the relative advantages of well-served locations over other places. New transport links, or being in the catchment area of a good school, dramatically affect the market value of homes in that location, because they boost the value of the land underneath those homes.

But the value of land is not only determined by its *current* use value. Because land is permanent, controlling land is also a means of securing the economic value that holding it will provide *in the future*. In other words, land is an asset as well as the provider of consumption goods (food, shelter), and land prices will reflect

---

5 House prices are thus a prime candidate for use in 'hedonic pricing' methods, a technique used by applied economists whereby price is determined both by internal characteristics of the good being sold and external factors affecting it.

people's expectations of future economic activity. The permanence and inherent scarcity of land make it a good asset for the storing of value (assuming no major changes to planning regulations). Most capital assets depreciate in value over time due to natural wear and tear but land tends to appreciate. This means people are often keen to convert other forms of wealth into land, including money which, although much more liquid, can lose value rapidly under conditions of consumer or asset price inflation. This dual function makes land challenging to neatly fit into economic theory since at any point in time land can be being used for different purposes.[6]

For similar reasons, land is also an excellent asset to act as security (or 'collateral') for extending credit and finance, the topic of Chapter 5. For the first few decades after the Second World War, restrictions were placed on lending against property because of concerns about excessive real estate bubbles. However, in the 1970s and 1980s the liberalisation of credit markets led banks to radically change their primary role in modern societies, switching from lending mainly to businesses for investment to lending to households for home purchase, taking land as collateral.

The regulatory constraints on the practice of lending against property assets are therefore a key determinant of the workings of the market in land and landed property and the macroeconomy more generally (Aron et al., 2012). Today the relative advantages that buy-to-let (BTL) borrowers have over first-time buyers in securing access to mortgage credit has helped to drive the increase in landlords' share of the total housing stock (Kingman, 2013). International regulatory moves since the 1970s have also incentivised banks to favour property-related lending over other types of loans and so contributed to keeping property and land prices up.

While there is a strong theoretical case for allowing land to be used as a form of collateral from an economic development

---

6 In this sense it is similar to money, which equally fulfils multiple and sometimes conflicting purposes. Money's functions include being a store of value, means of exchange and unit of account. Economic theories of money have typically isolated either the store of value or means of exchange function of money as its primary role and neglected the tension between the two roles (Dodd, 1994; Ingham, 2004).

perspective (De Soto, 2000), there is also strong evidence that rapid rises in real estate credit increase financial fragility and are strong predictors of financial crises and long-lasting recessions. More generally, a number of economists now argue that capitalist economies are characterized by a land–credit 'cycle', which may be longer and deeper that the standard economics textbook 'business cycle' (Aikman et al., 2014; Borio, 2014).

Figure 1.1 shows how house and land prices have developed over time in the UK over the last sixty years. We can see that since the 1960s land prices have become highly volatile, with three huge boom–bust cycles, corresponding to expansions in bank credit in the 1970s, late 1980s and 2000s. Discounting inflation, house prices have gone up five times since the end of the Second World War. But the price of the land needed to put houses on has increased in real terms by fifteen times over the same period. Research suggests that house price volatility is primarily driven by land values – which is to be expected, as the price of construction (labour and building materials) is subject to more standard and slow moving economy-wide factors. Importantly, land values tend to rise rapidly ahead of house price booms, showing how land markets present good opportunities for speculative investment to extract value.

Figure 1.1 Real land and house price indices UK 1945–2008 (1945 = 100) (*source*: adapted from Cheshire, 2009, 2014)

As noted by the American sociologist Thorsten Veblen (1899), landed property can also be seen as a 'positional good' which people use to demonstrate their social status. People will therefore be prepared to pay more for desirable locations than can be justified purely by rational economic calculations. As economies develop and become more informationally intensive and the costs of many goods and services – cars, computers, mobile phones – fall, locationally desirable land and property will be likely to eat up a larger proportion of people's incomes (Turner, 2015a, p. 70).

Relatedly, physical space is also highly desired and not subject to diminishing returns – as people get richer, they want more space. Estimates suggests that a 10% increase in incomes leads people to spend about 20% more on space in houses and gardens (Cheshire and Sheppard, 1998). In the economics jargon, land has a 'high income-elasticity of demand' – people will stretch their incomes to consume it.

This is why the rise of communications technology has not meant 'the end of distance' as some predicted, but has in fact driven the economic pre-eminence of a few cities that are best connected to the global economy and offer the best amenities for the knowledge workers and entrepreneurs of the digital economy (Florida, 2004; Thrift, 1996). The scarcity of these locations has fed a long boom in the value of land in those cities (De Groot et al., 2015).

The technological transformations of recent decades may not have abolished the significance of land in the economy, but they have accelerated a shift in the relative economic importance of different land uses, which was already underway. As Piketty's (2014) data demonstrates, the proportion of the total stock of wealth represented by housing has risen rapidly since the mid-twentieth century, while the value of agricultural land has dwindled to almost nothing as a share of GDP (see Chapter 6).

Piketty's data also shows that for around 270 years, in the UK and France residential property wealth varied between 60% and 180% of GDP (Figure 1.2). Since the 1980s, however, residential property values have exploded and are now over 300% of GDP in both countries. In the US, the expansion has been less dramatic but residential property values have still increased threefold since the beginning of the twentieth century as a percentage of GDP. Clearly,

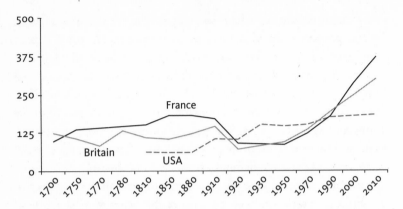

Figure 1.2 Residential property wealth as a % of GDP in advanced economies (*source*: Piketty and Zucman, 2013)

a fundamental shift has occurred in these economies, as housing has replaced farming as the primary economic use of land.

All of these factors complicate any assessment of the value of land, but in general they combine to make land a highly favoured investment class, and a perfect asset for speculation – provided, that is, it can be owned at all.

1.3 Landownership and economic rent

The main institution which has mediated the interaction between land and the economy in modern societies is via property owner-ship, the subject of Chapter 2. The idea of property ownership seems simple at first: you own a property and have exclusive rights to occupy that piece of land for a defined period of time (or the landowner grants you such rights as a tenant). In fact there are multiple forms of individual and collective forms of ownership possible, with modern exclusive individual homeownership a rela-tively recent phenomenon.

The history of landownership is important to explore for it demonstrates how the rules and customs that underlie private property – a cornerstone of modern capitalist economies – have actually very little to do with economics and much more to do with politics and power. This makes it an awkward phenomenon for mainstream economics which assumes, in general, that all economic relationships have been voluntarily entered into. The only 'power' that appears in most economics textbooks is the power of some sellers to influence the prices of products – i.e. 'market power' (Hill and Myatt, 2010, p. 251). In the real world of imperfect information and finite land, those with control over the latter have heavily influenced access to it and its value through legal and regulatory influence over the state.

It is not our aim in this book to tackle the philosophical or moral arguments for or against property ownership but rather to show how this phenomenon interacts with the economy and the financial system. What can be said is that property ownership has played a central role in the shaping of modern economies and brought significant benefits to many millions of people at certain points in history. But it is not at all clear that ownership is the superior form of tenure in terms of optimising social welfare or economic productivity at the aggregate level.

This fact is related to the inherently exclusionary nature of land-ownership given that land itself is scarce. This is true even if there are large quantities of 'empty' land that have not yet been brought into economic use, because more economically productive locations are *relatively* scarce, and the best of all are extremely scarce. Each location is more or less unique, so control of every piece of land is essentially monopolistic. As a result, landowners can command returns from those who must use their land based purely on their ownership of it, unrelated to their costs of bringing it into production or any efforts they have expended. Such returns are known as 'economic rent'.

The fixed supply of land for particular uses means it does not fit easily in mainstream economic theories where supply and demand set prices in a free market. If the demand for iPhones increases, Apple can increase the quantity of phones produced – at a cost to themselves – until an equilibrium is reached, whereby demand meets supply and the market 'clears'. Apple may instead choose to increase the price of iPhones; however they then face the risk that some consumers may choose to buy a different brand of phone. The idea is that market competition generates an efficient trade-off between quantity and price and economic rents are minimised.

But the quantity of land cannot be increased in the way the quantity of iPhones can. If demand for land increases, the price goes up without triggering a supply response. This problem may be exacerbated by planning regulations that restrict the supply of land over and above its natural scarcity (Cheshire and Sheppard, 2004) but, as we argue in Chapter 7, such regulations merely crystallise the problems of scarcity and rent, and make them more amenable to democratically controlled policy mitigation.

As David Ricardo (and later Henry George) identified, the ability to extract economic rent is so powerful it can effectively monopolise much of the growth created in an economy, the vast bulk of which will not have been created by the landowners themselves. In its simplest conception, as the economy grows, landowners can increase the rent they charge non-owners to absorb all the additional value that their tenants (such as workers, shopkeepers and industrialists) generate.

Rent-seeking seems intuitively unfair to many, but it is also inefficient. If the worker, the shopkeeper or the industrialist cannot benefit from their own efforts, but must watch it being extracted in the form of rent, why would they exert themselves or innovate? As is often noted by studies of the divergent economic health of different cities, successful urban centres around the world experience soaring land and housing costs, which ultimately threaten the very economic success of those cities, as valuable workers choose to move to less dynamic places where lower wages are more than compensated by much lower housing costs (Hsieh and Moretti, 2015). The ability to extract rent for little effort or risk also distorts investment decisions, as it encourages those with capital to over-allocate it to land and property purchases, rather than other productive uses (see Chapter 5).

The allure of rent extraction encourages those who can to accumulate land, and the monopolistic nature of private ownership of land enables them to preserve and expand their holdings. Historical evidence suggests that markets in private property tend towards concentration, and to absorb a disproportionate share of growth (George, [1879] 1979; Ricardo, 1817). The result is growing wealth inequality, acute poverty for some, and inefficient capital allocation which dampens economic growth (which we explore in Chapter 6). As Joseph Stiglitz has put it, rent-seeking involves directing effort 'toward getting a larger share of the pie rather than increasing the size of the pie' (Stiglitz and Bilmes, 2012).

1.4 Summary of chapters

The remainder of this book is laid out as follows. Chapter 2 describes the emergence of tradeable, privately owned landed property and the enclosure of previously common or feudal lands into private ownership. This is the key starting point for any understanding of the way in which land interacts with the economy in modern capitalist societies. We argue that there is a paradox at the heart of landownership. The spread of ownership of land has helped drive economic development, democratised power and spread wealth; yet, we argue, it equally has a tendency towards concentration and monopolisation of resources via excessive rent extraction with increasingly negative economic impacts at the aggregate level, even as the paper wealth of those owning property may increase. Landed property can thus be thought of as both 'freedom and theft'. The second half of the chapter summarises how states have attempted to address these challenges, through control over land and the subsidy and taxation of land.

Chapter 3 reviews the history of economic thought on land, with a particular focus on the classical political economists who first identified the economic rent that derived from agricultural land as a key challenge for the state and economics more generally. The chapter then examines how neoclassical economics emerged and sought to develop universal scientific rules that determined the distribution of income – marginal productivity theory – across all factors of production. Together with the shift away from agricultural to industrial production, this led to land being conflated with capital and its unique qualities were no longer identified in economic theory and policy.

Chapter 4 focuses on the economic transformation of land usage from agriculture, through industrial production and to the site of a consumption good – housing – in the twentieth century. This chapter uses the United Kingdom as an example by which to illustrate how the paradox of property ownership and the problem of economic rent was dealt with by various governments. We show how changes in taxation and subsidies for homeownership have increased the incidence of land rents in the latter part of the twentieth century.

Chapter 5 focuses on the relationship between land and finance. Although, as discussed, property has always been a source of collateral for the extension of credit, the last few decades have seen an extraordinary growth in credit related to real estate , particularly for mortgage lending: what we call the 'financialisation' of land. The chapter argues that the move towards homeownership as the preferred form of tenure and the liberalisation of the banking sector have led to the emergence of a feedback cycle between land and credit that has come to dominate modern economies. This has resulted in greater financial fragility and instability with consumption, the main contributor to economic growth in advanced economies, increasingly determined by the interaction between housing wealth and credit.

The liberalisation of property finance and the failure to tackle economic rent has important distributional consequences. Chapter 6 examines these dynamics via an exploration of the role of land in generating income and wealth inequalities in modern societies. It reviews different theories of inequality and shows how changes in land value are the primary determinant of modern inequalities but are largely ignored because of the failure of economic theory and national accounting frameworks to properly incorporate property wealth and economic rent.

Chapter 7, in conclusion, summarises the key ideas of the book and focuses on potential solutions to the problems that have been created by the neglect of land in economic theory and policy, in particular the problem of economic rent from land. These include changes to ownership, planning, altering the burden of taxation and structural changes to our financial system to break out of the land credit feedback cycle.

Our contention is that many of the economic challenges of the current era are rooted in a failure to properly consider the role of land in the economy. Nonetheless, landownership remains a key site of political conflict and regulatory intervention, from local battles over planning restrictions on development to global rules on the capitalisation of banks. A clearer understanding of how land operates in the economy is therefore essential for better policy, as well as better economics. We hope the rest of this book provides a small step towards this goal.

CHAPTER 2

· · · · · · · · · · · · · · · · · · · ·

Landownership and property

The first man who, having enclosed a piece of ground,
bethought himself of saying 'this is mine', and found people
simple enough to believe him, was the real founder of civil
society. From how many crimes, wars and murders, from how
many horrors and misfortunes might not anyone have saved
mankind, by pulling up the stakes, or filling up the ditch, and
crying to his fellows, 'Beware of listening to this impostor;
you are undone if you once forget that the fruits of the earth
belong to us all, and the earth itself to nobody'.

JEAN-JACQUES ROUSSEAU (1775, P. 84)

2.1 Introduction

To gain a full understanding of the economics of land, we must first
gain an understanding of landownership and private property as the
key institutions via which land interacts with the economy.

Modern societies are accustomed to thinking of land and the
buildings on it as simply another commodity that can be owned,
bought and sold much like any other. Such a view also pervades
mainstream economic theory. But in reality the ownership of land is
nowhere near as straightforward as the ownership of other goods or
assets. Indeed the very concept of 'owning' the land has proved highly
controversial throughout history.[1] No simple linear narrative of this
history is possible, as widely different concepts of land use, property
rights and ownership have come and gone over the centuries. This
chapter conducts a brief review of the origins of landownership and
property and then moves on to explore a fundamental paradox that

---

1 For an excellent account of landownership through history, see Andro Linklater's
  book *Owning the Earth*, published in 2013.

lies at the heart of landed property: that ownership is both a form of freedom and, because of its exclusionary nature, theft.

The second half of the chapter examines responses to this ownership paradox. This includes state acquisition of land, the imposition of laws governing tenure, trading and inheritance of land, regulations around the use of land (planning), and subsidies and taxes to influence land usage.

2.2 Landownership: origins of the theory and forms

The notion that land could be turned in to property was one of the key developments of enlightenment thinking in the seventeenth and eighteenth centuries in Europe and the United States. Thinkers such as Thomas Aquinas, Hugo Grotius and Samuel Pufendorf argued that property emerged out of the interplay between the individual and the state (Pierson, 2013, p. 165-188). According to these thinkers, God gave the earth to humanity in common rather than individually. However, as civilisation developed, it was justified for man to exercise a general right to seize land for his own needs and, once this had occurred, it became unjust to deprive anyone of what they had seized. The state played the role of upholding the right to property and ultimately, according to the theory of 'eminent domain', it could expropriate the right to property under extreme circumstances so long as the property holder was appropriately compensated (Ambaye, 2015, pp. 108–109).

However, modern economic theory draws more from the writings of John Locke, a follower of Pufendorf, who developed a theory of 'natural' property rights. Locke (1690) argued that private property was antecedent to and thus independent of the state, and that humans had a right to property when they invested in it with their labour as in doing so they removed it from the state of nature and improved it. By virtue of this labour expenditure, the labourer becomes entitled to its produce. Such activity was vital, in Locke's view, to create a civilized society freed from the insecurity and latent violence of the state of nature and also from absolutist monarchs. For Enlightenment thinkers, then, landed property was a form of freedom.

Although, as we shall see, Locke's natural rights theory of land was rejected by classical political economists, it can be seen to underpin mainstream (neoclassical) economic theory, which presents private market exchange and private property rights as 'natural', with their origins in universally accepted rules not subject to particular political or social arrangements. This appeal to natural law gives mainstream theory a significant advantage:

> The derivation of natural moral theory has provided the foundation for the use of economic theory to support specific ideological viewpoints ... this tendency has justified laissez-faire economic policies as if they were based on natural laws. Always behind the legitimization activities of economists is the belief that markets are 'natural' institutions and market outcomes are natural outcomes, and the institutions necessary for markets, such as private property rights, are 'natural rights'. (O'Hara, 1999, pp. 782–783)

Often overlooked in Locke's work, however, was the 'Lockean proviso' that property was only natural so long as there was sufficient common land for others to enjoy. Locke believed that there was plenty of unclaimed land in America, so that the rules for a time when land was *not* scarce applied to the time when he was writing, and he did not need to deal with the eventual scarcity of unclaimed land. Since in most advanced economies all land is owned, it is not clear the Lockean justification for private property in land still has legitimacy. The classical political economists that followed Locke and fellow Enlightenment thinkers rejected the 'natural law' argument (we discuss this more in Chapter 3).

Adam Smith, usually recognised as the founder of liberal economic thought and free markets, accepted the concept of natural rights but limited them to the notions of 'liberty and life'. In contrast, he held property to be an *acquired* right that was dependent on the state and its form (West, 2003, pp. 20–42). Smith believed that civil government could not exist without property and that its main function was to safeguard property rights. Like Locke, however, he had concerns about the inequalities that could arise from the relationship between the state and property, arguing that: 'civil government, so far as it is instituted for the security of property, is, in reality, instituted for the defense of the rich against the poor, or of those who have property against those who have none at all' (Smith, 1776, p. 167).

Marx viewed liberal theories of natural property rights with great suspicion. In Section *VIII* of *Capital* he develops the concept of 'Primitive Accumulation' as an integral part of the formation of English capitalism (Harvey, [1982] 2006, p. 359). Despite feudal law formally providing land entitlement to the peasantry, as Marx saw it, in reality aristocratic classes could forcibly remove peasants from their lands. These lands would then be used for commercial farming activity and peasants would be re-employed as labourers. These clearances were vital in creating a large, un-landed class which had to work for wages to survive.

Multiple forms of ownership

In fact multiple forms of individual and collective ownership are possible, and in practice many tend to coexist. The modern form of individualised, near-absolute property ownership is only one. As such, 'ownership' is a misleading term, as it implies outright, indefinite control. In reality, property is best thought of as a complex of overlapping tenure rights – rights to enter, pass over, use, use the fruits of, exclude others from, build on, pass on to inheritors, or sell land.

These rights have emerged and evolved over time, as increasing social and economic complexity have driven a transformation from 'possession' to 'property' as the guiding principle. Pre-modern tribal communities collectively regulated economic activity based on customs of reciprocity: they recognised rules of possession of land, governing who can use it and its products. And there are some modern-day non-capitalist societies that still operate along such lines (Berkes, 1987; Sillitoe, 1999). But such land cannot be considered property, as it cannot be sold, transferred or alienated. This can only happen once land has become *property*, a process that began in the early modern period and is not complete today (Heinsohn and Steiger, 2006).

In medieval Europe, most land was held either by the Church or by the Crown – the origin of the term 'real (meaning royal) estate'. Under feudalism, the Crown granted favoured nobles huge swathes of land that they could hold 'of the king' in return for allegiance and military service. The nobles could in turn grant different types of use rights over parts of their land to knights and tenant farmers, in exchange for loyalty and rent paid in kind or in labour. Each of these layered transactions came with rights and obligations on both sides, which were codified in a huge range of now-forgotten tenures such as 'soccage', 'burgage' and 'frankalmoin' in England (Pollock and Maitland, 1899). Multiple individuals and collectives could have specific rights to use land that was held by the Crown, Church or nobility – such as 'pannage' (the right to forage pigs) or 'turbary' (the right to cut turf for fuel) (DEFRA, 2015).

Monarchs also sought to control the way that land could be passed on to inheritors, used as security for lending, or traded. Some tenures could be inherited, others could not. In many places and times land could not be bought and sold at all, or only by certain classes of people, and the conditions under which debtors' land could be seized by lenders were constantly argued over and legis-lated for. Under various circumstances – such as a failure to provide military service, or dying without an heir – a noble's land would revert to the crown. In Heihnsohn and Steiger's (2006) conception, feudal systems did not recognise property, but only possession.

Even once the concept of private property in land began to emerge in sixteenth century England, it coexisted with these older forms for many years. Even today, landownership is never absolute. A field may be privately owned, but it may still have public rights of way across it. Landowners' freedom to develop their land, or change its use, is generally restricted by planning and environmental laws, and they have only a partial claim to any treasure or archaeological remains found on their land. Many countries have retained layered forms of landownership, like the English freehold/leasehold system. Around the world a huge range of tenure models, including many collective forms of ownership and use rights, continue to thrive, and remain a key subject of anthropological study and political contro-versy (Payne, 2004).

In all this rich diversity of land tenure, one key fact stands out: the structure of landownership is not natural, but is a matter of law and custom, and hence is inherently political. Compared to owning other assets, such as gold, controlling land over time requires a high degree of social acceptance of that control. Unsurprisingly, a large proportion medieval law concerned land use, tenure, trading, ownership and inheritance – demonstrating both the central importance of land use in the economy, and the legal nature of it.

These laws and customs have shaped the pattern of landownership, and hence are a major determinant of economic and political history. Much of the diverse evolution of different national economies can be attributed to their differing histories of landownership regulation and its interaction with political power (Linklater, 2013). Orthodox economics neglects these dynamics in assuming the nature of property rights is fixed and not a policy variable (Turnbull, 2007). It also assumes property rights are binary – you either own something or you don't – but in fact there are many gradations and cases of ownership for specific uses for specific amounts of time, as discussed above.

2.3 Landownership as freedom: secure title and economic growth

The concept of private landownership may be a relatively new one, but its introduction was transformational. When Henry VIII seized the lands of the monasteries in the 1530s he sold much of them on to the emerging lower gentry and richer mercantile class, who were desperate to achieve the social status and economic power associated with landownership. This, and a similar wave of land redistribution during and after the English civil war, created a new class of landowner who were often more mercantile in their outlook than the older nobility, and a new concept of land as a private, tradable commodity. Combined with the advances in trade, farming and finance of the time, this set the scene for land to be used far more extensively as collateral for borrowing, tying landownership firmly into the emerging capitalist economy (Linklater, 2013).

Owning land in this way – with secure title, and the right to sell it on to whomever you wish – is essential for it to be used as collateral for loans. Without these features, no lender would accept land as security, as it could not be sold to repay the debt in the event of the lender having to foreclose on the borrower. Once owners had clear and transferable land titles, supported by detailed surveys, standardised measurements and recognised legal institutions, it opened the way to vastly expand the creation of bank and other forms of credit. This change in the social, political and legal treatment of land was therefore a critical factor in the birth of modern finance, and a vital condition for the economic transformation of the industrial revolution and capitalist production. To this day, in many countries including the UK, lending against landed property (particularly as mortgage lending to homeowners) is the largest source of credit and money creation (see Chapter 5).

The role of individual ownership of land as property in economic and social change can be seen throughout modern history. It enabled early industrialists to raise capital to fund investment in new machinery, and played a central role in the post-war restructuring of national economies in Germany, Japan and Korea, where land redistribution and the grant of title to those who worked it (mainly in an agricultural context) spread access to capital (both credit and the means of production) to a much larger proportion of society than had existed previously. This in turn enabled the emergence of dynamic, capitalist economies and the long boom of the post-war era (Linklater, 2013).

In the UK and much of the Western world, the mid-twentieth century rise of individual homeownership also spread landownership to large sections of the population, with broadly beneficial consequences for economic growth, resilience and equality (Saunders, 2016), at least up until the 1970s.

The power of private property has also led some economists to identify it as the key to tackling entrenched poverty in developing economies. Hernando de Soto (2000) argued that granting poor slum dwellers legal title to their informally held homes and business properties would enable a massive transfer of land from the pre-modern state of possession to full private property and trigger

broad-based economic growth as the newly entitled owners leveraged their property to fund business expansion.

More intangibly, the independence – from community as well
from rulers – that individual landownership brings has made it a
moral aspiration for some. In English folk tales, most obviously
those of Robin Hood, it is always the 'stout yeoman' that is the
hero – while peasants, monks and lords are portrayed as lacking
the virtues of honest work that independent, freeholding yeomen
exemplified. Thomas Jefferson famously associated small-scale
landownership with the rugged virtues of the independent home-
steader that he modelled his vision of the United States upon. In
the twentieth century, politicians from right and centre-left alike
have extolled the moral qualities of homeownership as a means of
promoting a 'property-owning democracy' (Torrance, 2010).

2.4 Landownership as theft: power and economic rent

The emergence of private landownership also shaped the evolving,
and often highly conflictual, political histories of modern societies.
There has always been an uneasy relationship between the economic
and political power that landownership brings. Controlling land
brings wealth, and therefore power; but this wealth also motivates
impecunious rulers to target landowners for taxation and expropriation. Because landed wealth is immobile, rooted in one place, and
inherently embedded in the socioeconomic structure, it is particularly vulnerable to expropriation; therefore landowners tend to seek
political power to protect their property.

Property owners have often sought to control or limit the power
of the Crown or state over them, by seeking to control the state
itself. Once they have achieved this, typically through the development of parliamentary systems designed to represent the interests
of property owners, these owners tended to use the law to privilege their wealth and expand their estates. They reduce the tax
burden on their property and exclude others from landownership,
economic freedom and political power.

In England this process can be seen in the political settlement
after the civil war, which constrained the power of the Crown and

made Parliament the guarantor of the rights of property holders and of the Crown's creditors (Kindleberger, 1993). In the US, a nation built on the promise of individual landownership, differing conceptions of property rights were central to the intense arguments over the creation of the constitution.

These early assertions of political power on behalf of (relatively small-scale) landowners now seem to be broadly progressive, as they restrained the arbitrary power of central authority and enshrined the rights and freedoms of individuals. Indeed, the emergence of the concept of human rights was intimately bound up in debates about the nature of, and limits to, property rights (Linklater, 2013).

But the changing political economy of land over the centuries is not a linear historical narrative. The power that individual property in land released initially served to open up political influence to new groups beyond the feudal aristocracy, but then that same force was used by the new landowners to monopolise power and close off access to landownership to others.

It is an irony of history that the creation of a market in property required a fairly radical redistribution of land from feudal lords, Crown and church and towards a broader-based gentry and mercantile class, but once created, the market reverted to concentrated landownership in the hands of small numbers of dynastic families. This tendency of property markets towards concentration, combined with the new landowners' grip on political power, led to the rise of the eighteenth century landed estates in England. In turn, this contributed to the stagnation of parliamentary democracy into corruption and clientelism, as landowners were able to control the electoral process in their areas (Pearce and Stearn, 2000). Like feudal lords before them, estate owners used their power over the legislative process to enclose common land, prevent the break-up of their estates and progressively weaken the state's ability to tax or control their landholdings.

In the case of eastern Europe, the landed interest's stronghold on power went as far as to create serfdom, under which peasants were legally barred from moving off their lord's estate or even marrying without their lord's permission. An extreme example can be seen in the case of Poland, where a vibrant proto-democracy initiated by the landowning nobility in 1505 regressed into serfdom as the landowners exploited their power over the Crown to entrench their privileges at the expense of those who worked the land. The economic and political dynamism that had characterised early-modern Poland was choked off, to the point where the state was almost bankrupt by the late seventeenth century, and largely unable to resist Ottoman expansion into eastern Europe (Linklater, 2013, p. 114).

These tensions were again most visible in the US, where the dependence of southern landowners on slavery brought the clash between competing definitions of property into sharp relief. In all three cases, the result of landowners' dominance of the levers of power was political and economic sclerosis, and ultimately conflict and decline.

In the current era a similar process can be witnessed in the disproportionate political power wielded by homeowners. At a local level, those who own homes are often motivated to resist the construction of new homes, which they fear may reduce the value of their assets, or change their neighbourhoods in ways they do not like. Localised planning decisions give them the political levers to prevent development, making NIMBYism (not-in-my-back-yard) a powerful force in the UK. This is despite the fact that, in aggregate, the failure to provide sufficient homes is a major drag on economic growth and a driver of growing inequality.

Again, this dynamic is rooted in the nature of land: homeowners who oppose development are by definition highly concentrated in a single place, and hence able to exert localised democratic power. Those excluded from ownership – or even from housing at all – and who might stand to benefit from the provision of new homes, have little or no effective representation in the democratic process.

At a national level the electoral dominance of homeowners (and those who identify with them) has led successive governments to prejudice the interests of owners above those of non-owners. In recent decades, tax policies, planning, public spending decisions and regulatory systems have all been skewed towards boosting and maintaining house prices, to preserve the asset wealth of existing homeowners (see Chapter 4). Despite the stated policy goal of extending the opportunities of homeownership to more people, when trade-offs between different interest groups have to be made, government policy has invariably entrenched the growing divide between those who own homes and those who do not (see Chapter 5), with the result that homeownership has been in absolute decline in the UK since 2003 (DCLG, 2016). Ultimately, in its policies towards land and property, the state has legitimised what would be described in economic terms as 'rent-seeking' behaviour.

2.5 Hypothesis: property is liberty, property is theft

It would seem that the transformation of land into private property brings both economic advantages and disadvantages. Thinkers have wrestled with this problem since the birth of political economy (the forerunner to economics) as a subject of study. It is not just that the individual ownership of land can be seen to have both beneficial and damaging consequences for economies and societies. It also poses fundamental philosophical problems about the nature of ownership itself.

Once land is owned privately, much of the additional value created by society is captured by landowners, even if they have done nothing to earn that value. Liberals like David Ricardo, John Stuart Mill and Henry George objected strongly to this ability of landowners to make unearned windfall gains at the expense of the rest of society, even though they firmly believed in the principle of private property. For them, the key was to solve the problem of economic rent precisely in order to prevent it from undermining the legitimacy of landed property itself.

Many early civilisations objected to private ownership of land, often basing their critique in religious concepts of the earth being entrusted to humanity in general by a divine creator (Pierson 2013; Linklater, 2013). Others, like Thomas Paine, were critical of private ownership from a secular conception of natural law. Under this view, the earth in the original state of society is seen as the common property of mankind, and each person should have an inalienable right to an equal share of this common inheritance. 'The earth, in its natural uncultivated state ... was the common property of the human race' and 'it is the value of the improvement only, and not the earth itself, that is individual property' (Paine, 1797, p. 8).

Whatever one thinks of these moral arguments, in economic terms it is undeniable that owning land is exclusionary: to become a landowner, one must exclude others from the use of that land (at least to some degree). This might be relatively unproblematic if land holdings are small, and if more entirely uninhabited land is up for grabs, but this almost never happens in reality. Much of the theorising on these points was done in the era of the colonisation of the United States, where 'free' land was indeed abundant – provided the claims of the native population were ignored, which they generally were. Any recognition of the rights of previous occupiers and users of land makes it almost impossible to articulate a sound moral basis on which someone can transfer land from a state of un-owned, collective possession to one of individual private property, especially as such exclusion has tended to require force – and even genocide.

Philosophers from John Locke (1690) to Robert Nozick (1974) have tried to develop moral justifications for property ownership from first principles, but none have really succeeded (Ramsay, 1997). It is hard to avoid the conclusion, most trenchantly made by the French thinker Pierre-Joseph Proudhon (1840), that property is theft. But Proudhon also agreed with US founding father Thomas Jefferson that property is liberty. Our hypothesis is that both these statements are broadly true, and that the tensions between them drive the constantly changing balance of economic and political power in modern societies.

Looking at the history, there seems to be a natural cyclical pattern. Up to a point, the rise of individual private property ownership (in land, homes and other buildings) can democratise economic power and enable economic development, boosting productivity and reducing wealth inequality (Saunders, 2016). But beyond a certain point, the entrenched power that landownership brings starts to work in the opposite direction, enabling landowners to monopolise the surplus generated from growth, and increasing inequality. Eventually, these processes stifle economic growth and undermine the political legitimacy of the private property system itself. As the number of those excluded rises towards a critical mass, political and economic crises threaten to destroy the social compact necessary for property ownership to exist.

Historically, such crises have taken the form of economic collapse and war, which in turn prompt a redistribution of property and a reformulation of the rules of property ownership, so that the cycle can begin again. Piketty sees the First and Second World Wars as just such a crisis: after a prolonged period of growing wealth concentration, the destruction of warfare obliterated much accumulated property wealth, and much of what was left was appropriated by states to fight the wars. This radical destruction and redistribution of property (and other) wealth reset the system, allowing a new phase of dynamic growth to begin.

In neoclassical economic theory, private property and homeownership has generally been thought of as beneficial. However, a number of empirical studies find a positive relationship between the growth of homeownership and increasing unemployment in a given area or country (Blanchflower and Oswald, 2013; Laamanen, 2013; Oswald, 1996). Oswald ([1999] 2009, pp. 47–49) argues that there are five explanations for this phenomenon: (1) homeowners are less mobile than renters and hence more vulnerable to economic downturns; (2) high ownership levels block unemployed people's and young people's ability to enter an area to find a job; (3) in an immobile economy, workers end up doing jobs for which they are not well suited, lowering overall productivity; (4) areas with high ownership levels may feature more restrictive planning legislation (more NIMBYism) that may put off entrepreneurs wishing to start new businesses; and (5) homeowners are likely to commute for longer distances, leading to transport congestion and higher costs across the economy.

While the rise in homeownership in advanced economies in the period from 1945 to the 1970s certainly coincided with important economic developments, since the 1970s, growth rates have fallen, inequality of wealth and income has risen and financial instability has increased, despite the continued increase in homeownership. It seems likely that the benefits of homeownership are not universal but rather contextually and historically specific. Beyond a certain point, it may be that increases in homeownership may not continue to support economic development.

However, studies of homeownership and labour markets also generally find that homeowners themselves do not see a worsening of their labour market position. Rather it is that increases in homeownership push up the costs of changing location *in aggregate* across the economy and make labour markets less fluid. There may thus be a 'fallacy of composition' problem, common in macroeconomic theory, which insists on micro-foundations: while for any particular individual, owning a home may not materially affect their economic prospects, or, with rising house prices, actually benefit them, in aggregate across the economy higher levels of homeownership can be associated with lower labour market flexibility and productivity. Of course, there are also many other reasons why individuals may rationally prefer homeownership at the expense of productivity – such as security, status and the ability to live rent-free in older age.

Exactly where the natural limit to the growth of private landed property might be remains impossible to say, not least because so many factors are in play. For example, the nature of the political and legal system will be a major determinant of how economic tensions play out. This book argues that it is the interaction between homeownership and other factors, such as the supply of land and the role of credit, that ultimately determines the impact on the economy – points further discussed in Chapters 4 and 5. But clearly no economy has ever achieved complete conversion to private property, as myriad other forms of collective and individual possession have continued to coexist in even the most property-orientated societies. It seems fair to assume that such limits do exist, even if they cannot be precisely defined.

This is not to assume that ownership must inevitably be absolute and individual, or that a dramatic cycle of growing wealth concentration and conflict is inevitable. As noted above, throughout history a wide range of tenure arrangements have come and gone, and it may well be that the particular form of private property that emerged in the sixteenth century will run its course, and be replaced by other forms.

For instance, it is perfectly possible for the freedoms of property ownership to be limited to a minimum needed to incentivise investment and enable the leveraging of finance. Nor do we mean to assume that the model of private property can easily be extended to places where it does not currently predominate. Evidence suggests that mass titling programmes are doomed to failure, as the success of private property relies on lots of other factors in the economy and society being in place – such as a well-established culture of entrepreneurialism, a financial sector prepared to lend to the new owners, and sufficient legal and political oversight to prevent those with insider power from exploiting the poor (Payne, 2004).

In this hypothesis, the current era can be seen as another such emerging crisis that began in the 1970s. Widening homeownership during the post-war growth phase increased the relative power of property owners, so Western governments increasingly prioritised their interests in tax, housing and planning policies. As the trajectory of post-war growth began to falter they sought to reignite the growth phase by liberalising credit markets and subsidising marginal homeownership at the expense of support for other tenures. Yet these attempts have at best only pushed the natural limits to property slightly further, and by doing so may have deepened the negative effects of private property in land, and increased the severity of the correction now required (see Chapter 4).

2.6 Responses to the ownership paradox

Throughout the history of modern economies, the rules governing landownership, inheritance and trading have been powerful determinants of economic and social structures. In other words, the rules of the game matter. And because these rules are inherently political, they themselves are subject to political pressures. In the complex political economy of land, there are many opportunities for political power to change the dynamics and influence the outcomes.

The state's objectives in regulating and intervening in the property market have varied widely over time, including (but not limited to) controlling territory, raising armies, securing the loyalty of particular social groups, raising money, improving agriculture, promoting commerce, improving public health, providing infrastructure and boosting homeownership.

Broadly, policy interventions in the land economy can be divided into two groups, depending on their primary purpose. There are those interventions deemed necessary to mitigate the imbalances created by property markets themselves and reduce the social harms created by the problem of economic rent – such as planning regulations on the development of land, or tax policies designed to tackle excessive rents. And then there are interventions into the land economy designed to achieve other goals entirely – such as land use laws to promote public health, or property taxes designed to raise revenue.

Of particular interest here are those interventions that seek to achieve both types of purpose, such as those designed not to abolish the creation of economic rents, but to capture them for the benefit of the public in general, as opposed to enriching individual landowners. Mechanisms for 'land value capture' therefore seek to socialise economic rent, often to pay for the infrastructure that generates much of the value of land. But there is always a tension inherent in these twin objectives: the more effectively such interventions reduce the prevalence of economic rent, the less revenue they raise. And to succeed in capturing significant benefit for the public, they must perpetuate the incidence of economic rent.

In practice, the tools for public intervention in the land economy vary widely, but the main policy levers come under seven categories.

State acquisition, ownership and distribution of land

While Crown lands were originally a source of royal wealth and hunting services, the most common purpose of permanent public landownership today is to prevent private property ownership from imposing excessive negative externalities on society. So the US National Parks Service owns some 340,000 square kilometres of land in order to protect it as national heritage, and local councils in England own over 1.6 million homes that are let out at submarket social rents. Direct public ownership of land can therefore dramatically reduce the problem of rent, provided of course that public landowners choose or are compelled not to extract maximum economic rents from their assets. In practice states and monarchs have often sought rents as vigorously as any private owner: few people would guess that Regent Street in the heart of London's West

End shopping district is owned by the Crown Estate, as it is run on entirely commercial lines.

Public authorities can also take temporary ownership of land for political purposes, or to deliver public goods. Medieval monarchs could seize the lands of traitors or those who died intestate and redistribute them to secure the loyalties of supporters. Modern laws enabling the compulsory purchase[2] of land enable public and private infrastructure and development projects to go ahead without being held to ransom by landowners unwilling to sell. This ability of the state to forcibly acquire land can also be used strategically to acquire large amounts of land for development and capture the uplift in value created by the state provision of infrastructure, as the example of the UK New Towns Programme shows (see Chapter 4).

The very existence of such powers can also change the incentives on landowners – for example, to encourage them to invest their land into publicly sanctioned development partnerships rather than face compulsory purchase.

Laws governing land tenure, trading and inheritance

As discussed above, much of the common and codified law of Europe, from ancient times to the present day, is devoted to governing the use, ownership and transfer of landed property. Most advanced economies today place few restrictions on who can own landed property – but most require the formal registration and recording of property title deeds and/or transactions. Official registration makes it much easier for property titles to be legally enforced, and hence to be treated as tradable economic assets. So standardised are these processes that there is little collective memory of the extensive restrictions that have existed on who could own what property – on grounds of class, race, religion and gender. For example, Jews were banned from owning land in most of medieval Europe, while married women in the UK did not secure the legal right to own property until 1870.

Nor is the extent to which tenure law has varied across time and different countries well recognised in economic studies, despite the

---

2 Known as 'eminent domain' in most US states and 'expropriation' in many other countries.

central importance of these institutions to economic history. For example, eighteenth century France's peasant agricultural economy was far more productive than Britain's, but generated far lower surpluses and a much weaker tax base, because the traditional feudal tenure model that survived there up until the revolution did not allow for land to be traded or used as collateral, or incentivise profit-seeking, in the way that Britain's private property system did (Linklater, 2013).

The huge variances in the housing systems of otherwise similar countries today can similarly be seen in differing tenure regulations: for example, in England the minimum length of a private tenancy is six months; in France it is three years; in Germany it is indefinite (Scanlon and Kochan, 2011).

Planning and other regulatory controls on land use and construction

Regulations on land usage date back at least to early modern times. Often they are driven by the desire to preserve land and buildings from unwanted development (such as conservation areas that protect historic neighbourhoods), or to achieve public health goals (such as Queen Elizabeth I's ban on building within three miles of London, to limit the spread of plague). These systems vary widely between different countries, but all developed economies now impose some form of legal restriction on the development and use of land (Bramley, 2003).

Planning regulations also have a major impact on the pricing of land and the returns achieved by different types of land use (Cheshire and Sheppard, 2004). In modern economies, especially in urban environments, the value of a piece of land depends almost entirely on what can legally be built on it. For example, during the height of the Japanese property bubble in the late 1980s, the site of the Imperial Palace in Tokyo was said to be worth more than California – if it had been permissible to build offices on it (The Economist, 2007). As palace gardens its value was far lower.

This feature of planning regulations allows them to indirectly address the problem of rent: requiring or banning specific uses of land planning allows the law to limit landowners' ability to externalise costs and internalise benefits. For example, in the UK, local authorities can require the provision of affordable housing within developments by private developers, as the price of securing planning permission. This reduces the ability of landowners to extract rents resulting from the scarcity of affordable homes by capturing a share of land value for public goods, and also lowers the market value of land.

Subsidies to support certain types of land use or certain groups

Most advanced economies have a long history of protecting domestic agriculture and industry with tariffs and subsidies, typically in order to protect the interests of agricultural landowners (Chang, 2007). Throughout the sixteenth to eighteenth centuries the government acted to protect its farmers and merchants through trade barriers and subsidies in order to maximise exports and minimise imports. This mercantilist approach to the economy was dominant until the repeal of the Corn Laws in 1846 (see Chapter 4).

In recent times, agricultural subsidies in Europe have been controlled by the European Union's Common Agricultural Policy (CAP). The CAP is an EU-wide system of payments to farmers and land managers aimed at supporting European agriculture. Introduced in 1962 it is by far the EU's single largest common policy, today accounting for over 40% of the entire EU budget. Substantial reforms over the years have moved the CAP away from a production-oriented policy towards the current single farm payment system which is based on size of holding. This has led to criticisms that the CAP is structurally regressive, with critics pointing to numerous high-profile cases of notoriously wealthy individuals receiving millions of pounds in annual subsidies.[3] Others have argued that the CAP system causes oversupply, artificially high food prices and stalled development in poorer countries (Matthews, 2011).

---

3 Prominent examples include the Queen, the Duke of Westminster and Prince Bandar of Saudi Arabia, all of whom received between £250,000 and £750,000 of CAP subsidies each in 2011.

Since the end of the First World War successive governments have accepted that some form of public subsidy is necessary to ensure people on low incomes can afford adequate housing. For much of the past century this primarily took the form of capital grants which subsidised the construction of affordable homes. Over the last thirty years or so, however, supply-side capital subsidies have been steadily replaced in favour of demand-side subsidies which aim to increase households' incomes to enable them to access accommodation (see Chapter 4).

Microeconomic arguments were deployed to support this shift: recipients of cash subsidies are able to exercise more choice, and it is easier to avoid dead-weight losses with cash transfers that can be carefully targeted and adjusted as the recipients' circumstances change. But cash subsidies that enable non-owners to subsist in an ownership economy clearly cannot deal with the problem of economic rent – indeed, they may exacerbate it by providing additional cash income to be paid to landowners, as evidenced by the spectacular growth in the UK housing benefit bill since the 1980s (Webb, 2012).

Taxation of property ownership, occupation and transfer

The immobile and productive nature of land has long made it a natural site of taxation, and for centuries differing types of land tax were a primary source of public revenues. As well as raising revenue in cash or in kind, land taxes can also be used to reduce the incidence of economic rent, making them a favoured policy solution of political economists from Adam Smith onwards (see Chapter 3). In the modern era, as the economic importance of land shifted from the production of food and other consumption goods, so the importance of land taxes for state revenue has declined, and has only partially been replaced by taxes on property such as business rates and housing transaction taxes (see Chapter 3).

Ongoing taxes on the value of land – such as the land value tax advocated by Henry George ([1879] 1979) – remain many economists' preferred mechanism for reducing economic rents (see Chapter 7). Land value tax clearly has many theoretical advantages, in that it reduces rather than increases distortions on investment decisions, lowers property prices by reducing speculative pressures on them, and forces the owners of landed property to make rational decisions about the amount of property that they wish to hold based on the ongoing costs. In practice few modern states have successfully levied such taxes, mainly because the political barriers to introducing them are considerable (Brooks, 2005). This may be particularly true now that owner-occupied housing is the primary site of land values, because these homes do not readily generate cash flows, despite the huge economic value that owning them brings. Exemptions for homes, or allowing homeowners to defer payment until sale, may reduce the political difficulties of land taxes.

Governments have therefore generally found it easier to levy taxes on property transactions and development. Economists tend to reject transaction taxes as they distort incentives to trade, and so worsen the already poor allocative efficiency of land. Tax authorities tend to like them, as they raise large sums relatively easily. Development taxes are more theoretically robust, especially when combined with strong land use planning policies, as they allow the state to capture a proportion of the land value increase generated by the state's grant of planning permission (sometimes called 'betterment').

However, these taxes suffer from practical drawbacks that have limited their efficacy at reducing economic rent. Firstly, although theoretically the burden of taxation ought to fall on landowners rather than developers, in order to buy land from its owners, developers must compete with each other on price, and so have a limited ability to pass this cost on. Development taxes are also politically vulnerable, as both developers and landowners tend to resist them strongly – to the extent of delaying development and waiting for the repeal of the tax (Ambrose, [1986] 2014).

2.7 Conclusion

The use and ownership of land has been at the heart of economic history – if not economic theory – because land is uniquely vital to all economic activity. Special features of land make it highly effective as a store of value and as collateral for finance, but also generate economic and social problems, especially the problem of economic rent. Legal frameworks are essential both to enable land to fulfil its beneficial economic roles, and to mitigate its negative impacts, making the regulations around landownership critical to determining the economic structure of modern societies.

Inevitably, these rules are contested and deeply political. They are also highly complex and vary widely across different jurisdictions and time periods. In the current era, the primary economic role of land is as housing – which is largely, but by no means entirely, held by individual owner-occupiers.

In modern economies, the predominant rules of landownership treat land as private property, although this concept has by no means completely replaced older and more complex forms of property and land use rights. The evolution of private property in land has been at the heart of the development of modern capitalism, and the concomitant development of liberal theories of individual and human rights. Yet despite this central importance in economic history, the role of land has been largely erased from economic theory. The reasons for this are explored in the next chapter.

CHAPTER 3

· ·

The missing factor:
land in production
and distribution

A captious economist planned
to live without access to land.
He nearly succeeded,
but found that he needed
food, water, and somewhere to stand.

LIMERICK, SOURCE UNKNOWN, QUOTED IN GAFFNEY (1994A, P. 96)

As soon as the land of any country has all become
private property, the landlords, like all other men,
love to reap where they never sowed, and demand
a rent even for its natural produce.

ADAM SMITH (1776, P. 56)

3.1 Introduction

Economics can be understood as the study of the production, distribution and consumption of goods and services. Production itself is the process of combining various physical and non-physical inputs in order to create something that can be consumed and has societal value (the output). Physical inputs include materials, for example wood and iron, while non-physical inputs include knowledge and skills. Economists use the term 'factors of production' to describe these inputs.

The three most recognised factors of production are capital, labour and land. 'Capital', although the subject of considerable controversy in economic theory,[1] generally refers to any humanly produced thing that can enhance a person's power to perform productive work and increase the efficiency of the production process, such as machinery, plant or information and communication technologies. 'Labour' refers to effort undertaken in conjunction with the ability and knowledge to do work. Finally, 'land' refers not only to physical sites or locations where production takes place but also to other inputs provided by nature (minerals, water, fish in the ocean, the frequency spectrum, etc.).

It should already be clear from this description that land is an important factor of production. As the limerick suggests, production cannot take place in a vacuum – the process must happen somewhere at some point in time. The earliest known school of economists, the French *Physiocrats*,[2] had as their defining belief the idea that all wealth derived from land and nature. A harmonious society would be one where the state should not interfere with the operation of 'natural' economic laws but rather complement such laws. They studied and lived in predominantly agrarian societies and attacked the other main school of economic thought, *mercantilism*, for its focus on trade and exchange, instead arguing that the source of true value and profit lay in the agricultural surplus. Seeing land as the source of all surplus, they proposed that the French government should obtain all of its revenue by taxing land, rather than by taxing trade and industry, which shrank when taxed. The classical political economists that shaped the birth of modern economics gave more weight to labour and capital but equally considered land to be the most appropriate source of taxation.

---

1 The definition of capital has been argued over for many years by economists, with different schools offering different definitions. In conventional (neoclassical) economics 'capital' is often used to refer to money or a financial instrument as well as to capital goods but this view has been challenged for being logically inconsistent – see, for example, Cohen and Harcourt (2003) and, more recently in relation discussion of Thomas Piketty's work Lavoie and Seccareccia (2016). In this book, we will focus primarily on the relationship between land and capital, itself the subject of controversy.

2 The seminal physiocratic work was François Quesnay's *Tableux Economique* (1972).

3.2 Classical political economy: land and economic rent

All of the classical economists, including Marx, Smith, David Ricardo and John Stuart Mill, viewed land as a vital factor of production. But it was recognised that land had special qualities that distinguished it from capital and labour, in particular that it was in fixed supply and had no cost of production. All else being equal, this means any increase in the demand for land will only be reflected in an increase in its price not its quantity. Whoever owns the land upon which this increased demand is placed is in a unique position economically: they possess a good that is not subject to the normal laws of market competition. The ownership of such a resource allows the owner to benefit from additional unearned income, what the classical economists called 'economic rent'.

'Rent' in common parlance refers to a payment made by one party to another for the temporary use of something – for example, a flat, a car or a machine tool. In economics, however, rent (or 'economic rent') has a related but different meaning. It generally refers to any benefit that is derived from exclusive possession of a scarce or exclusive factor of production, in excess of the cost of bringing that factor into production. Those that earn such rents are often referred to as 'rentiers' (from the French) or the 'rentier class'. Economic rent should not be confused with normal profit or producer surplus, both of which involve productive human action.

David Ricardo was the first economist to bring the concept of rent in to wider usage in the context of land and location. Ricardo (1817, ch. 2) argues that the 'rent' of a site of land is equal to the economic advantage obtained by using this site relative to the advantage obtained by using the best unused (i.e. rent-free) land for the same purpose, assuming the same inputs of labour and capital. So a field with a proper irrigation system and proximity to a main road could attract a higher rent than one without. Ricardo argued that a labourer's bargaining power would never dip below this rate; a labourer would never agree to be paid less since they could create the same output on the rent-free land for that additional amount. Thus wages were related to the productive capacity of marginal land, and not the productivity of labour. Ricardo's 'law of rent' challenged established theories of wages that existed at the time, in particular the belief that as the population of a country increased, wages would inevitably fall to just above that which was required for sustenance. This was the 'iron law of wages' associated with Thomas Malthus (1872).[3]

One important aspect of Ricardo's argument is that the land-owner is not free to choose the economic rent they charge for the use of their land. This rent will change over time as land is developed around any particular plot, out of the control of any individual landlord. But equally, economic rent is not related to the investment the landowner has put into the land. In other words, rent is determined by *collective* rather than individual investment and activity. As Adam Smith noted in *The Wealth of Nations* (1776, p. 162):

> The rent of land, therefore, considered as the price paid for the use of the land, is naturally a monopoly price. It is not at all proportioned to what the landlord may have laid out upon the improvement of the land, or to what he can afford to take; but to what the farmer can afford to give.

Economic rent in an urban context: locational value

Ricardo and Smith were mainly writing about an agrarian economy. But the law of rent applies equally in developed urban areas dominated by industrial and service sector activity. Over time, if an economy develops and its population expands, the un-owned land available for improvement will become scarcer and eventually there will be no 'rent-free' land left. The rent then becomes determined by *locational* value.

In his classic text *Progress and Poverty* ([1879] 1979, pp. 95–101), land reformer Henry George describes an 'unbounded savannah' with a single settler, who, though blessed with all the gifts of nature and an abundance of free land, is actually materially poor for there is little he can do on his own to raise himself beyond subsistence. Over time, as more settlers arrive, the settlement develops around

---

3 Malthus was a contemporary of Ricardo with whom he engaged in long debates (see e.g. Ricardo, 1973, vol. II).

the original settler and the collective efforts of the increasing population enable economic growth. The original plot of land the settler
claimed becomes extremely valuable, for it lies at the centre of what
is now a city:

> Our first settler's land being the center of the population, the
> store, the blacksmith's forge, the wheelwright's shop, are set upon
> it, or on its margin, where soon arises a village, which rapidly
> grows in to a town, the center of exchanges for the people of the
> whole district. With no greater agricultural productiveness than
> it had at first, this land now begins to develop a productiveness
> of a higher kind. To labour expended in raising corn, or wheat,
> or potatoes, it will yield no more of those things than at first.
> But to labour expended in the subdivided branches of produc-
> tion that require proximity to other producers and especially to
> labour expended in that final part of production which consists
> in distribution, will yield much larger returns ... The productive
> powers that density of population has attached to this land are
> equivalent to the multiplication of its original fertility by the
> hundred fold and the thousand fold. And rent, which measures
> the difference between this added productiveness and that of
> the least productive land in use, has increased accordingly. Our
> settler, or whoever has succeeded his right to the land, is now
> a millionaire. Like another Rip Van Winkle, he may have lain
> down and slept; still he is rich – not from anything he has done,
> but from the increase of population.

George was writing at the end of the nineteenth century. But the
same dynamics apply in our modern, information and communication dominated economies. Take a digital media agency, for
example. Despite the fact that they do not create any physical
output, locating in the middle of a city gives them access to better
transport links, means they are closer to some of their key clients
and complementary firms (for example digital design or IT service
firms) and makes them a more attractive place to work for talented
staff. There are well-known 'agglomeration' efficiencies and
network effects from city centre locations and clustering of similar

types of company in the same areas (Feldman and Florida, 1994; Porter and Clark, 2000).

The difference in the rent such companies will be prepared to pay between the city centre location and a location on the outskirts of the city reflects the fact that they will have to invest more time and money in travel, maintaining relations with clients and firms or salaries for high calibre staff. It is this difference that is the economic rent the landowner of that central plot of land – let us call her Mrs Briggs – is able to charge.

Economic rent does not stand still. In our example, Mrs Briggs might have purchased her plot ten years ago, when the city was smaller and the city centre less desirable. During that ten-year period, Mrs Briggs may have invested a small sum of money in the upkeep of the physical building that lay on top of her plot of land, perhaps having the roof repaired or the windows double glazed. But considerably more investment might have gone into the surrounding area as a result of other private and public investment. The regional government might have built a new train line with a station near to her plot. Entrepreneurs might have opened attractive organic cafés, town councils improved drainage and invested in local schools, developers built desirable flats or family homes. All of this investment will increase the value of Mrs Brigg's plot of land relative to all other areas of the city and indeed any region which has received less investment.

This increase in land value can and most likely will be realised by Mrs Briggs via the charging of a higher rent for the use of the property on that land (some of which may be taxed by the state, of which more in section 3.3). The return to Mrs Briggs over and above that need to keep her property in a state of good repair is economic rent. It is an unearned, or windfall income; it in no way reflects any investment of her time or labour or productive investment. It was simply her luck to have bought a plot in an area that received a lot of investment.[4]

---

4 Of course land prices can also fall as economies deteriorate and indeed when an economic shock hits land prices can fall more rapidly than economic growth – further explored in Chapter 5.

All of the above applies equally to land that is used for domestic residence. There will always be greater demand for attractive, well-connected city centre locations for residents. The land values underneath such properties will rise at a rate that bears no relation to the investment in the physical property made by the landlord. And as demand for that location rises, so the economic rent the landlord can charge for residential occupancy will rise. There is no reason the increase in the value of land should be aligned with the growth of median wages – we can see that much from cities like London, New York or Tokyo.

For Ricardo and other classical political economists, excessive economic rent derived from landownership was viewed as leading to dangerous levels of inequality and to distortionary effects on economic growth. Ricardo warned that rising land rents would allow Britain's landowners to monopolise the gains from economic growth. To prevent this, he argued that Britain should end its agricultural tariffs which protected the high prices landowners could charge for their products and import cheaper crops from abroad. Prime Minister Robert Peel eventually followed Ricardo's advice when he repealed the infamous Corn Laws in 1846 (Hudson, 2008, p. 2) – we develop this story further in Chapter 4.

Others argued that economic rent should be tackled at source. Since the main source of rent was land, the privatisation of property constituted a form of arbitrary enrichment at the expense of wider society. Nineteenth century socialists such Ferdinand Lassalle and Pierre-Jean Proudhon argued that private property should be abolished and that 'property is theft' (Proudhon, 2005, p. 55). They argued that property should only exist when it was being actively occupied and used. This contrasted with later socialists who, following Marx and Lenin, argued for the state nationalisation and collectivisation of land.

The key point is that there was broad agreement among all these nineteenth century thinkers on the principle that economic rent should not accrue to private individuals; the disagreements were on the appropriate solution.

Box 3.1 Other forms of economic rent

In this book we focus mainly on landownership as a form of economic rent. But economic rent equally applies to other factors of production that are provided by nature. For example, energy companies that are given an exclusive licence to extract oil in a defined area are able to extract economic rent equivalent to the difference between what they charge for oil and the nearest alternative source of licensed oil production (which could potentially be many hundreds of miles away). Or, if oil companies organise themselves into a cartel, as with OPEC (Organization of the Petroleum Exporting Countries), their rent will be determined by alternative sources of energy (the US discovery of fracking appears to have forced OPEC to reduce oil prices). Because oil and other natural resources (including land) are naturally fixed or scarce, economic rent will inevitably emerge – supply cannot meet demand and the price difference that is realised fills the gap.

Patents also provide access to economic rents since they provide individuals or organisations with a monopoly over the production of goods or services: for example a type of pharmaceutical drug that others could produce but are not legally permitted to. Patents can be seen to make goods artificially scarce. The justification for creating patents is to drive entrepreneurial behaviour and innovation – entrepreneurs will be less willing to invest or take risks if their successful inventions can be copied as this will significantly reduce their profits. Economic rent can also take the form of licensing fees for the provision of a TV, radio or broadband spectrum.

Economic rent is also a feature of the financial sector. Banks are underwritten by the state – via deposit insurance – which gives their credit IOU's (bank loans) the equivalent status to money issued by governments or central banks (Ryan-Collins et al., 2012, pp. 75–77). Profits banks generate from the charging of interest on their loans or other financial activities is often considered to be economic rent, particularly where the loan itself does not contribute to economic growth (for example a loan to a financial corporation to make a bet on a currency or buy existing financial assets). We discuss this further in Chapter 5.

3.3 Land tax or separation as a solution to the problem of economic rent

The British classical political economists' strongly held belief in private property as a formative institution in a liberal society led them towards taxation as the most appropriate solution.[5] This for them resolved the inherent tension between private property and social justice. Indeed Adam Smith, John Stuart Mill and later Henry George argued that economic rent should form the basis of the national tax base, rather than taxing labour or capital, both of which contributed to economic growth. Mill (1884, pp. 629–630) put it as follows:

> Suppose that there is a kind of income which constantly tends to increase, without any exertion or sacrifice on the part of the owners: those owners constituting a class in the community, whom the natural course of things progressively enriches, consistently with complete passiveness on their own part. In such a case it would be no violation of the principles on which private property is grounded, if the state should appropriate this increase of wealth, or part of it, as it arises. This would not properly be taking anything from anybody; it would merely be applying an accession of wealth, created by circumstances, to the benefit of society, instead of allowing it to become an unearned appendage to the riches of a particular class.

The idea was that taxing economic rent should actually increase growth since it would increase the incentives for capitalists and landowners to invest in and generate profit from capital and labour rather than non-productive land. To take our example of Mrs Brigg's plot of land, if the majority of economic rent that she could generate on that land was taxed away via an annual land value tax, she would have more incentive to, for example, build an extension or improve the appearance of her building so she could charge more

---

5 The classical economists were building on a long tradition: ancient civilisations taxed land and property for thousands of years before consumption, income or corporation taxes were invented (Blöchliger, 2015, p. 6).

contract rent. Indeed, she might eventually decide to sell up the land completely if her future streams of economic rent were to be taxed away, allowing the land to be used for potentially more productive or socially useful activity.

Henry George's *Progress and Poverty*, first published in 1879, was the most significant publication on the topic of land and tax. George's central question in the book is how it is possible for society to make such huge leaps of progress through technological and social advances – including education and social services – yet still be dogged by poverty, inequality and unemployment and damaging economic cycles. His explanation, following Ricardo, is that such advances, while benefiting mankind, also increase the value of land and thus the amount of economic rent that can be demanded by the owners of land from those who need to use it.

The natural tendency of the price of land and the rent charged for its use to increase faster than wealth can be produced to pay for it, George argued, has the result of lowering the proportion of growth remaining for wages and investment. Thus the landowner monopolises the proceeds of growth. Eventually, a tipping point is reached, leading to the collapse of enterprises at the margin that can no longer afford to pay their staff and this may lead to a more widespread economic downturn with rising unemployment, banking crises and foreclosures. This natural tendency of economic rent to crowd out productive investment is, according to some, the true cause of the businesses cycles that plague advanced economies (Anderson, 2009; George, [1879] 1979, pp. 102–110).[6]

The solution, for George, was a comprehensive 'single tax', a land value tax (LVT), levied annually on the value of land held as private property. It would be high enough to end other taxes, especially upon labour and production, and would finance beneficial public investment in transport and provide improved social

---

6 Rent extraction may also overshoot and capture even more than the true change in land values because of information asymmetries and price stickiness. For example, there is evidence that landlords do not lower rents when economic growth declines or when their costs fall (for example with interest rate cuts that reduce their mortgage payments). However, when their costs increase (e.g. tax changes) they insist they have to pass on the cost to tenants.

services, including a basic income for every citizen as a form of comprehensive welfare provision (see for example Van Parijs, 1992; Reed, 2016). George argued that LVT would give landowners an incentive to use desirably located land more efficiently, increasing the demand for labour and creating wealth. This would lead to higher wages and ensure the end of poverty.

Box 3.2 The secret origins of the Monopoly board game

Monopoly is one the world's most famous board games and also a great tool for helping children understand the nature of capitalist economies and the dangers of concentrated wealth. As all players will know, the game involves players competing for limited properties or utilities and ends with one monopolist controlling the properties and utilities on the board, having expropriated all the other players' money holdings through the charging of rent.

But the origins of the game lie with the American anti-monopolist Elizabeth J. Magie Phillips, who created 'The Landord's Game' in 1904 as a means of explaining Henry George's single tax theory to the public. The game operated along similar lines to its successor, Monopoly, but had an alternative set of rules that allowed players to cooperate with each other and pay rent into a common pot rather than to individual landowners, therefore securing prosperity for all players. The game spread around America and adopted various forms and names. Eventually Charles Darrow (the 'official' inventor of the game) patented his version in 1932 and sold the rights to game maker Parker Brothers, making millions.[7]

Progress and Poverty was hugely influential at the time, selling several million copies and exceeding sales of all other books except the Bible during the 1890s. It was translated into thirteen different languages and gave birth to a major social reform movement – the 'Single-taxers' – who advocated a shift to George's land value tax.[8]

---

7 See Orbanes (2007) for a detailed historical account of the game.
8 See Gaffney (1994, pp. 35–39) for a description of the legacy of Henry George.

Yet while the idea of a single tax was hugely popular, it was never implemented, although in the UK Lloyd George came close.[9] We examine the reasons in section 3.6. There are, however, some successful examples of property and land taxes being implemented, as we shall discuss in Chapter 7.

What is more surprising and more important for this book is why the economics profession did not embrace George's and the classical political economists' arguments for a land tax as the most efficient basis for reducing rent-seeking behaviour. It is to this question that we now turn for the remainder of this chapter.

3.4 Neoclassical economics and the conflation of land with capital

We explained in section 3.1 how the classical political economists saw a clear difference between land, capital and labour as factors in the production process. Land was recognised as a vital constituent but one quite separate from 'capital'. However, neoclassical economics, which now dominates the teaching of economics and informs government policy, conflated the concept of land and capital. Or, to put it another way, the neoclassical notion of 'capital', in contrast to the classical political economists, incorporated land.

The reasons for this departure appear to lie in the desire of a group of scholars at the turn of the nineteenth century to identify universal or 'natural' rules that could be applied to economics as a discipline, thereby enhancing its status as an objective 'science' (Gaffney, 1994b).[10] This contrasted with the normative frameworks used by the classical political economists, which argued that economic outcomes were the result of political as well as natural market dynamics. John Bates Clark was one of the leading economists of the time and is generally recognised as the founder of

9 Lloyd George's 'People's Budget' of 1909 proposed to introduce a 20% land tax (see Chapter 4, section 4.3).

10 For a detailed account of the development of neoclassical economics' concept of capital from a pro-Georgist perspective, see Gaffney (1994b). For a more general but critical account of the development of neoclassical economic theory in the US, see Tobin (1985).

neoclassical capital theory. Clark (1891b, pp. 144–145) argued that Ricardo's law of economic rent generated from the marginal productivity of land (section 3.2) equally applied to capital when conceptualising the economy at a static point in time:

> For a study of the static income of society we must take the invested wealth existing at a single instant of time, as a fixed amount expressible in dollars. We must conceive of it as business men conceive of it, abstractly, as a sum or fund of value in productive uses, without regard to the concrete things in which the fund is invested. Buildings, tools, materials, land, etc., embody the capital of which we speak; but for the time being we disregard the nature of these concrete things, and treat the capital as a business man does when he puts it on his inventory as a certain number of dollars. It is a quantum of productive wealth ... The earnings of these funds constitute in each case a differential gain like the product of land ... Let the working force of the isolated community be constantly equal to that of a hundred average men, and let capital be introduced unit after unit. We might, in imagination, strand the men on a bare rock in the sea and give to them first a little loam, a seed or two and a pool of water, and then more loam and a series of working instruments. For the present, however, we need to forget the particular forms of the invested fund, and to remember only the fact that, as the fund increases in amount, it adapts itself in quality to the needs of those who are to use it. Give to the men, then, one unit of capital, and it will be marvellously productive. Give them two, and the product per unit will be less. Give them a hundred units, and the last one will earn normal interest without a surplus.

Clark then takes this argument a step further and suggests that marginal productivity theory applies equally to labour. Given a fixed stock of capital (including land), each additional worker will contribute marginally less profit. A firm will maximise profit at the point where the marginal cost of an additional worker is equal to the marginal revenue they obtain. Clark develops the notion of a 'fund' of 'pure capital' that is homogeneous across land, labour and capital goods (1891b, p. 145). 'Pure capital' can move between capital goods or from capital to land by 'transmigration' and 'transmutation' (Clark, 1890, quoted in Gaffney 1994b, p. 53).

Despite the slightly mysterious qualities of Clark's notion of 'pure' capital, early twentieth century English and American economists adopted and developed it as integral to a comprehensive theory of distribution of income and economic growth. The famous English economist Philip Wicksteed (1914, pp. 6–7), for example, here makes a clear statement that any factor of production, including land, is, in the long run, interchangeable with any other:

> Land, manifold apparatus, various specialised faculties of the hand, eye, and brain, are essential, let us say, to the production of some commodity valued by someone ... for some purpose ... None of these heterogeneous factors can be dispensed with, and therefore the product in its totality is dependent upon the co-operation of each one severally. But there is room for wide variety in the proportions in which they are combined, and whatever the existing proportion may be each factor has a differential significance, and all these differential significances can be expressed in a common unit; that is to say, all can be expressed in terms of each other, by noting the increment or decrement of any one that would be the equivalent of a given decrement or increment of any other; equivalence being measured by the neutralising of the effect upon the product, or rather, not upon the material product itself, but the command of generalised resources in the circle of exchange for the sake of which it is produced.

Clark's work had a huge influence on twentieth century economics. Despite the strong emphasis placed on land and its distinctive qualities by the classical economists, macroeconomics largely abandoned land as a separate topic for analysis. Clark's model of aggregate production become the basis for the seminal neoclassical 'two-factor' growth models in the 1930s (Harrod, 1939), and 1950s and 1960s (Solow, 1956). These adapted Clark's static model and generalised it into dynamic steady state growth models (see Tobin, 1985, p. 31). The standard aggregate 'production function' is made up simply of capital and labour with one substitutable for the other; land is absent.

Land still features in microeconomic theory but as a factor of production with the same essential properties as capital or labour. Pick up any microeconomics textbook and you will find a series of graphs showing supply curves intersected by downward sloping demand curves for an individual firm, representing the different factors of production: labour, land and capital. There will be little or no difference between the graphs for the different factors – each factor is subject to the same rule of diminishing returns and marginal revenues that fall as more output is produced.[11] Holding other factors equal, as Clark suggests above, an additional unit of capital, land or labour will provide proportionately less profit. In each case, profit maximisation will occur where the marginal cost of the factor equals its marginal return (or 'marginal revenue product', to use the economics jargon) (Sloman and Wride, 2009, pp. 258–289). Wages and prices will be determined by these dynamics in perfectly competitive markets.

3.5 Problems with the neoclassical account: fundamental differences between land and capital

The theory of marginal productivity briefly outlined above has been subject to criticism over many decades.[12] However, the bulk of this criticism has been on challenging the idea that both labour and

---

11 See, for example, the well-established undergraduate textbook *Economics* by Sloman and Wride (2009, pp. 258–259). The authors dedicate four pages to a discussion of the role of land in the economy out of a total of 793 under the microeconomic theory section of the book (Chapter 9: 'The theory of distribution of income'). On page 58 they discuss the 'non-human factors of production' – i.e land and capital – and present two graphs showing the 'profit maximizing employment of a factor', arguing that the same equation, '*marginal cost = marginal revenue of product*', applies whether the factor is land, capital or labour.

12 Most famously in the twenty-year 'Cambridge controversy' between academics at the British university and Cambridge, Massachusetts, home of the Massachusetts institute of Technology (MIT) in the 1950s and 1960s. See Cohen and Harcourt (2003) for a discussion.

capital should be theorised as being subject to the same dynamics, in particular the idea that market prices generate the distribution of income between the two factors as opposed to the distribution of income determining prices (Cohen and Harcourt, 2003; Keen, 2011, pp. 142–157). Much less attention has been paid to the role of land and whether it makes sense to merge land into the concept of capital.

At first glance, neoclassical economics' conflation of land and capital does seem to follow a certain logic. It is clear that both can be thought of as commodities: both can be bought and sold in a mature capitalist market. A firm can have a portfolio of assets that includes land (or property) and shares in a company (the equivalent of owning capital 'stock') and swap one for another using established market prices. Both land and capital goods can also be seen as store of value (consider the phrase 'safe as houses') and to some extent a source of liquidity. Although land itself is clearly not as liquid as shares in a company, land has always been a preferred source of collateral for bank credit and in recent decades mortgage-backed securities have become an important financial instrument (we develop this argument in Chapter 5).

In reality, however, land and capital are fundamentally distinctive phenomena and to conflate them is to undermine the usefulness of both concepts in understanding the process of production and distribution.[13]

Land is permanent, capital is temporary

Firstly, land is permanent, cannot be produced or reproduced, cannot be 'used up' and does not depreciate. As discussed in Chapter 1, land in an economic sense is physical space: the soil on top of it may erode or deteriorate but the land beneath it remains. None of these features apply to capital. Capital goods are produced by humans, they depreciate over time due to physical wear and tear and innovations in technology (think of computers or mobile phones) and they can be replicated. In any set of national accounts, you will find a

---

13 The below account draws heavily on an excellent paper by Mason Gaffney: 'Land as a Distinctive Factor of Production' (1994a).

sizeable negative number detailing physical capital stock 'deprecia-tion': *net* not *gross* capital investment is the preferred variable used in calculating a nation's output. When it comes to land, net and gross values are equal.

Much of economic theory, in particular microeconomics, neglects the different effects of *time* on land and capital by compressing time into two types: the short run and the long run (Keen, 2011, pp. 175–202). In the short run it is generally assumed that some factors may be fixed – for example, you cannot immediately build a new factory or develop a new product to respond to new demands or changes in technology – and others variable. However, in the 'long run' it is assumed there are no fixed factors of production. Instead all factors, including land, are equally variable and thus there are no constraints on changes to the output level via alterations to the capital stock or entering or leaving an industry. In the long run, firms – the main object of analysis for microeconomics – plan ahead and reach minimum long-run average costs which in equilibrium will be equal to long-run marginal costs. The permanently fixed nature of land and the fact that it cannot be converted into capital or labour are ignored in the long run (Gaffney, 1994a, p. 58).

The argument is that by removing the complexities of dynamics, the true or pure functioning of the economy will be more clearly revealed. Microeconomic theory generally deals with relations of coexistence or 'comparative statics' (how are labour and capital combined in a single point in time to create outputs) rather than dynamic relations. This has led to a neglect of the continued creation and destruction of capital and the continued existence and non-de-preciation of land.

Indeed, although land values change with – or some would say drive – economic cycles (see Chapter 5), in the long run land value usually *appreciates* rather than depreciates as capital does. This is inevitable when you think about it; as the population grows, the economy develops and the capital stock increases, land remains fixed. The result is that land values (ground rents) must rise.

Indeed, there is good argument that as economies mature the demand for land relative to other consumer goods increases. Land can be viewed as a 'positional good' (Hirsch, 2005), the desire for which is related to one's position in society vis-à-vis others and thus not subject to diminishing marginal returns (Veblen, 1899). As technological developments drive down the costs of other goods, so competition over the most prized land rises and eats up an increasing share of people's income (Stiglitz, 2015a; Turner, 2015a, pp. 176–178).

Similarly, the land element of residential real estate increases in value much faster than the physical building stock (Knoll et al., 2014). Relatedly, household demand for space is highly elastic, unlike many other consumption goods. As an illustration, how many people would feel that they were overconsuming grossly if you increased the size of their home by 50%? This suggests that quantity of supply alone can never account for prices – or provide a viable solution.

Human beings cannot create land or the atmosphere or sunlight or water, we can only acquire the rights to use it or (temporarily) improve or worsen its condition. Land, unlike capital, can be used for different purposes over time, ranging from waste disposal to high-rise commercial property to railway tracks. Land thus has an *opportunity cost* attached to it: it can at any time be used for multiple different purposes. If cities expand and occupy land with houses and factories, this leaves less land for other uses, such as food production or the preservation of wildlife or space for leisure activity.[14]

While land might be seen as a store of value for the individual, its aggregate capacity to operate as a store of value cannot be augmented by individual action – the individual consumer can only tap this store by selling their land to another. In contrast, an individual or firm can increase their individual capital and aggregate capital by saving or investing or innovating, without reducing the capital of anyone else. Physical capital in most cases has only one use – other than being used for scrap when it becomes obsolete.

In summary, capital requires both space and time to exist; land *is* space and is time*less*.

---

14 Although it is possible to have multiple uses for land – for example an area of wetlands might serve as a wildlife sanctuary, a site of leisure and a flood defence.

Land is immobile, capital can move and change

Secondly, land is immobile. Capital, in contrast, 'turns over', changing form and location as capital depreciates and businesses reinvest their profits or their tax allowances for capital appreciation in new technologies, or move to improved locations, or sell or recycle old equipment. If you live in a city you are likely to see this very clearly: new shops open and close, new buildings are erected and knocked down, pavements and roads are dug up and reconstructed, all on the same plot of land which changes not at all.

Land is also fixed within politically, not economically, defined jurisdictions. These boundaries are easily crossed by capital – capital is mobile and it migrates. If you are a multinational company and wish to avoid high corporation tax in France, you can easily move your production operations to a tax haven in the Caribbean. But if you need excellent transport networks or to be close to particular producers of complementary goods, or to have easy access to a supply of highly skilled French-speaking staff, or to operate in a certain time zone to give traders access to markets, you may think twice. These phenomena are fixed in space – they are 'land'.

The Bank of England (2016a) statistics department records loans as either 'secured' or 'unsecured': the former are loans collateralised with property. They make a considerably larger part of total credit than unsecured loans in the UK and most advanced economies and enjoy considerably lower interest rates than unsecured loans (a story developed further in Chapter 5). Location, fixity and permanence are valued highly by financial institutions – try getting a bank to accept a computer as collateral!

Land provides a steady flow of services over time to its users, but this flow cannot be stored up or controlled or saved for future anticipated increased demand as with capital goods. Land not used is land services down the drain. Alfred Marshall, one of the founding fathers of neoclassical economics, recognised this, arguing that the public value of land is derived from three things that are external and uncontrollable by the owner of land: the 'gift of nature', public services and spillovers (positive or negative) from the use of nearby private land (Marshall, 1920, pp. 300–307, quoted in Gaffney, 1994b, p. 49).

Marginal productivity theory assumes that in the long run all factors of production – whether land, capital or labour – will be subject to the same variable marginal returns (Wicksteed, 1914, p. 7). This is based on the idea that all factors can be reduced to equivalent physical quantities: if a firm adds an additional unit of labour or additional capital good to its production process, it will be homogeneous to all previous units. But this is not the case with land. It is impossible to add homogeneous land to a firm since each unit of land has a unique location and each new unit of land added to a city will be further from the centre of production.

Economic rent from land does not increase investment or production

If the rate of return on capital investment[15] rises, this will draw in additional capital flows – at a given interest rate – until the rate of return drops to a common level, i.e. the excess returns are competed away. In other words, increasing profits, dividends or interest gained from capital investment will increase the demand for more investment and potentially push up interest rates. These general rules do not apply to land. When land rents rise, the excess returns are reflected in higher land prices, which are treated as fixed costs of production. But this is circular reasoning – it is not that the value of land has pushed up fixed costs, but rather that the value of land has absorbed the additional return that was generated via production. As a result, rising land costs do not increase productivity or demand for capital; rather they do the opposite. High land prices and rents eat into and reduce the return to capital (Gaffney, 1994b, p. 65).

Capital and land are in competition for the same, limited, spending power of the firm. If land values increase, the firm will be left with less funds for capital investment and profits will fall, all else being equal. The firm can substitute capital for land, for

---

15 'Return on capital' or 'return on invested capital' is typically calculated by dividing the net operating surplus minus taxes divided by invested capital for a particular period, usually a year.

example by constructing high-rise buildings or digging out basements to save land costs.[16] But substitution can only go so far and is
not the same as conversion. A firm cannot convert land into capital
as neoclassical economic theory appears to assume, since capital
cannot exist without land – it cannot exist without space and time.
The converse does not apply: land can exist without capital. In addition, while it may be true that a single firm (or household) can at
the margin obtain additional land, including to substitute it against
capital, firms as a whole cannot, because the total supply of land is
fixed, at least the supply of land of a desired type.

The cost of money – i.e. interest rates – also tends to have inverse
effects on land and capital. Lower interest rates make capital investment cheaper but an increase in capital spending tends to drive up
land prices and the economic rent attaching to it as productivity
increases and economies grow. In addition, lower interest rates can
help create higher land prices as more credit flows into mortgages
for domestic and commercial real estate (elaborated further in
Chapter 5).

In summary, to understand the processes that determine capital
and industry more generally, it is necessary to understand, separately, the dynamics of land and economic rent.

3.6 Political reasons for the disappearance of land from economic theory

Given the fundamental differences between land and capital
outlined above, it may seem remarkable that neoclassical economics
was eventually successful in eliding the two together in the theory
of marginal productivity. Some scholars argue that the real reason
for the success of Clark and those that followed was that they
were representing and supported by vested – and landed – interests
opposed to land taxation (Gaffney, 1994b; Hudson, 2010).

---

16 The London Borough of Kensington and Chelsea, where house prices are some
of the highest in the UK, received 450 planning applications for basements in
2013, compared to 46 in 2001 (Dowling, 2014). The local council decided to ban
multi-storey basement excavations in 2014 due to residents' complaints (Ward,
2014).

As well as seeking a universalising theory of capital to turn economics into a true science, the neoclassical theory of 'capital' can be seen as a political response to Henry George and the growing movement for a single tax in the late nineteenth and early twentieth centuries. By obfuscating land's particular role in the process of wealth creation, by eliding it with capital goods, George's opponents could thwart policy makers and progressive politicians in their efforts to isolate the value of land and tax it accordingly. Clark and his followers were funded by big businesses at US universities such as Columbia, which were losing their religious roots and becoming funded by wealthy business and financial interests towards the end of the nineteenth century (Gaffney, 1994a, pp. 50–53).

There is evidence that Clark was motivated by George's (and Ricardo's) theory of economic rent as relating to land. Gaffney (1994b, p. 48) notes twenty-four articles or books published by Clark targeted against Henry George over a span of twenty-eight years (1886–1914). The following quote, from the preface of his seminal book *The Distribution of Wealth*, is an example:

It was the claim advanced by Mr. Henry George, that wages are fixed by the product which a man can create by tilling rentless land, that first led me to seek a method by which the product of labour everywhere may be disentangled from the product of cooperating agents and separately identified; and it was this quest which led to the attainment of the law that is here presented, according to which the wages of all labour tend, under perfectly free competition, to equal the product that is separately attributable to labour. (Clark, 1899, p. viii)

More broadly, Clark and the marginal utility theory that was blossoming in Europe can be seen as a reaction to the writings of both George and Karl Marx's (1867) labour theory of value. Both emphasised the economic rent and exploitation of workers derived from private ownership (of the 'means of production' in Marx's famous term).

Although presented as an objective theory of distribution, in fact Clark's version of marginal productivity had a strong normative element. He explicitly argued that having rewards determined by marginal contribution to output was fair because 'what a social class gets is, under natural law, what it contributes to the general output of the industry' (Clark, 1891a, p. 319). Every unit of capital or labour has its own 'marginal product' and any attempt by the firm to pay less than this will, under conditions of perfect competition, lead to other firms paying more, bidding prices back up to equilibrium levels. Clark's 'natural law' 'if it worked without friction, would give to every agent of production the amount of wealth which that agent creates' (Clark, 1899, p. v). Here Clarke treats the social class of landowners as contributing what land contributes to production, without acknowledging that he is doing so.

Marginal productivity and marginal utility theories ultimately lead to a world where, so long as there is sufficient competition and free markets, all will receive their just deserts in relation to their true contribution to society. There will, in Milton Friedman's (1975) famous terms, be 'no such thing as a free lunch'.

Marginal productivity theory says nothing about the distribution of the ownership of factors of production – not least land. Landed property is assumed to be the most efficient organisational form for enabling private exchange and free markets with little questioning of how property and tenure rights are distributed or of the gains (rents) that possession of such rights grants to its holders. Ultimately, this limits what the theory can say about the distribution of income, particularly in a world where such economic rents are large (Robinson, 1973).

3.7 Land and socialism

Although neoclassical economics can be said to have dominated the past fifty years of economic thought, Karl Marx's powerful legacy and its continuance in socialist regimes across the world from 1918 to 1990 in the first sixty years of the twentieth century maintained a focus on the economic rents that can be derived from ownership of the means of production. Social democratic regimes in Europe in particular were successful in advancing an interventionist role for the state in preventing the worst abuses of monopoly via competition laws, as well as using progressive income taxes to support advanced welfare states. Even in the United States, where socialism and public ownership of enterprise never took off, powerful anti-trust legislation dealt a blow to big business monopolists that controlled the railroads, the telegraph and oil businesses. The progressive era policies of Roosevelt led to huge public investment in order to provide affordable housing and public infrastructure free of *rentier* charges.

The economic rent from land enjoyed much less attention. One potential reason is that George himself and the single tax movement failed to form a broad alliance with the growing socialist movements of the late nineteenth and earlier twentieth centuries because of their fixation on land rent – and taxation as the solution – above and beyond other forms of economic rent. According to Hudson (2008, p. 4) the narrow focus on land tax

> isolated George from reformers who came to view the land tax as being so sharp a challenge to the propertied interests that they turned to more readily achievable public regulation and more general tax reforms ... George ... opposed socialist ownership of capital and even refrained from advocating industrial and financial reforms. George's intolerance in rejecting these reforms helped push his single tax advocacy to the outer periphery of the political spectrum.

In the United States, where land was not in great shortage at the time George was writing, there was a strong argument that the real rents were being extracted by business monopolies such as the railroads who controlled the movement of capital across the country (Patten, 1891, p. 361). Taxes were also imposed locally in the US and a national land tax imposed by the federal government would have been a much greater political struggle than national reforms of the business and labour sector, including the breaking up of business monopolies.

In Europe, where land was less available and the inequalities between landowners and labourers were more stark, George's ideas had perhaps greater potential influence, particularly given Ricardo's legacy in Britain. However, Ricardo's analysis, essentially shared by George, with its emphasis on the marginal productivity of agricultural rather than urban land, was becoming less influential as industrialisation and huge improvements in farming led to a decreasing proportion of labour working on agricultural land. We discuss these important developments in more depth in Chapter 4.

Marx, whose influence grew through the nineteenth century, viewed the land tax with suspicion, seeing it as a policy to support industrial capital and the urban bourgeoisie in their battle with landed interests while doing nothing to prevent the exploitation of labour by these groups (Marx, [1847] 1995, quoted in Hudson, 2008, p. 13). For Marx, only the full-scale nationalisation of the capitalist means of production and land would enable labour to earn its full and fair share of the economic surplus. The political aim of Ricardo's rent theory was to buttress the programme of taxing land rather than industry and was 'a last attempt to save the capitalist regime'.[17]

George was opposed to taxing capital and income (George, [1879] 1979, pp. 125–126), although he favoured government ownership of natural monopolies, and saw industry as a wealth generator. This position antagonised socialists, who increasingly saw the exploitation of labour as having little to do with capitalists' control over land and more to do with governments' failure to properly regulate industry or tax excessive incomes.

Equally, George placed less emphasis on reform of the financial sector, which was viewed by socialists, in particular those that followed Proudhon (1840), as a major source of rentier profit and the reason for the build-up of public and private debts beyond that which the growth of the economy could handle. George largely neglected the ability of banks to capitalise on the economic rent derived from increasing land value via interest paid on mortgage credit (Hudson, 2008, p. 20), a phenomenon we explore in more depth in Chapter 5.

Ultimately, the socialist movement for the regulation of industry and taxation of capital and labour had considerably greater success

---

17 Marx wrote this in a letter to John Swinton who had sent him a copy of *Progress and Property* in 1881. It was published in Engels (1887, quoted in Hudson, 2008, p. 41).

than the land tax movement. Under social democratic governments in Europe, tax has come to fall upon capital income and labour rather than the unearned income deriving from landownership or, to a considerable extent, money interest (see Chapter 4).

3.8 Consequences of the conflation of land and capital today

That economic policy has failed to properly incorporate the differential properties of capital and land can be evidenced by current policies pertaining to property, not least tax policy.

If you are a buy-to-let landlord in the UK you are given a tax 'allowance' for the 'capital' depreciation of the physical furniture in your home. But at the same time you are supposed to pay a 'capital gains' tax when you sell your home (assuming you don't live in it). Clearly the furniture in your home can depreciate in value – as do the bricks and mortar – at the same time as the total value of the home goes up. In fact, it is actually the land underneath it that increases in value for all the reasons explained in section 3.2. We confuse these two effects by referring to both as 'capital', even though the tax system recognises the difference.

More generally, in the UK, unearned rental income from the letting out of rooms or homes is taxed at the same rates as income from productive activity (i.e. for work). As land values rise faster than wages, so landowners are in a position to increase rents at a faster rate than wage growth. Combined with rapid capital gains, there is a perverse incentive to invest in land rather than capital. Until 2015 in the UK, interest payments on mortgages for buy-to-let homes could also be offset against tax at up to 45%: a subsidy for landlords estimated to cost the Treasury around £6.3 billion a year (This is Money, 2015).[18]

For policy makers following neoclassical free-market maxims, the policy challenge of rising property prices is to ensure that the market for land and housing is free and competitive and that

---

18 In his 2015 Budget, Conservative Chancellor of the Exchequer George Osborne slashed mortgage interest tax relief for landlords from 45% to the basic rate of 20% (This is Money, 2015).

consumers of housing have as much information as possible. This should lead to conditions where the market for land clears at an appropriate price, with relatively few frictions. Rising house prices or rents (relative to incomes) can be attributed to insufficient supply of homes or land.

Mainstream policy debate has become focused precisely on this issue: calls are repeatedly made to build more homes or allow more land to be made available for home building. As with other policy challenges, such as unemployment, the focus is on the supply side. Housing demand is assumed to be subject to the same rules that drive desire for any other commodity: its marginal productivity and utility. The distribution of land and property wealth across the population, its taxation and the role of the banking system in driving up prices through increases in mortgage debt (Chapter 5) are neglected.

Human beings do not and cannot 'make' land in the way they can make commodities if more is demanded. Rather, we occupy scarce land in the process of production and consumption. If this resource is not appropriately managed it can easily become misallocated and wasted through speculation. As land has become relatively scarcer in countries like the UK, so have house prices risen, and owning a property has become the goal of households, not for its use value as a home but as a financial asset.

The neglect of land in economic theory and policy has also had implications for the measurement of land values. In many advanced economies land values are not properly measured and tracked over time. For example, access to the information held by the Land Registry for England and Wales is not free, making the land market highly opaque. This problem is worsened by the near total absence of publicly available data on the value of land or property. Despite a plethora of generalised indices of house prices, the only official index of land prices was discontinued in 2011, and the datasets on the value of commercial property held by the Valuation Office Agency for the levying of business rates are not publicly available. This paucity of market information creates significant inefficiencies and barriers to entry (see Chapter 4) and restricts the ability of public bodies and citizens to scrutinise the activities of landowners and developers (Jefferys, Lloyd, Argyle, et al., 2014).

Property prices tend to be a poor proxy for land values since, as mentioned, materials prices and labour costs bear little relation to land values. This makes it impossible for economists to analyse the economic significance of land prices and land rents even if they wanted to. Belatedly recognising this problem, Eurostat and the Organisation for Economic Co-operation and Development (OECD) (2015) are working with national governments to improve land valuation practice and incorporate land into national accounting frameworks.

3.9 Conclusion

The classical economists of the nineteenth century were conscious of the key role of land as a factor of production and the means via which economic rent could be extracted from the economy. But the theories and policy solutions of Ricardo, Mill, Smith and George were gradually erased from economic theory and public policy during the early twentieth century. A confluence of factors – the shift to urban production and industry and away from agriculture, the failure of Henry George and his followers to form an alliance with European socialists focused on other forms of economic rent, and the rise of neoclassical economic theory – led to the eventual disappearance of land and economic rent from modern theories of production and distribution.

But land is not capital, nor is it just another commodity. It is fixed in its supply and fixed in time and space. Yet it is central to production. For these reasons, ownership of land grants the opportunity for the extraction of economic rent as businesses and households seek out the most attractive location, stretching their spending power as far as it will go. The scarcity of desirably locational landed property means its income elasticity is higher than parity – as their incomes increase people will be prepared to spend relatively more on it than other goods and services. Conversely it is also price inelastic compared to most commodities: rising prices relative to incomes will lead to consumers taking on more debt and more speculative purchases, rather than seeking alternatives (explored further in Chapter 5).

Today's economics textbooks describe 'income' narrowly as a reward for one's contribution to production. Wealth is understood as 'savings' due to one's productive investment effort, not as unearned windfalls from being the owner of land or other naturally scarce sources of value. Mainstream economic theory pays little attention to the role of institutions, including systems of land-ownership, property rights and land taxation that are historically determined by power and class relations. In fact it is these inherently political, social and cultural developments that determine the way in which economic rent is distributed. We now turn to the key institutional and political-economic developments of land through modern history to the present day, with the United Kingdom as our main case.

CHAPTER 4

Land for housing:
land economics in the modern era

That, when they should have occasion to enlarge their city by
purchasing ground without the town, or to build bridges or
arches for the accomplishing of the same, not only were the
proprietors of such lands obliged to part with the same on
reasonable terms, but when in possession thereof, they are
to be erected into a regality in favour of the citizens.

KING JAMES II ON THE PROPOSED BUILDING OF EDINBURGH'S
NEW TOWN, 1680S, QUOTED IN GRANT (1880, VOL. II, P. 335)

4.1 Introduction

So far this book has presented a generalised historical and theoretical overview of the role of land in the economy and in economic
thought in the modern Western world. Yet because land is geograph-
ically fixed and its economic use heavily determined by social and
legal structures, the ways in which this role has played out have
varied considerably over different countries and in different sectors
of the economy. It is impossible to do this varied history justice
in one book, which could potentially cover the colonial real estate
markets of Australia, the frontier economy of the expanding USA,
early experiments with land-backed monetary reform in France, or
the evolution of the peasant economy of China, to name but a few.

Rather than seek universal coverage, in this chapter we explore
the history of housing in Britain[1] as one tangible example of the

---

1   That is, the UK excluding Ireland and Northern Ireland. Discussion of more
    recent times tends to focus on England, as housing markets and policies have
    varied widely across the nations of the UK, particularly since devolution around
    the turn of the millennium.

way that the role of land in the economy has played out. We use this case study as it is relevant both to the general argument and contemporary social problems. Britain was one of the first countries to develop a modern market in land and to industrialise, and many of its institutions were exported around the world in the era of colonialism, making its economic history relevant to land economics more widely. In recent decades the experience of Britain's housing economy has been a precursor of trends in other developed economies: countries around the world have recently experienced the high and volatile asset prices, affordability crises and widening wealth inequality that have marked Britain's housing economy for decades (Woetzel et al., 2014).

This chapter explores the different instantiations of the problem of rent that have manifested themselves in the British housing system over the centuries – and the varied policy interventions that have sought to address these problems. These responses include land use regulation; public land acquisition, ownership and privatisation; taxation policies; housing tenure regulations; housing subsidies; and the direct provision of non-market housing. We therefore consider the British housing economy to be a useful lens through which to examine many of the universal themes of land economics – in particular the inherently political ways in which societies have attempted to address the problem of rent in different times.

This chapter begins with the economic transformation of the Industrial Revolution and the accompanying phenomenon of urbanisation in the nineteenth century, before outlining the emergence of the modern housing market in the twentieth, and the difficulties it has encountered in the twenty-first. The following chapter then describes how this new asset class of privately owned family homes became central to the liberalised financial system that emerged from the late 1970s onwards. As a result of these economic changes, public, political and academic attention has become increasingly focused on the housing market, while the critical underlying role of land itself has been largely obscured.

4.2 The Industrial Revolution and the growth of cities

By the mid-eighteenth century the evolution of private ownership, enclosure and clearances in the UK had removed almost all vestiges of the feudal system, and created a pattern of private landownership that was highly concentrated compared to the landowning democracy of the United States, or even the peasant economies of France and Italy – although not as concentrated as the serf economies of eastern Europe (Linklater, 2013).

However, during the late eighteenth and early nineteenth centuries the Industrial Revolution transformed economic life across Britain. Scientific innovations and technological improvements contributed to the advancement of agriculture, industry, shipping and trade, causing an unprecedented expansion of the economy and dramatic changes to power relations and living conditions.

While agriculture had dominated the British economy for centuries, the explosion in productive capacity during the Industrial Revolution saw capital come to replace land as the dominant factor of production. This marked the beginning of the decline of agricultural land as the primary source of wealth, and gave rise to a new class of prosperous industrialists, shipowners and merchants.

Between around 1650 and 1850 the development of new tools, fertilisers and harvesting techniques led to greatly improved agricultural productivity, which enabled farmers to produce much greater quantities of crops. Throughout the medieval period wheat yields stayed at around ten bushels[2] per acre, whereas by the eighteenth century farmers in Britain were yielding twenty-five bushels of wheat per acre (Linklater, 2013). This increase in the food supply contributed to a rapid growth of the English population from 5.7 million in 1750 to 16.6 million in 1850. By 1900, the population of England reached 32 million (Overton, 1996).

This improvement in agricultural productivity meant that rural workers were freed up to work in other sectors of the economy, and many moved to urban centres in search of employment. Here

---

2   A bushel is an old unit of volume which was used mostly for agricultural products
    such as wheat.

they found work in burgeoning new industries which had been transformed following the invention of steam power and other new technologies. Among the most important industries were coal, which was needed to power the new steam engines, and iron, which was often converted into steel and used to expand the country's infrastructure and transportation networks. The textile industry also grew rapidly following the mechanisation of the textile mills, which revolutionised the industry and put the north of England at the centre of the global cotton industry (ONS, 2013a).

By 1850 only 22% of the British workforce worked in agriculture; the smallest proportion of any country in the world (Overton, 1996). By 1900 the urban population had grown to 20 million, up from 2 million only a century earlier (Clive Turner, 2015). The shift from agrarian to industrial economies saw land's economic significance take on a new dimension. Whereas previously land's primary economic role was in food production, the Industrial Revolution saw land take on a new economic function as the site of capitalist industrial production.

This also reduced the importance of agricultural land for taxation purposes, and created new opportunities to tax other aspects of the industrial and urban economy. In 1700, taxation from land represented around 35% of the national revenue. Over time this proportion fell to some 17% in the 1790s, 11% by the 1820s and just 2% by the end of the nineteenth century. Income tax was first introduced in 1799 in order to pay for weapons and equipment in preparation for the Napoleonic Wars, but much of the burden of taxation fell upon domestically produced commodities that were in high demand, such as beer, spirits, bricks, salt and glass, and imported goods such as tea, sugar and tobacco (Mathias, 2013).

In 1815 the Corn Laws were enacted, which imposed restrictions and tariffs on imported grain. The laws were intended to keep grain prices at a high level to protect English landowners from cheap foreign imports of grain following the end of the Napoleonic Wars. The laws proved controversial and provided one of the first examples of the growing tension between the old landowning class and the new wealthy industrialists. While landowners strongly supported the policy, it was bitterly opposed by industrialists, who saw high food prices as a barrier to cutting wages and boosting profits.

The laws were eventually overturned in 1846 after popular movements such as the Anti-Corn Law League succeeded in turning public and elite opinion against the laws. This was seen as a defeat of mercantilist economic thought and a triumph for classical economists such as David Ricardo. It was also evidence of the declining political power of the landowners, as the power of industry and cities rose. The two great political reform acts of 1832 and 1867 further shifted the balance of power in parliament in favour of new urban middle and even working classes. By the end of the nineteenth century, as land was slipping out of mainstream economic thinking (see Chapter 3), the political power of the landowning class was diminishing too (Linklater, 2013).

Housing supply and tenure

The rapid increase in urban populations created a huge demand for accommodation in Britain's major cities, most of which were not prepared for this increase in population. Large houses were turned into flats and tenements, and multiple families were crowded into already crammed houses by often unscrupulous landlords who saw an opportunity for quick profit. During this time those who ran the dominant industries in the city often wielded significant power, and much of the housing needs of the new urban workers were met by factory owners who built accommodation near their factories. This housing was cheap and often low quality; there were few building regulations during this time and those that did exist were frequently ignored. Neither older cities like London nor new ones like Manchester had sufficient infrastructure to support such high density urban populations well, and life under these conditions was often harsh. Small open rooms or apartments were frequently greatly overcrowded and lacked any sanitation or fresh water. This, combined with poor food and hygiene, contributed towards a proliferation of slum-like conditions (Wise, 2013). In London, poor sanitation allowed cholera to spread, killing over 43,000 people between 1832 and 1866 (Clive Turner, 2015). Throughout the nineteenth century London's death rate exceeded its birth rate: that its population grew so fast was due entirely to the scale of in-migration from the British countryside and the wider world (Ackroyd, 2001).

This grim portrait of urban life was not universal, however, and did not go unchallenged. Other trends ran concurrently, both in direct reaction to the growth of the new industrial cities, and drawing on entirely different economic and cultural roots. Firstly, from the earliest days of the industrial period there was a flowering of privately sponsored town planning schemes for the wealthier classes. Developments such as Bath, Brighton and the Edinburgh New Town were designed with quality and social amenity in mind. Strategic and coordinated planning, made possible by unified landownership, enabled these towns to be developed with good infrastructure and a coherent look, characterised by residential squares and crescents comprised of grand terraces (Haywood, 2009).

Secondly, some enlightened factory owners and wealthy philanthropists took it upon themselves to address social ills by providing a good living environment for the new working class. One such example was Richard Arkwright, the wealthy textile industrialist, who built high-quality homes for his workers that still stand to this day. He believed that a healthy workforce would benefit everyone, as in addition to enjoying a higher standard of living his employees would also work more effectively. Other examples of wealthy factory owners who cared deeply about improving the quality of life for workers were the chocolatiers George Cadbury and Joseph Rowntree, and the textile industrialists Titus Salt and Robert Owen.

More direct attempts to solve urban poverty and squalor via the provision of better homes were pioneered by the likes of Octavia Hill and American merchant and banker George Peabody (Hanley, 2007). These philanthropists invented the concept of social housing: modest, but high-quality urban homes that would be built and owned in perpetuity by charitable trusts, to be let out to working families at rates that would allow them a decent standard of living. In this they were drawing on the older tradition of almshouses, which had provided homes for fixed numbers of the 'deserving poor' associated with specific trades since medieval times. But Hill and others went further in making mass housing provision a tool for social reform and progress, rather than just charity, and used modern methods of finance, organisation and construction to create dynamic organisations that would grow and shape whole neighbourhoods for decades or even centuries to come.

Thirdly, there was the emergence of cooperative, mutual, self-organised housing provision in the form of building societies from 1775 and building clubs from the early 1800s, which provided mutual help with the financing and construction of houses respectively. Later, other forms emerged, such as the tenant co-partnership model in 1904; co-ownership in the 1960s; shared ownership co-ops in the 1970s (Birchall, 2014); and Community Land Trusts today (see Chapter 7). Although the contribution of cooperative housing to the UK housing system has never been widely acknowledged, it has been influential among movements for urban reform, including the Garden City movement, which sought to combine new design principles with cooperative and mutual traditions (see Box 4.1) (Rowlands, 2009), and the housing association movement that has largely replaced local councils in providing social housing (see below).

Finally, there is also a long, and often supressed, history of self-organising land use – from the common lands of the feudal era through to the 'plotlands' movement of working class self-builders that thrived up until the Second World War. At the most marginal end of the scale, the conflict between exclusionary legal ownership and the universal need for access to land has always fostered a degree of squatting – occupying land and property illegally (Ward, 2002). Some have occupied and managed property use for generations, often acquiring collective and customary rights over it in the process, such as the squatting community of Headington Quarry, outside Oxford, where irregular landownership supported a trading economy and a welfare network outside of the official system of poor relief well into the twentieth century (Ward, 2004).

Yet while they undoubtedly made a difference to many places and millions of people, none of these responses were sufficiently resourced or widespread to overcome the structural problems of the new industrial cities. The need for better urban infrastructure finally prompted the state to act, overcoming the ideological preference for minimal intervention in the market. Grand public works like Bazalgette's immense sewer system, which finally ended cholera, required state action and subsidy via a series of Public Health Acts (Clive Turner, 2015). By the turn of the twentieth century housing standards in the major cities had begun to improve, as mains sewers, flushing toilets and regular waste collections became commonplace, and new building codes prevented the construction of substandard housing.

The need to stop individual landowners being able to block the construction of new railways prompted the emergence of the compulsory purchase regime. This gave the state the power to acquire rights over land, or to buy it outright, without the current owner's consent, in return for compensation. Initially this was done through individual Acts of Parliament, although by the late nineteenth century powers of compulsory purchase slowly became more consolidated and transparent (Gray and Gray, 2011). In the heyday of laissez-faire liberalism itself, it became apparent that only collective intervention into the land market could provide the infrastructure that society and the economy required.

Following these interventions to provide better infrastructure, state attention began to turn to the problems of poor quality housing in cities, where slum conditions still proliferate alongside the most valuable real estate. The prevalence of such overcrowded urban slums is often regarded as an indicator of poverty and economic failure, but in reality they represent the relative economic attractiveness of certain locations, which is sufficient to attract ever more people despite increasingly unsanitary conditions. In fact, slums like London's famous Old Nichol were often the most valuable real estate, as the rental yield on slum properties with a family in each room was typically higher than on high-end properties accommodating one wealthy family and their servants (Wise, 2013). Slums are therefore an expression of the problem of economic rent: the benefits of economic growth accrue to slum landlords, who can capture much of the income of their tenants and externalise the costs onto society at large. The Old Nichol was eventually redeveloped by the new London County Council into the pioneering Boundary Estate: the alleys and crumbling tenements replaced with mansion blocks of social housing built to an ordered street pattern, often described as the first council housing in the world. This represented a new attempt to address the problem of rent by providing quality housing for the working poor at below-market rents, with the capital cost of construction met by the state.

But although these multiple efforts to clean up cities, provide infrastructure and give ordinary people better homes made significant improvements to urban life and mitigated the worst effects of the problem of rent, the fundamental structure of the land economy remained largely unchanged. By the end of the nineteenth century the vast majority of people rented their home from private property owners, while poor conditions persisted. Sources usually say around 90% of homes were rented (Heath, 2014), including those of the urban middle classes. Leases were often sold for the lifetime of the tenant, giving an appearance of permanence, but landlords were clearly able to extract a high degree of economic rent: the Royal Commission on the Housing of the Working Classes (1885) found that almost half of working class households were paying 25–50% of their income on rent alone (Samy, 2015). In part, this was due to the lack of transport, which required industrial workers to live near to the factories that employed them.

In the new, urban and industrial economy that had been created, the problem of rent was still alive and well. But now it found its strongest expression in the housing market, rather than in the agricultural fields that Ricardo had originally used to explain his theory.

4.3 1900–1970: world wars and the golden age of capitalism

By the dawn of the twentieth century there was an increasing awareness among social and political elites that the social problems of industrial, urban Britain were rooted in the economic and physical organisation of land and property, triggering interest in how these problems could be overcome at a more systemic level (Simpson et al., 1992). During the turbulent decades that followed, governments and other actors would make repeated attempts to reform the land economy using the growing number of tools available to democratic, developed societies.

Edwardian experiments

One of the most prominent figures to emerge from this period was the stenographer Sir Ebenezer Howard, who founded the influential Garden City movement in the early twentieth century (see Box

---

Box 4.1 Sir Ebenezer Howard's garden cities

In the 1880s Sir Ebenezer Howard became deeply concerned about the deteriorating conditions in large cities due to the rapid influx of large numbers of people. In response he proposed the founding of 'garden cities' – suburban towns of limited size, planned in advance, and surrounded by a permanent belt of agricultural land. Howard's vision, outlined in his book *Tomorrow: A Peaceful Path to Social Reform* (later republished as *Garden Cities of tomorrow*) was of towns which would enjoy the benefits of both town and country and which would be managed and financed by the citizens who had an economic interest in them (Howard, [1898] 2010).

In 1903 Howard sought to put his vision into practice at Letchworth, thirty-four miles north of London. Four thousand acres in two farms were bought with money donated by philanthropic enthusiasts, and ownership of the land was transferred to a new 'cooperative land society' in which people who moved to Letchworth were given a mutual stake. Over time a thriving community emerged that was committed to developing Letchworth along the lines of Howard's garden city model. A key part of the model was the funding mechanism which saw the increment on land values that arose as the community developed from rural to urban collected and then continuously reinvested in community improvements. Howard subsequently went on to lead the development of nearby Welwyn Garden City in the 1920s.

Although Howard's garden city proposal was never more widely adopted, his ideas are recognised as having influenced urban planning throughout the world. And despite a famous attempt to privatise the land in the 1960s, to this day the community-controlled Letchworth Heritage Foundation is the largest landowner in the town, using income generated from the estate to fund its charitable objectives and provide services for the community.

4.1). Howard's proposal was to use the community ownership of land to provide public benefits like decent housing and a healthy environment, in perpetuity. As such, the Garden City movement was as much about economic reform to address market failure as it was about design principles. Its model of holding land in perpetuity for the benefit of the community was an explicit attempt to solve the problem of rent by capturing economic rent for the community itself.

An entirely different attempt to address the problem of rent systemically came in the form of taxation. Like much of the early twentieth century enthusiasm for economic and social reform, this also stemmed partly from a desire among elites to prevent unrest which might lead to more radical demands for reform. In 1909 the Liberal government, led by Chancellor of the Exchequer David Lloyd George and his young ally Winston Churchill, attempted to introduce a range of radical social welfare programmes and redistribute wealth among the British public through the passing of a 'people's budget'.

The budget's stated aim was to 'wage implacable warfare against poverty and squalidness', and among the proposals was a 20% tax on increases in land value payable each time land changed hands. Influenced by the ideas of Henry George, the proposal sought to capture the 'unearned increments in land' which arose not from the skill or effort of the landowner, but from the endeavours of the community as a whole. This debate gave a new prominence and rhetorical force to the problem of economic rent. As Winston Churchill described in a speech made to the House of Commons:

> Roads are made, streets are made, services are improved, electric light turns night into day, water is brought from reservoirs a hundred miles off in the mountains – and all the while the landlord sits still. Every one of those improvements is effected by the labour and cost of other people and the taxpayers. To not one of those improvements does the land monopolist, as a land monopolist, contribute, and yet by every one of them the value of his land is enhanced. He renders no service to the community, he contributes nothing to the general welfare, he

contributes nothing to the process from which his own enrichment is derived. (Churchill, 1909a)

The proposals for land taxation were met with fierce opposition in
the House of Lords, whose membership comprised many aristocratic
landowners who would be adversely impacted by the proposals.
The budget was ultimately rejected by the House of Lords, triggering a constitutional crisis and a general election (Dolphin, 2009).

This newfound fervour for social and economic reform was
soon brought to an abrupt end by the outbreak of the First World
War in 1914. War immediately killed off the political drive to tax
landownership, but also prompted other forms of reactive intervention in the land economy. As house building ground to a halt and
demand for housing far exceeded supply, the profiteering of some
landlords led to rent strikes and unrest which threatened to undermine the war effort itself. In response to this, the government passed
the Increase of Rent and Mortgage Interest (War Restrictions) Act
1915 which restricted rent increases for private tenants and froze
the rate of interest that landlords paid on their mortgages. These
new rent controls were originally intended as a temporary measure
due to expire six months after the end of the war. However, they
were repeatedly extended in response to the continued shortage of
housing (Kemp, 2002).

In a democracy with many more renters than landlords the political appeal of rent control as a means of tackling the problem of
rent is obvious, especially as it is a solution that seemingly costs
the state nothing. Rent controls of some form endured in Britain
for much of the twentieth century, until private rents were fully
deregulated in January 1989. The evidence on the effectiveness of
these rent controls is mixed, and today many economists oppose
rent controls on the grounds that they create shortages in the rental
housing market, and reduce the quality of the stock by discouraging
private investment (Jenkins, 2009; Heath, 2014).

The interwar years: 1919–39

In the aftermath of the devastation suffered during the First World
War, the British government viewed the provision of good-quality,

affordable homes for men returning from war as essential for maintaining social harmony and boosting the lagging economy. It was also viewed as a means of staving off the threat of industrial and political unrest following demobilisation of the armed services. Fearful of contagion from the 1917 Russian Revolution, Prime Minister Lloyd George said of his proposed housing plan, 'even if it cost a hundred million pounds, what was that compared to the stability of the state and the threat posed by Bolshevism' (Jones and Murie, 2008, p. 9).

This led to the introduction of the Housing, Town Planning, &c. Act 1919 (also known as the Addison Act) which, together with the first Labour government's 1924 Housing Act (also known as the Wheatley Housing Act), marked the start of a period in which local authorities would build houses and make them available to people at low rents (Clive Turner, 2015). The effect of this was a significant shift within the rental sector from private to social renting. Although 77% of households were renting in 1918, only 1% of households were doing so from social landlords (either councils or the charities established by reforming philanthropists). As a result of direct state action to build council homes, by 1939 the percentage of households socially renting had risen to 10% (ONS, 2013b).

The interwar period also saw the beginnings of the growth in homeownership that was to continue for the rest of the century. While in 1918 23% of households were owner-occupiers, by 1939 this had increased to 32% (ONS, 2013b). In the 1930s low interest rates, rising living standards and greater availability of affordable mortgages – mainly from mutually owned building societies – created a boom in private sector housing development. This was the period when the speculative model of private house building got going: relatively small-scale builders could buy agricultural land around cities and towns, and develop it as new suburban retail and housing for sale (see Box 4.2 below).

New development in this period was characterised by a significant expansion of cities into the suburbs, encouraged by new transport infrastructures and a weak and patchy planning system (Barlow, 1940).

Land was widely available around towns and cities and could be bought at relatively low prices. Cities expanded outwards, some doubling their footprint in a decade, as huge swathes of land were brought under development for the first time. As a result, during the 1930s many single-earner families found that they could buy a new family home with a mortgage of only three times an ordinary worker's salary. This supports the theoretical argument in Chapter 1, that the problem of rent can be temporarily avoided (though not permanently overcome) when new marginal land is abundant. But these conditions are rare, short-lived, and rely on the externalisation of the costs onto other groups or society as a whole. In the case of the suburbanisation of cities, these costs can be seen today in the prevalence of low-density, car-dependent neighbourhoods and the resulting road congestion, economic and environmental costs (Litman, 2015) – although these impacts are far less pronounced in Britain than in many other developed economies, thanks to the much greater constraints on urban sprawl imposed after the Second World War.

The combined effect of increased social housing and new private development meant that by the time war broke out again in 1939, an additional 4 million homes had been built since 1918 (Marshall, 1969). This period marked the beginning of the next major shift in land's economic significance as it became the site of what has come to be regarded as a near-universally entitled consumption good: the family home.

The post-war recovery: 1940–69

Bombing throughout the Second World War caused destruction across Britain on a scale never witnessed before. Half a million homes were destroyed and a further 250,000 were badly damaged (Lund, 2011). After the war ended the government embarked on an ambitious programme of new social housing in order to provide homes for returning soldiers and those who had lost their homes in the war. Achieving this would require a new approach to the problem of rent, in the particular form of 'betterment': the uplift in land value created by the grant of planning permission. The question was simply, how much of the betterment should go to the owner of the land, and how much can reasonably be claimed by the planning authority itself? And conversely, how much compensation were landowners entitled to if public policy prevented them from developing their land?

This problem was already well understood, thanks to the failings of the Town and Country Planning Act 1932, which required local authorities to compensate landowners for any development value lost if the authority restricted their right to develop, and was seen to have enabled landowners to extract too much economic rent. But in 1942 the matter was urgent, because of the need to repair the war damage to much of urban Britain. If landowners were able to capture all of the gains from public-funded reconstruction, it would leave too little to pay for public amenities and trigger a land price boom that would further undermine the viability of development.

The Uthwatt Committee into Compensation and Betterment (Uthwatt, 1942) proposed tackling this incarnation of the problem of rent head-on by compulsorily acquiring land for reconstruction at 1939 values – a move that was strongly resisted by the landowners and ultimately rejected by Churchill (Ambrose, 2014). The system created by the Labour government in 1947 sought to balance public and private interests: property would stay in private hands, but the right to develop it was nationalised – meaning that landowners and developers must apply to their local authority for planning permission to build new property or convert existing buildings from one use to another (Clive Turner, 2015).

One-off compensation would be given to landowners for value lost, but a development charge would capture the betterment caused by the granting of planning permission. Where the state chose to develop land – for reconstruction, industrial development or to provide better housing – it would compulsorily purchase land if necessary, but the owners would be compensated at the full market value. Green belts around major cities would prevent the suburban sprawl of the 1930s and focus private investment on the war-damaged inner cities, while the state would ensure an adequate supply of land for new homes via slum clearance and the New Towns Programme (see Box 4.2). Just as King James II noted in relation to the first proposals for building Edinburgh's New Town in the quotation at the start of this chapter, the key to delivering the new settlements was to acquire the land at low cost. If the landowners were able to extract too much economic rent in the form of land prices there would be insufficient value to pay for the infrastructure and quality needed to make the result 'in favour of the citizens' (Grant, 1880). The combination of low-cost land acquisition, strong plan-making and the power to determine planning applications proved to be a powerful means of overcoming the problem of rent.

Box 4.2 The New Towns programme

The New Towns programme built thirty-two new towns in Britain between 1946 and 1970 under the powers of the New Towns Act 1946 (and later acts). The programme was designed to relocate populations in poor or bombed-out housing following the Second World War. They had in common the statutory mechanism used to develop them, involving the creation of an appointed public corporation serving each new town that had extremely strong powers as a delivery vehicle (TCPA, 2014).

The new towns were built on agricultural land beyond the designated green belts of the older cities they surrounded. Each New Town Development Corporation purchased land compulsorily at agricultural prices, laid down a comprehensive masterplan for the town, and built the necessary infrastructure with Treasury bond finance. They granted planning permission on the sites they now owned, and sold many of them on to private house builders, using the uplift in the value to repay the loans (DCLG, 2006). Other sites were sold to local authorities for council housing and community facilities.

Although many of the new towns have poor reputations today, this is partly a reflection of the contemporary preference for dual carriageways, roundabouts and concrete, and partly due to the fact that many are now thought too small to be economically successful. But these criticisms belie the successful delivery record of the programme. The development corporations were largely self-financing, thanks to their ability to borrow cheaply and to capture the uplift in land value they created. Today the new towns are home to over 2.76 million people – around 4.3% of UK households.

Much of this post-war package of land market intervention survives today, particularly the planning system. The major exceptions are the commitment to ensure sufficient land supply for new homes and the development charge. The latter was widely criticised as unfair and unworkable by individuals seeking to build their own homes as well as by larger landowners. Many landowners withheld their sites from development, hoping that a future government would repeal the charge – which the incoming Conservative government duly did.

The 1951 Conservative government was elected on a promise to build 300,000 houses a year. Part of the Conservative vision was to dramatically increase homeownership and transform the country into a 'property owning democracy' (Bogdanor and Skidelsky, 1970). The 1950s and 1960s saw house building in Britain reach its peak, with over 425,000 homes being built in 1968 alone – a figure that has never since been surpassed (see Figure 4.1). This unprecedented rate of building was partly offset by large numbers of demolitions, as decaying or war-damaged urban terraces made way for new estates.

The combined effect was a rapid decline in private renting and a dramatic rise in owner-occupancy and, to a lesser extent, social housing. By the late 1960s, more households were renting socially than privately, and by 1971 the number of owner-occupiers roughly equalled those who were renting (see Figure 4.2). This represents a watershed moment as, from this point onwards, owner-occupancy would be the most common type of housing tenure in the UK.

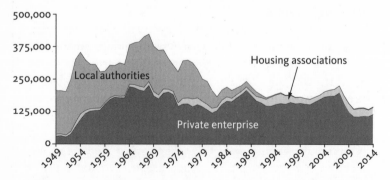

Figure 4.1 New houses built by tenure (United Kingdom) (*source*: Office for National Statistics, 2016a)

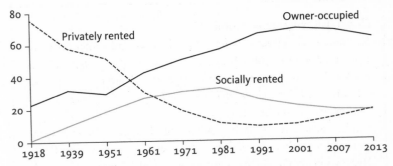

Figure 4.2 Trends in tenure type from 1918 to 2013 (Great Britain) (%) (*source*: Office for National Statistics, 2016b; figures for 1918 and 1939 are for England and Wales only)

Post-war Britain – along with much of the developed world – enjoyed high levels of economic growth, moderate rates of inflation and full employment. Economic policy making was dominated by Keynesian thought (see Box 4.3) and the pursuit of bold social reforms such as the establishment of the welfare state, the nationalisation of the railways and the creation of the National Health Service. This period is often described as the 'Golden Age of Capitalism', and lasted until the collapse of the Bretton Woods fixed exchange rate regime in 1971.[3]

In the mixed economy of the Keynesian era, state-sponsored house building by councils coexisted with development by private firms, and to a much lesser extent by non-profit housing associations. The years in which the state built most were also those in which the market built most, suggesting that state supply caused little if any crowding out of private investment. If anything, the opposite was true, as relatively small regional and local building

---

3 The Bretton Woods system was developed at the United Nations Monetary and Financial Conference held in Bretton Woods, New Hampshire, from 1 to 22 July 1944. The major outcome of the Bretton Woods conference was the introduction of an adjustable pegged foreign exchange rate system whereby all currencies were linked to the US dollar which, in turn, was made convertible to gold at a fixed price. The conference also saw the creation of two global institutions that still play important roles today – the International Monetary Fund (IMF) and the World Bank. The system disintegrated on 5 August 1971 when US President Nixon abandoned the US dollar's convertibility to gold.

Box 4.3 Keynesian economics

Keynesian economics gets its name, theories and principles from British economist John Maynard Keynes (1883–1946), who is regarded as the founder of modern macroeconomics. His most famous work, *The General Theory of Employment, Interest and Money*, was published in 1936.

The central tenet of this school of thought is that government intervention can stabilise the economy. During the Great Depression of the 1930s, existing economic theory was unable either to explain the causes of the severe worldwide economic collapse or to provide an adequate public policy solution to jump-start production and employment. The prevailing idea that free markets would automatically adjust and provide full employment had failed.

The main plank of Keynes's theory is the assertion that aggregate demand measured as the sum of spending by households, businesses and the government is the most important driving force in an economy. Moreover, prices, and especially wages, respond slowly to changes in supply and demand, resulting in periodic shortages and surpluses, especially of labour. Keynes asserted that free markets have no self-balancing mechanisms to counter this and achieve full employment, and therefore justified government intervention through public policies that aim to achieve full employment and price stability.

Keynes' ideas became widely accepted after the Second World War and provided the main inspiration for economic policy makers in Western industrialised countries. However, Keynesian economics began to fall out of favour in the 1970s as many economies experienced slow economic growth, high unemployment and rising inflation, a phenomenon which is often referred to as stagflation.

firms were able to take contracts to build homes for the council, while financing a few speculative homes for sale themselves. If credit was hard to come by, or sales slow, these builders could keep themselves in business and their staff in work by continuing to build for the council. State supply thus not only supported private investment, it operated counter-cyclically by smoothing the peaks and troughs inherent in the speculative business model employed by private house-building firms.

This mixed economy in both housing supply and tenure was supported by strict financial regulations which restricted the amount of credit that could flow into the private housing market (see Chapter 5), and a tax regime designed to balance the economic position of homeowners and renters. Between them, these measures constituted the most comprehensive attempt yet to address the problem of rent. Taxes, financial regulations and rent controls prevented property owners from extracting excessive rents, while state intervention in the land market and council house building reduced market volatility and provided low-cost alternatives. But some of these critical mechanisms of the Keynesian land economy had already been undermined towards the end of this period.

Firstly, a number of changes to taxation shifted incentives dramatically in favour of homeownership. In 1963 'Schedule A' income tax, a tax on imputed rental income, was abolished. Imputed rent is the 'in kind' income that homeowners receive from their property, and is calculated as the rent that would be paid for a similar property in the private rented sector. The concept of imputed rent rests on the idea that owner-occupiers benefit from housing services they would otherwise have to pay for by renting a property. While imputed rent from owner-occupancy is no longer subject to taxation, landlords' rental income is still subject to income tax. Many economists maintain that the tax-exempt status of imputed rental income makes it more attractive to receive income in this form than in other forms, which has the effect of distorting investment decisions, attracting excess capital into the housing market (Callan, 1992). In conditions of low price elasticity of supply this in turn drives up house prices, excluding others from buying and increasing the gap between those that own property and those that do not. The value of this tax exemption was estimated at £8.3 billion in 2012–13 (National Audit Office, 2014).

Secondly, when capital gains tax was introduced in 1965 an exemption was made for primary residencies. Capital gains tax is charged on gains realised due to the disposal of assets, calculated as the difference between the cost of acquiring the asset and the income acquired due to the disposal of that asset. This tax exemption means that, relative to people who choose to invest in other assets, those who treat their home as an investment will benefit when selling that home. This is particularly relevant in the UK where real house prices have risen considerably, with owners enjoying windfall gains that have gone untaxed. The value of this tax exemption was estimated at £10.4 billion in 2012–13 (National Audit Office, 2014)

Thirdly, in 1969, the government introduced mortgage interest relief at source (MIRAS) which provided tax relief for interest payments on mortgages. MIRAS enabled mortgagors to claim back debt interest costs at the basic rate of income tax, and this gave a clear financial incentive to get a mortgage and buy property. The rate of relief was gradually reduced from 1994 until it was abolished completely in 2000. Although mortgage interest relief is no longer available for owner-occupiers, some relief remains in place for buy-to-let landlords.

Finally, governments began to support various forms of 'low-cost homeownership', starting with mutual co-ownership in 1964 (Martin, 2001). Together, these changes created a major bias in favour of owner-occupation, and contributed towards the continued rise in homeownership in the 1970s and 1980s – against the headwinds of rising house prices.

4.4 1970 onwards: the emergence of 'residential capitalism'

The 1970s was a period of huge change, socially, politically and economically. While an immediate shortage of housing was no longer a major concern following the large-scale building in the post-war era, the UK economy faced multiple challenges as the dynamics of the global economy were transformed following the collapse of the Bretton Woods system. These included runaway inflation, oil price shocks, high interest rates and increasing tensions between industry and trade unions. This ultimately led to the election of Margaret Thatcher as prime minister in 1979, along with the emergence of monetarism and a more market-orientated approach to social and economic policy (see Box 4.4). Seen in retrospect, the economic and political upheavals of the 1970s have overshadowed some of the dramatic changes to the housing landscape. This was the era when homeownership reached majority status, and when the now-familiar pattern of house price booms and busts was born.

Box 4.4 Monetarism

Monetarism is mainly associated with Nobel Prize-winning economist Milton Friedman, whose seminal work *A Monetary History of the United States, 1867–1960* was published with Anna Schwartz in 1963. Monetarism maintains that, in the absence of major unexpected fluctuations in the money supply, markets are inherently stable and will adjust to disruptions quickly. Monetarists believe that the objectives of monetary policy are best met by targeting the growth rate of the money supply, and assert that other forms of government intervention can often destabilise the economy rather than help it.

Monetarist economists typically believe that the provision of housing should be left to the private sector and oppose government interventions such as social housing, subsidies and rent controls. Although generally supporting minimal taxation, monetarists favour property taxes on the basis that they are the least distortionary taxes. Milton Friedman famously supported the taxation of land as advocated by Henry George on the basis that it was the 'least bad tax'.

Although monetarism gained influence in the UK and the USA in the late 1970s as both countries battled high inflation, within a few years monetarism had fallen out of favour with economists as the link between different measures of money supply and inflation proved to be less clear than monetarist theories had suggested. Today central banks have largely abandoned setting monetary targets, choosing instead to target inflation by setting interest rates. However, the monetarist support of free markets and opposition to state intervention had a lasting influence on economic theory and policy making.

The advent of the house price boom

As will be discussed in detail in the next chapter, the early 1970s and 1980s saw the deregulation of mortgage lending. Prior to this, mortgage lending had mostly been carried out by building societies – mutual organisations operated for the benefit of their members. But the liberalisation of credit markets encouraged banks to enter the housing finance markets. This helped triggered the first boom and bust in house prices, with the average price of a house doubling between 1970 and 1973 before falling sharply again in real terms. Lending limits were re-imposed on banks after this but the Conservative government that gained power in 1979 pushed back on these. The result was a second house price boom and bust which occurred between 1978 and 1982. In both cases nominal house prices never actually fell – the fall in real values was driven by nominal prices not keeping up with general price inflation.

Partly as a result of the fiscal crises of the 1970s, public house building fell significantly, though this was also due to the fact that, after twenty years of record house building and modest population growth, it was widely felt that supply was simply no longer a problem. This view, and growing political concern about the decline of inner cities, spelled the end of the New Towns programme after the founding of Milton Keynes, and the redirection of funding to urban regeneration programmes (Hall and Ward, 2014). At the same time, court judgments on compensation (particularly the Myers case of 1969) reinstated the principle that landowners should be able to claim 'hope value' on any land compulsorily purchased, reducing the ability of the New Towns model to deliver cheap land for new housing. These two related changes were hardly noticed at the time, but in effect they removed one side of the 1946–47 settlement on land supply and planning, leaving the other side (development control and the green belt) firmly in place (Aubrey, 2016).

The drive for homeownership

Following the election of Margaret Thatcher's Conservative government in 1979, the huge state house-building programme that had characterised the post-war era came to an end. Inspired by the party's strategy in the 1950s, the newly elected government sought to dramatically increase homeownership and achieve the long-held Conservative goal of transforming the country into a 'property owning democracy'. The first step towards this came in October 1980 when the government passed its first Housing Act, launching its flagship 'Right to Buy' policy, compelling councils to sell social homes to their occupiers (see Box 4.5).

Further reforms completed the transformation of the housing sector. Much remaining council housing was transferred to the housing association sector, largely driven by the political desire to keep official public sector borrowing down. The stage was set for the revival of the private rented sector by the Housing Act of 1988's removal of rent regulation and introduction of the Assured Shorthold Tenancy. Under this new form of rental tenure, private landlords would be able to evict their tenants at will, without having to show grounds, and tenancies could be as short as six months.

Meanwhile, further financial deregulation drove a greater allocation of credit to house purchases, fuelling a new house price boom (see Chapter 5) that would burst spectacularly in 1990 when interest rates were raised to keep the value of the pound within the bands of the European Exchange Rate Mechanism.

Finally, in recognition that moving towards market housing would leave some people unable to adequately house themselves, the complex systems of individual housing subsidies were amalgamated and Housing Benefit was born (Malpass and Aughton, 1999). The new benefit regime was part of a dramatic shift away from subsidising 'bricks and mortar' and towards subsidising individuals (Webb, 2012). The effect of this shift to a system of 'subsidised individualism' was to allow for a greater role for market forces in the provision of housing for lower income households (Forrest and Murie, 1986). Whereas in 1975 more than 80% of housing subsidies were supply-side subsidies intended to promote the construction of social homes, by 2000 more than 85% of housing subsidies were on the demand side aimed at helping individual tenants pay the required rent (Stephens et al., 2005).

In effect, the reforms of the 1970s and 1980s marked a reversal of the package of economic policies of land and housing that had

Box 4.5 The Right to Buy

The Right to Buy allowed public housing tenants to purchase their homes at a heavily discounted price. During Margaret Thatcher's time in office 1.5 million publicly owned houses were privatised in what she described as 'one of the most important revolutions of the century' (Linklater, 2013). This led to a significant rise in owner-occupancy throughout the 1980s and 1990s and a marked decline in the number of people living in the social rented sector.

The Right to Buy was controversial from the start and the effects of the policy are still debated today. Some hail it as a great success which provided ownership and an asset with appreciating value to many who would otherwise have been prevented from gaining access to property (Stephens et al., 2005). Others have criticised it for weakening the ability of government to meet objectives relating to housing need. In many cases shortages of social housing have led to longer waiting lists and the housing of families in unsuitable or more expensive properties. The policy has also led to an increasing divergence between the types of property that are in the private sector and the social sector. In the years following the policy's introduction there were proportionately fewer purchases of less popular types of housing such as high-rise flats, and as a result local authorities were generally left with homes of lower quality (Forrest and Murie, 1986).

Moreover, as wealthier tenants were better placed to take up the Right to Buy, the social rented sector saw a greater concentration of the poorest and most disadvantaged households. While in 1979 20% of households in the top decile of the income distribution lived in social housing, by 2004–05 this had fallen to close to zero (Hills, 2007). This phenomenon has been described as the 'residualisation' of the social rented sector (Stephens et al., 2005).

Right to Buy has also been criticised for representing poor value for money for taxpayers who funded the initial building of the council houses, subsidised the substantial discounts offered to tenants and then – once the homes were sold – missed out on the rental income that would otherwise have been received. Many of these criticisms of the policy would have been avoided if the homes sold had been replaced. Certainly the money raised from the sales, even after the discounts, could have financed the building of much new social housing, but government rules largely prevented councils from building new stock, and the proceeds of the sales were mainly appropriated by the national Treasury for general fiscal purposes. This decision was driven by the government's desires to reduce state expenditure and public debt, cut back the role of local government, and change the tenure balance away from social housing.

emerged after the First World War and reached its zenith after the Second. No longer would the state seek to actively intervene in the market to ensure land supply for development, provide large amounts of non-market housing for rent, or restrict the ability of landlords to set rent levels or evict their tenants. Instead, deregulated credit and the privatisation of publicly owned assets would extend opportunities for homeownership to more people, while cash benefits would support the small number who could not house themselves in the newly liberated market. Under this new, liberal settlement the problem of rent would not be tackled directly at all, but the ability to be on the winning side of the equation would be offered to a greater proportion of society than ever before.

4.5 The new political economy of housing

By the end of the millennium direct state involvement in house building had largely come to an end, social housing was in decline and homeownership was on the rise. These changes would permanently alter the political economy of housing in Britain and have lasting consequences for political behaviour, public policy and macroeconomic outcomes.

One important effect has been on the interests and aspirations of the electorate: the last thirty years have witnessed an expansion in the number of voters who have a vested interest in the buoyancy of the housing market, and a marked decline in the constituency of voters with an interest in social housing. This has triggered a shift in political attitudes on issues of housing and resulted in a much greater focus on meeting homeowners' aspirations.[4]

Overall these factors represent a profound shift in the way that land and property has been perceived in British society. Whereas 100 years ago houses were mostly regarded as simply somewhere to live, today homeownership is promoted as an investment opportunity which offers long-term financial security in the face of stagnating wages, dwindling pensions and reduced state welfare provision. To politicians and much of the general public alike, houses are no longer perceived as universal consumption goods but rather as vehicles for accumulating wealth. Homeownership has become perceived by many as 'the essential step to obtain membership of an expanding middle class for whom housing equity was pivotal in a broader lifestyle of credit based and housing equity fuelled consumption' (Forrest et al., 1999).

As we will examine in Chapters 4 and 5, underpinning this has been a deregulation and liberalisation of the financial sector and a rapid increase in income and wealth inequalities. This marks the final major shift in land's economic significance, as high levels of owner-occupation, a deregulated housing finance system and growing inequalities have combined to create a system of 'residential capitalism' (Schwartz and Seabrooke, 2008). In turn, the political dominance of homeowners – both in national elections and in local planning decisions – has ensured that their interests have been protected and subsidised by government policy (Keohane and Broughton, 2013).

But the realisation of this vision of a property-owning democracy remains necessarily incomplete, and the new political economy of land has proved to be inherently unstable. As would soon become apparent, the new model of state-supported private wealth accumulation via mortgaged homeownership did not resolve the older contradictions of the land economy – it merely gave them a new and broader field to play themselves out on.

---

4 Some scholars have cited the example of the Labour Party's reversal of its opposition to the sale of council houses and subsequent enthusiasm for homeownership as evidence of this (Forrest and Murie, 1986).

Supply: house building into the new millennium

From its peak in the 1960s, the steady withdrawal of the British state from the housing supply system has had profound consequences. Not only has it changed the tenure balance firmly in favour of the market, it has also entrenched the dominance of the speculative model of private house building (see Box 4.6).

As part of the move away from building traditional social housing, the 1990s and 2000s also saw the rise of a new means of subsidising affordable housing.[5] Section 106 of the Town and Country Planning Act 1990 allows local planning authorities to enter into legally binding agreements with developers, with the latter having to provide certain public benefits as part of the development – particularly the provision of a proportion of affordable housing within the development (or sometimes via a commuted sum paid to the authority). This cost falls on the developer, so S106 can be seen as a form of development tax, negotiated on a case by case basis, even though it is not framed as such legally, and cash rarely changes hands. It is also a form of direct subsidy for affordable housing via the planning system. Perhaps because it has evolved gradually, and because each obligation is negotiated separately, S106 has not suffered the same fate as the various attempts to introduce development taxes since the Second World War. Nonetheless, along with the planning system as a whole, it has come under attack from free-market economists and developers, especially when they feel the percentage of affordable housing required by planning authorities is too high.

The 'mixed funding' model for supporting housing associations' development or acquisition of affordable housing that has emerged since the 1990s consists of three main pillars: planning subsidy (Section 106); direct grant paid to housing associations; and commercial borrowing by associations. This model has been successful in reducing the amount of direct government subsidy per home, and at integrating market and affordable homes in mixed-tenure communities, but it has exposed affordable housing supply

---

5 The term 'affordable housing' is used from here on to refer to the growing number of submarket, subsidised tenures that have joined traditional social housing as targets of government policy. As housing policy became increasing devolved to Wales and Scotland from 1998 onwards, the focus from here on is on England.

Box 4.6 The speculative house builder model

The speculative, or 'current trader' model of house building is essentially a cyclical process of raising finance, buying land, securing planning permission, constructing the homes and finally selling them (Callcutt, 2007). Most of these functions will typically be carried out by specialised contractors – land agents, planning consultancies, construction contractors, marketing agencies – although some may be carried out in-house by the developer (meaning the company that initiates this process). The developer is said to be acting speculatively, because they are not building for a known purchaser or at a known price, but with the intention of selling on the open market to whomever is prepared to pay the most. Under this model, the developer retains no long-term interest in the property, but moves on to redeploy their capital in further speculative cycles. This contrasts with the development of commercial property, which is typically carried out by asset-holding companies seeking rental income from their property.

The developer's profit will be the margin between the sale price achieved, and the total amount spent on the entire development process. There are long time lags in this process, with typically many years elapsing between land acquisition and sale of the finished homes. Developers must deploy large amounts of capital during this process, and therefore take on significant risk. The biggest risks are around securing planning permission, and the market price for the homes that will be achieved at the end of the process. These risks are typically borne by the developer itself, whereas the various contractors in the process typically only take on the smaller risks of delivering on the agreed contract. Correspondingly, contractors typically charge fixed fees or margins of around 6%, whereas the developers target returns of around 20% and may make far more in a rising market.

Several important features of the British housing system are the product of this model. Because development is risky, uncertain and requires a lot of capital, developers prioritise strategies that can reduce their risk, such as holding strategic land banks, financing each scheme separately, and seeking to dominate localised new-build markets to reduce competition. Risk, and a high level of demand for homes, discourages innovation in the industry, which prefers to stick to tried and trusted technologies and product designs.

Because of the time lags inherent in development, and its vulnerability to housing market price cycles, development is highly cyclical. When house prices fall, developers suspend land acquisition and cut build-out rates swiftly to reduce expenditure and avoid selling into a falling market. When house prices are rising, developers must compete to secure suitable land, driving greater volatility in land prices.

Because land acquisition is usually the largest single cost, and often the first one to be incurred, the price that the developer pays for the land determines much of what happens later in the process (see Box 4.7). The difficulties and costs of securing land also create major barriers to entry for new firms.

The combination of high risk, cyclicality and barriers to entry drives concentration in the industry through business failures and mergers. This is only partially offset by the need for detailed local knowledge to secure the best sites at good prices.

Because the developer does not retain an interest in the scheme, and because the developer has far more knowledge than the buyer (who is typically the consumer or an amateur investor) there is little incentive on the developer to prioritise quality.

It is worth noting that most of these aspects of the speculative model stem from the interaction between private firms and the planning system – specifically the weakness of the system's ability to determine appropriate land use in advance, which creates uncertainty. Countries with stronger plan-led systems do not seem to experience such high degrees of speculative behaviour (Needham, 2014).

to multiple market and political risks and uncertainties. It also makes determining the precise subsidy actually required to provide affordable homes extremely difficult, as each scheme is different and the value of S106 is hard to quantify accurately (University of Reading et al., 2014).

Housing associations' ability to invest depends on lenders' willingness to lend to them, which in turn depends largely on the perceived security of the associations' future income stream, which in turn depends largely on welfare policy (as around 60% of social tenants rely on housing benefit). Cuts to housing benefit, and uncertainty about the likelihood of future cuts, therefore increase the cost of housing association borrowing.

At the same time, growing reliance on S106 means that affordable housing provision became more directly linked to market production, so it is liable to stop when private house building stalls. Affordable house building is therefore less able to provide the countercyclical stabilising impact that it used to, potentially worsening the severity of market downturns (Katz et al., 2003).

Each of the three periods of private supply growth that have occurred since 1970 have ended in a dramatic downturn in market house building, which is to be expected given the nature of the speculative house building model. While each drop in supply has been very rapid, the recovery after each slump has been slow, and each new peak in supply has been lower than the last. The effect of this asymmetric relationship between demand and supply is that total market house building has ratcheted inexorably downward since the high-water mark of 1966 (Jefferys and Lloyd, 2015).

A further effect of the pattern of housing market boom and bust is that speculative house building has become an increasingly risky business. When the market turns rapidly, smaller developers find themselves facing calls on their bank loans incurred to buy land at inflated prices, just as sale prices and volumes collapse. Inevitably, in the absence of countercyclical public investment or council construction contracts to tide them over, many go bust or are bought up by their better capitalised rivals. With each turn of the cycle, the house building sector has become more and more concentrated into fewer, larger national firms.

These national house builders operate on a business model that focuses on controlling and trading land in high-demand areas, as this is both an essential survival strategy and the source of the greatest profits. While media and policy attention typically focuses on developers' 'current' land banks (i.e. those with planning permission), these only account for around five years of future housing supply, while it is estimated that 82% of all the land held by developers is strategic (i.e. without planning permission) (Office of Fair Trading, 2008). Developers often control strategic land via the use of options agreements, which are private contracts with landowners such as farmers, and are generally not publicly disclosed.

This restricts the ability of rivals to acquire suitable development sites, and presents a major barrier to entry into the house building industry, further entrenching the dominance of the existing large firms (Griffith, 2011). These land market conditions effectively give 'monopoly power to developers who own particular patches of land where large proportions of development [are] being made available' (Cheshire, 2011).

The concentration of the industry and barriers to entry have lowered competitive pressure, and militated against product innovation, with the result that new homes in Britain are widely seen to be unattractive and poor quality, with only 18% rated as being of good or very good design. Fully two-thirds of home buyers say they would not even consider buying a new-build – an extraordinary indictment of the quality and size of home that the industry produces (Neale, 2009). While design quality may be partly subjective, the evidence on space is more clear-cut. New homes in the UK are smaller than the existing stock and those built in comparable countries: new homes in the land-constrained Netherlands are on average 53% larger, and in Denmark 80% bigger. Even Japan builds homes 21% larger than the UK (Robert-Hughes et al., 2011).

Poor quality development in turn feeds two distinct vicious cycles. Firstly, in a highly localised, discretionary planning system, local people are more likely to successfully resist development proposals they perceive to be undermining the quality of their environment, worsening overall supply rates (Garvie, 2013). Secondly, in the context of high house prices, supply shortages and a liberalised mortgage market, market pressure to make homes smaller and raise densities helps to drive land prices upward. As developers must compete on price for development sites, in conditions of uncertainty, there is a significant risk of overpaying for land. This pushes up land prices and landowner expectations, fuelling the

Box 4.7 Residual land valuation

Because land is not fungible, the value of each site is unique to it at a particular moment in time: there is no generic price of land. Indices of land value are therefore at best descriptive averages, rather than accurate expressions of actual market prices. Each plot of land must be valued separately to ascertain its potential price. While non-developable land is typically valued based on its use value – how much income it generates – valuing development land is more complex, as its value depends on what can be built on it and what sale value or rental income that property will command.

Developers, as buyers of land for housing, typically employ a residual valuation methodology to arrive at an offer price. This process essentially works by estimating the final sales value that the developer expects to get from the homes (or other property) built, and then subtracting all of the costs expected to be incurred in building them, to leave a residual amount. Whatever the developer decides to offer for the land must come from this residual.

This process is highly uncertain, as there are a huge number of unknowns which the developer must estimate. It is also competitive, as the landowner will typically accept the highest bid offered. Several critical features of the housing supply system flow from this process:

- Rising house prices feed directly back to rising land prices, so landowners receive much of the increase in property values.
- Any cost imposed by public policy, such as taxes on development, restrictions on what can be built, or benefits in kind like affordable housing, effectively comes off the land price, as the developer will include these costs in the residual valuation.
- In a competitive market for land, the developer that makes the most bullish expectations of sales prices, and/or projects the lowest costs, will typically be able to offer the landowner most and secure the site. This drives development towards lower construction costs and higher densities – meaning smaller, poorer quality homes.
- Once the land has been paid for, the developer is exposed to the risk that costs may be higher, or sales values lower, than

expected, which eats into the developer's profit. If the developer's profit falls too far, the scheme will be deemed 'non-viable', construction will halt and the developer may go bust. The higher the land price paid, the higher this risk: competition for land therefore means that development is likely to be close to the margins of viability.

speculative pressure on land and further undermining the viability of development (see Box 4.7).

Despite repeated reviews and policy initiatives to reform the planning system and boost private house building (Barker, 2004; Callcutt, 2007; Lyons, 2014), total supply remains far below the levels achieved under the post-war mixed economy.

Demand: boom without the bust?

Today, both the housing market cycle and the obsession with home-ownership are firmly entrenched in Britain, to the extent that it is often assumed that both have always been with us. But despite the damaging impacts of housing market crashes on many households and the wider economy, the three major booms and busts between 1970 and 1995 did nothing to dampen the British public's desire for homeownership, or politicians' enthusiasm for promoting it (Saunders, 2016). In fact, once prices had stabilised and both buyers' and lenders' appetite had returned, each crash brought prices within reach of a new generation of homeowners. In the mid-1990s, the ratio of house prices to earnings was five, as it had been in 1969 (see Figure 4.3), while the proportion of homeowners had gone from around 50% to nearly 70%.

But the fourth price boom that began in the mid-1990s was different. This time, consistently low interest rates and low inflation enabled prices to triple in the ten years up to 2007, sending the price/earnings ratio up to over ten (Jefferys and Lloyd, 2015). The severity of this decline in affordability was masked, for a while at least, by low mortgage rates, which kept monthly repayments within reasonable bounds for those buyers able to find

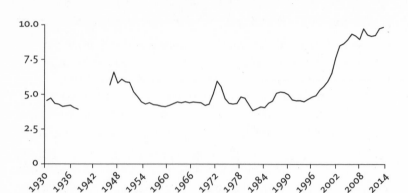

Figure 4.3 Ratio of house prices to gross average earnings (*source*: Bank of England, 2016d; DCLG, 2010)

sufficient capital for a deposit (Wilcox, 2006). Policy responses to the mounting affordability pressure therefore focused on helping first-time buyers over the deposit barrier through a series of low-cost homeownership initiatives, while the market response was to offer mortgages on ever higher loan-to-value rates – peaking at over 100% in some cases. The credit crunch and subsequent monetary easing reinforced this picture of high house prices and low mortgage rates, while the withdrawal of high loan-to-value mortgages raised the deposit barrier ever higher. As affordability pressures worsened and first-time buyer rates plummeted government resorted to ever more generous subsidies for marginal homeowners (Wilson and Blow, 2013).

As we discuss in Chapters 5 and 6, the consequence of the long house price boom was a huge increase in both the asset wealth of homeowners and the amount of mortgage debt outstanding. The financial crisis triggered a rapid reduction in new mortgage lending, but only a modest correction in house prices, which has since been reversed in most parts of Britain. Domestic demand may have been curtailed by lenders' attempts to deleverage, a trend reinforced by a new regulatory regime requiring lenders to inspect borrowers' ability to repay far more closely, but the global nature of the financial crisis also opened up new sources of demand, as anxious foreign capital sought the relative safety of UK property, joining the flood of buy-to-let investment (see section 6.4).

The financial crisis and the response to it also had profound impacts on the housing supply industry and the land market. After 2008 the mortgage lending banks, the major developers and government all had an interest in maintaining artificially high book values of developers' land banks. If land prices had been allowed to crash, as they had after previous market busts, many developers would have faced bankruptcy. Despite many developers breaching their bank covenants, or coming close to it, in the main it suited the banks not to foreclose on their assets, as this would have hastened the downward spiral in land values. In practice, the market largely froze, as developers cut back their outgoings and sought to recapitalise. This sustained relatively high land and house prices, and preserved the developers and banks, but at the price of transactions and output plummeting. There was no clearing of the market, no rebasing of land and house prices as after the last three booms, no opportunities for new entrants to enter the market, or for a new cohort of owner-occupiers to buy.

In the absence of a market clear-out, the new government resorted to ever more massive demand-side subsidies to help push a few more middle-income households over the line into homeownership. The new land economy settlement that had emerged by the end of the 1980s – minimal supply-side intervention and demand-side support for homeownership – was being pushed to its limits.

Tenure: the limits to homeownership

Just as redistribution of agricultural land had broken open monopolies on political and economic power in previous eras, and in the reconstruction of the losing countries after the First World War, so the spread of homeownership during the twentieth century brought many benefits (Linklater, 2013). Not only did it give millions of people the prospect of a secure, decent home for the first time (including the ability to live rent-free in retirement), it also gave them a capital asset and created a new channel for converting wealth into current consumption (see Chapter 5).

But rising homeownership also seems to create the conditions for its own demise, as rising prices choke off effective demand from first-time buyers.

As outlined above, house builders have become increasingly geared towards building for the private market, making supply levels highly vulnerable to housing market falls, yet very slow to pick up during house price booms.

Rising levels of homeownership also impact on the politics of housing, which in turn have reinforced the pattern of rising prices and sclerotic supply.

As homeownership in the UK has increased over time, the proportion of the electorate whose personal wealth is tied to the housing market has also grown. A substantial increase in the housing stock would likely put downward pressure on house prices, so a political tension has arisen between resolving the problems of supply and affordability on the one hand, and maintaining the asset wealth of homeowners on the other. Keohane and Broughton (2013) describe this as a negative feedback loop between homeownership and house prices, leading to a 'low-supply equilibrium' (see Figure 4.4).

The evolution of taxation policy follows a similar trajectory: as homeowners become electorally dominant, elected governments since the 1960s have rolled back property taxes (see Box 4.8), and started to subsidise house purchase and homeownership.

This has been further reinforced by a more individualised approach to welfare and a reduced dependency on state housing provision or

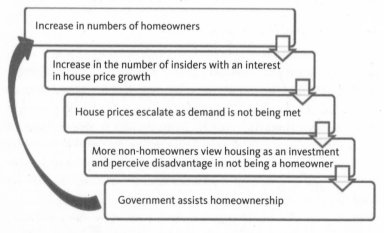

Figure 4.4 Homeownership and a 'low supply equilibrium' (*source*: Keohane and Broughton, 2013, p. 6)

land market intervention. Governments have increasingly sought to encourage the personal accumulation of assets such as housing equity as a means of meeting the cost of social care and retirement needs in an ageing population (Doling and Ronald, 2010). The move towards asset-based welfare has intensified under successive British governments on both sides of the political spectrum (Watson, 2009), but accelerated further once the Conservatives returned to power in 2010.

As a result of all these factors, the golden age of homeownership now seems to have been remarkably short. In fact, by the 1980s the ownership surge triggered by the Right to Buy already masked a deeper pattern: that the steady post-war rise in homeownership was fizzling out. As house prices started their volatile but inexorable upward march, and fewer and fewer of the middle classes were left renting, the gap between house prices and the incomes of those left behind grew ever larger. Lower mortgage costs following deregulation and Right to Buy discounts were able to cover this widening gap for a while, but by the early 1990s there were simply not enough prospective buyers who could afford to buy, and the proportion of mortgaged homeownership plateaued. The demographics of an ageing society meant that the rising number of older, outright owners continued to push total homeownership gently upwards for a further ten years, even as the number of younger first-time buyers fell away (DCLG, 2016). But this effect could only last so long: by 2003 total homeownership peaked at 73%, and has been in decline ever since (see Figure 4.2).

With traditional social housing in decline, but ownership increasingly out of reach, an increasingly large proportion of households found themselves without good housing options, particularly in the economically buoyant cities of the South East and a few others like Manchester, increasing the intensity of the housing pressures in these areas.

Despite new subsidy schemes aimed at aspiring homebuyers, both middle earning and poorer households have increasingly found themselves with little choice but to rent privately, producing a dramatic shift in the tenure pattern. The private rented sector, which had declined more or less steadily throughout the twentieth

Box 4.8 Taxes affecting residential property in the UK
Historically land was the primary source of taxation in the UK, but over time there has been a shift away from the taxation of land towards flows of income and of expenditure (Mirrlees and Adam, 2011). However, land and property taxes continue to form an important part of the tax base in the UK and most advanced economies.

- *Council tax:* a recurring tax levied on households by local authorities. The tax levied is based on the estimated value of the occupied property as at 1 April 1991 in England and Scotland and 1 April 2003 in Wales.
- *Capital gains tax:* a tax on the gain or profit made on the sale or disposal of assets such as shares or property. Primary residencies are exempt from capital gains tax.
- *Inheritance tax (IHT):* a tax paid on the net value of a person's estate transferred at death above a nil-rate band (currently £325,000) after deducting any exemptions and reliefs. The rate is currently 40%.
- *Stamp duty land tax (SDLT):* a tax which is payable on the purchase or transfer of property or land in England, Wales and Northern Ireland where the amount given is above a certain threshold. SDLT is charged as a percentage of the amount paid for the property. In Scotland there is a similar levy called land and buildings transaction tax (LBTT).

By some measures, the UK receives the highest proportion of tax from property in the OECD, amounting to 12% of total revenues (OECD, 2015). However, this is mainly due to the council tax, which can be said to be a highly ineffective property tax since taxable values bear little resemblance to current market values, and in any case is levied equally on those that rent their homes (Andrews et al., 2011). The reality is that under the UK tax system homeownership is treated favourably relative to other forms of investment.

One of the reasons for this is the exemption of primary residencies from capital gains tax and the tax exemption of imputed rental income, as discussed above. More recently, changes to inheritance tax have further enhanced the tax treatment of housing compared with other assets. In the 2015 summer budget the chancellor of the exchequer announced a new transferable main residence allowance which will gradually increase from £100,000 in April 2017 to £175,000 per person by 202021. This will effectively raise the tax-free allowance from £325,000 to £500,000 per person for estates that include a house, and to £1 million for married couples.

Evidence suggests that the favourable tax treatment of home-ownership relative to other forms of investment has an impact on wider macroeconomic outcomes. Oxley and Haffner (2010) examine the systems of housing taxation in the UK, Denmark, Germany, the Netherlands and the USA and compare the impact on house price volatility, distributional outcomes and the choice of tenure. They conclude that the UK tax system stands out as being more favourable towards homeownership over other forms of tenure, and that these tax advantages bring significant distri-butional advantages to homeowners, who benefit from rising real values compared with those who rent. They also find that the UK's comparatively high house price volatility is linked to a lack of countercyclical property taxation such as those targeting capital gains and imputed rents.

century, began to pick up again following the abolition of restric-tions in 1988, and took off in the late 1990s once lenders spotted the opportunity to finance buy-to-let investment (see Chapter 5). Most of these investors were homeowners who had already accumulated significant wealth from the rising housing market (Lord et al., 2013). They also tended to be individual amateurs, rather than professional property firms, and they tended to favour existing homes rather than new builds. This new source of demand therefore helped keep house prices high and rising during the long boom from 1996 onwards, but did little to support new development.

In effect, the buy-to-let boom provided rented accommodation for the very generation increasingly shut out of homeownership by rising prices and from social housing by dwindling supply. And as private rents rose to absorb an increasing proportion of wages, it became ever harder for renters to save for the deposit needed to buy a home, creating a rent trap for a widening section of society (see Chapter 5).

Inevitably, this has meant the overall cost of housing benefit has increased significantly over time. In 2014–15 the government spend £24.3 billion on housing benefit, more than was spent on the police, roads and buying military equipment combined. The increase has been driven by a combination of changes in the number of claimants and changes in spending per claimant. The late 1980s and early 1990s saw large increases in spending driven in part by the deregulation of the private rental sector which led to rapid increases in private rents. After a period of stabilisation in the late 1990s, spending on housing benefit grew rapidly in the 2000s as the number of claimants and spending per claimant increased (Adam et al., 2015). Today nearly one in five households in Britain is reliant on housing benefit,[6] despite repeated attempts by government to scale it back.

4.6 Conclusion

As a result of these changes to the housing landscape since 2000, two sets of lines on the tenure graph have now crossed. Firstly, the decline of mortgaged homeownership among younger generations, coupled with low interest rates and increased life expectancy among older people, has meant outright ownership has overtaken mortgage-holding. And secondly, private renting has overtaken social renting for the first time since the 1960s (Figure 4.5).

Projecting these trends forwards, it would seem that the nineteenth century picture of the land economy is beginning to reassert itself in the twenty-first: sooner or later, the majority will find themselves renting from a small, wealthy minority of property owners. In this light, the twentieth century begins to look like an excep-

---

6 In 2014–15 4.9 million households claimed housing benefit out of approximately 27 million households (DWP).

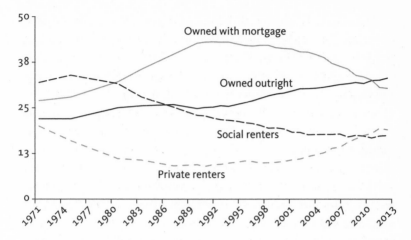

Figure 4.5 Tenure change in England, 1971–2015 (%) (*source*: Savills analysis of DCLG/analysis of English Housing Survey and Labour Force Survey data by Neal Hudson; pre-1981 data interpolated from unweighted responses for 1971 and 1975)

tion, during which successive waves of policy intervention – into land, housing and finance markets – allowed millions to achieve the dream of a decent, secure home. But as homeownership reached its limits and government abandoned attempts to address the problem of rent, the dynamics of the land market have reasserted themselves once again.

The quest for a way out of the rent trap led millions to become homeowners, and to start experiencing the benefits of rent extraction themselves. Today, the beneficiaries of the rentier economy are not a tiny handful of landed aristocrats, but a huge number of ordinary homeowners, including a smaller but growing subset who have used the wealth in their homes to acquire multiple properties to let out to those excluded from ownership. Nonetheless, their role in the economy is directly analogous to the landowners of the eighteenth and nineteenth centuries.

In an era of majoritarian democracy, governments have seen fit to slant public policy in favour of these new, domestic landowners, deepening the divide between those that do and do not own landed property. As a result, the government now finds itself paying out huge subsidies to mitigate housing problems, yet seemingly unable to address the fundamental drivers of those problems in the land economy. The policy response to date has been to continue to promote marginal homeownership, with limited success and at an ever rising cost in individual subsidies. Supply in all tenures remains stubbornly far below all measures of what is needed. Created by volatility and risk in the housing market, and supported by the politics of homeownership, the low supply equilibrium seems thoroughly entrenched.

The long history of the private property system suggests that, sooner or later, either a crash in property values will reset the market or housing market failure will weigh down ever more heavily on the economy, until the growing frustration of those paying ever larger proportions of their wages in rents triggers a political crisis, with unpredictable consequences.

Before going on to explore these impacts of the land economy on inequality in Chapter 6, we need to understand the critical factor that has driven the explosive yet persistent growth in house prices and housing wealth in recent decades: the vital link between land and finance.

CHAPTER 5

· ·

The financialisation
of land and housing

In most advanced countries, the share of mortgage lending
relative to other lending has increased dramatically over the
past century. With very few exceptions, the banks' primary
business consisted of non-mortgage lending to companies
both in 1928 and 1970. In 2007, banks in most countries
had turned primarily in to real estate lenders.
OSCAR JORDA ET AL. (2016, P. 16)

[T]he US and UK economies … turned their populations in to
highly leveraged speculators in a fixed asset that dominates
most portfolios and impairs personal mobility.
MARTIN WOLF (2008)

5.1 Introduction

In Bishops' Avenue, a grand street in a desirable part of North
London, a third of the mansions on the road are empty (Booth,
2014). Many have fallen into a state of disrepair and been unoc-
cupied for many years. This is striking. How could once beautiful
buildings on a plot of land so well located in one of the world's
fastest growing cities be left to rot? Clearly, these places are no
longer 'homes' in any meaningful sense of the word.

The owners of these buildings care little whether they are occupied or about their physical condition precisely because it is not
these features of these properties that make them valuable. Rather
their value lies in the prime real estate – the land – underneath them.
One of the mansions is on record as selling for just under £1 million
in 1988. They are now being sold for £65 million.

This example is an extreme one. But increasingly in parts of the United Kingdom and other advanced economies, the distinction between the *use* value of land or property as shelter for domestic or commercial residence and its *market* value as a financial asset that enables unearned capital gains – and rent extraction – is becoming blurred. But as land and house prices rise faster than incomes over a lengthy period of time, people increasingly view property not just as a place to live but as financial investments: for retirement, for their children, as an asset to borrow against and/or simply as a speculative financial asset. Similarly businesses and national and international investors are coming to view land as an attractive asset, particularly in a low interest environment.

How has this situation come to pass? We saw how different political economy regimes shaped and were shaped by the dynamics of land up until the 1980s in the last chapter and how the collapse in affordable home building drove up land prices in the UK. In this chapter we focus on the role of finance and how, in particular in the last thirty years, deregulation of credit and developments in information and communication technologies and households' expectations of speculative gains have increasingly become important drivers of rapid rises in land and house prices.

Today it is the *interaction* between land, property and the financial system that shapes the macroeconomy. Land has become 'financialised' (see Box 5.1), the object of speculative lending and investment, resulting in land and house prices separating themselves from growth and incomes in the wider economy. This fact is increasingly recognised by a number of eminent economists as a central problem for modern economies – for example John Muellbauer (2012), Adair Turner (2015a) and Joseph Stiglitz (2015a) – but is yet to be addressed by policy makers.

One reason policy makers have failed to recognise the issue is that mainstream economic theory lacks a coherent analysis of land and its role in the production process and the problems that can arise if economic rent is not addressed, as outlined in the previous two chapters. But just as importantly, mainstream economic theory fails to properly conceptualise the role of the banking system in the economy and the flows of credit and stocks of debts it creates.

In neoclassical economics, credit and money are considered a 'veil' over the real economy, which is made up of the exchange of 'real' goods and services in production and consumption (Schumpeter, 1954, p. 277). Banks' role is to oil this process by recycling pre-existing savings to borrowers (non-financial businesses) to invest in productive businesses creating goods and services. Fluctuations in the supply of money and credit may cause short-term shocks in the economy but in the long run they are assumed to be neutral, with economic growth primarily determined by changes in technology and labour productivity.

In fact, when a commercial bank makes a loan it does not 'recycle' money from elsewhere in the economy, rather it creates new money and purchasing power (McLeay et al., 2014). In addition, banks do not only create money for businesses to invest in production. They also create money for existing property and land purchase.

If banks create credit and money against existing land, as with the majority of home mortgages, this can inflate house and land prices.[1] Rising prices mean households and firms must borrow more to become home- or landowners. Therefore the supply of bank credit can be seen to create its own increased demand for even more credit, assuming a fixed supply of land. The demand for land can then stretch well beyond people's incomes or firms' profits – and the growth rate of the economy – in particular if people expect house prices to continue to rise faster than incomes. As debt-to-income ratios build up, this will have non-neutral long-term 'real' economy effects; people may start to reduce their consumption as more and more of their income is taken up in mortgage repayments.

Similar dynamics apply to commercial real estate, the subject of repeated credit-driven bubbles through the twentieth century, including in south-east Florida in the mid-1920s (Ballinger, 1936), in Japan in the late 1980s and many states in the US in the 1970s (the latter driven by commodity price shocks) and in South East Asia in the 1990s (Kindleberger and Aliber, 2005, pp. 29–30).

---

1 Banks can and do also create credit and money for the purchase of existing financial assets, such as shares and bonds or to help companies purchase existing firms. Again, in such cases the likely effect is to inflate the prices of these financial assets (Werner, 1997; Bezemer, 2014).

These dynamics have been missing from the debate on rising property prices in the UK and other countries. Credit, and particularly real estate or mortgage credit, is the 'elephant in the room' when it comes to understanding the behaviour of house prices, land prices and consumption in advanced economies (Muellbauer and Williams, 2011). A further distinctive feature of the UK property system in recent years is its role as a recipient of funding from non-banks such as insurance companies and international funds as the era of globally low interest rates and recent monetary policy leads even more conservative investors to seek out higher yielding assets.

In this chapter we examine the relationship between land, the financial system and the wider economy. We will show how deregulation of the financial sector led banks to transform into property lenders and contribute to excessive house price inflation. Credit liberalisation also led to land prices and property wealth coming to play an important role in determining consumption demand, the main contributor to economic growth in advanced economies today (around two-thirds of GDP growth is driven by domestic consumption in the UK). This process has led to the emergence of a feedback loop, with ever rising house prices and ever increasing household debt making our economy highly vulnerable to economic shocks.

5.2 House and land prices, income and bank credit

The UK has experienced some of the highest increases in house prices of any advanced economy over the past two decades and considerable house price volatility (swings in prices). Figure 5.1 shows an index of how the average house price to average disposable income ratio[2] – a widely accepted measure of housing affordability – has changed since 1987 in five major advanced economies. In the UK and Australia, there has been close to a 40% increase in this ratio. In contrast, in other countries including Japan and Germany there have been significant decreases in the house price to income ratio.

---

2 Examining house prices as a ratio to income gives a better picture of affordability than simply looking at changes in the nominal value of property. Disposable income means after taxes, pensions and other benefits have been subtracted from gross income. This is a widely used proxy for purchasing power.

The UK and the US have also both experienced major swings in the affordability of house prices, swings much larger than changes to economic growth.

The vast majority of these increases in housing wealth and house prices have come not from increases in building costs, which have remained relatively flat, but from increases in *land* prices. A recent study of fourteen advanced economies found that 81% of house price increases between 1950 and 2012 can be explained by rising land prices, with the remainder attributable to increases in construction costs (Knoll et al., 2014, p. 31). In the UK, the figure was 74%. Figure 1.1 in Chapter 1 showed how land prices are much more volatile than house prices and, since the early 1990s in particular, land price increases have been far greater than the increase in house prices.

How do we explain these differences in land and property prices between countries? The diversity of experiences across economies at similar levels of development suggests that universal, catch-all arguments, such as 'low interest rates have caused high house prices', are not convincing. These countries have experienced similar central bank interest rates over time but house prices have diverged considerably.

It seems more likely that there may be deep-rooted country-specific and institutional dynamics at work, a finding that academic research supports (Muellbauer 2014a). One explanation that we have already touched on in Chapter 4 is that these countries have very different supply-side drivers of house prices, including different planning rules and different kinds of land and construction markets. We might expect a country like the UK, which has a relatively complex and slow-moving planning system, to have experienced higher house price rises than a country like Germany where there is greater regional and local autonomy over planning. Yet Australia and the US also have relatively decentralised planning systems but they have both experienced periods of very rapid house price inflation.

Another question when looking at Figure 5.1 is how do people afford to buy homes when they become so expensive relative to incomes? Why don't housing and land markets 'correct' more quickly after experiencing rapid rises, such as the UK and Australia experienced between the late 1990s and the mid-2000s? In an advanced

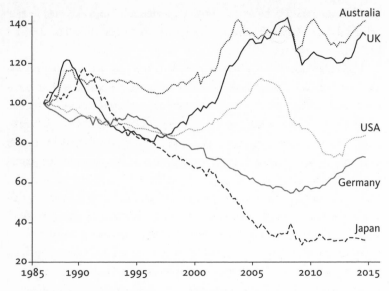

Figure 5.1 Index of house price to disposable income ratios in five advanced economies (base year = 1987) (*source*: OECD, n.d.)

market economy, it is generally unusual for any commodity or service to experience the kind of increases and variations we have seen in house prices.

The answer here lies not with the supply of homes but with the *demand* for those homes. The demand for homes and land is not limited in advance by people's incomes or the amount of money circulating in the domestic economy at any one particular time. This is because people can access credit – mortgage loans from banks – to finance the purchase of homes and land. When you get a mortgage, money is not taken from the existing supply of money in the economy and hence does not immediately reduce economic activity somewhere else.[3] When a bank makes a loan, it creates new credit and money – new purchasing power is added to the economy (see Box 5.1). Via bank lending (credit creation), households are thus able to purchase property even as property prices increase faster than their incomes.

---

3 Although the loan does need to be paid back, which, depending on the interest rate, may reduce spending going into the future, other things being equal.

Box 5.1: Credit and money creation by the banking system[4]

When a bank makes a 'loan' it creates a new asset and a new liability upon itself at the same time. The bank's asset is created by it simply typing into its account that the borrower owes it a sum of money: the loan. The bank's liability is created because it also types into the customer's account that s/he has a bank deposit of the same amount. No other customers' deposits are altered in any way. Bank deposits are created by banks mainly on the basis of their own confidence in the capacity of the borrower to repay the loan.

The borrower then spends that loan somewhere else. After the loan has been spent, it ends up in another (or even the same) bank as a deposit. An efficient electronic payments system then ensures that these liabilities can function as money: most payments can be settled by electronically reducing the balance of one account and increasing the balance of another, without any physical transfer of cash.

When a loan is repaid, the opposite process occurs. Both the loan (the bank's asset) and the deposit (the bank's liability) is reduced; money is destroyed and the money supply shrinks. Therefore, at any one moment in time, the money supply is determined by the amount of new loans being created minus those being repaid. In the UK, banks create 97% of the money supply via their lending activity with the remaining amount created as cash by the Bank of England and Treasury.

As shown in Figure 5.2, mortgage debt outstanding has increased from around 30% of real disposable income in 1987 to almost 100%, helping to drive up average house prices from four times disposable income per household to ten times. This of course disguises large regional variations – in more desirable areas such as London and the South East the ratio is up to twenty times (ONS, 2015c). Recent research shows that when housing costs (including

---

4   For a detailed exposition, see Ryan-Collins et al. (2012) and the Bank of England's *Quarterly Bulletin* article 'Money Creation in the Modern Economy' (McLeay et al., 2014).

- Ratio of house prices to real disposable income per capita (left-hand side)
- Mortgage debt outstanding (stock) as % of real disposable incomes (right-hand side)

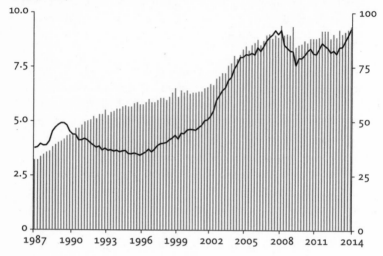

Figure 5.2 House prices and mortgage debt compared to income in the UK (*source*: ONS, Nationwide and Bank of England; data deflated using 2010 prices)

mortgage debt and rents) are included in an assessment of changing living standards since 2002, over half of UK households across the working age population have seen falling or flat living standards (Clarke et al., 2016).

The impact of rising housing costs is not distributed equally across populations of course. In 2013, 1.17 million households had mortgage debts amounting to more than 4.5 times their disposable income – representing nearly one in seven (13.2%) households with mortgages (ONS, 2015a, p. 1). We turn to inequality in the next chapter.

There are of course multiple reasons for increases in house prices, including incomes and population outpacing the housing stock, with the latter falling not just because of a lack of supply but also increases in household formation (e.g. more people choosing to live alone – see Dorling, 2014) and people generally seeking more space. In addition, money has come into the country from outside the UK for the purchase of land, particularly in the South East of the country where there has been a marked increase in cash-only buyers.

But it's clear that a major driving force in UK house price increases in the last thirty years has been a relatively elastic supply of credit meeting a fixed supply of land along with increased speculative demand for homeownership. Without the existence of a credit- and money-creating banking system, it is impossible to envisage how such huge increases in prices would have been possible given the slower pace of income growth.

The relationship between mortgage credit and house prices also applies internationally. An International Monetary Fund (IMF) study of thirty-six advanced and emerging economies (including the UK) found that a 10 percentage point growth in mortgage credit as a percentage of GDP was associated with a 16 percentage point higher growth of real house prices (IMF, 2011). Of course, correlation is not causation and it is likely that rising house prices, potentially driven by other factors, lead to an increase in demand for mortgage credit which itself helps to drive up house prices (Goodhart and Hofmann, 2008).

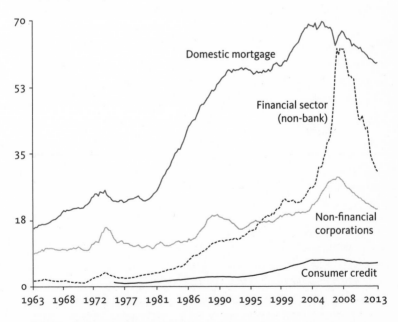

Figure 5.3 Disaggregated nominal credit stocks (loans outstanding) as % of GDP in the UK since 1963 (*source*: Bank of England, GDP from ONS; credit series are break adjusted)

Figure 5.3 shows how, since the early 1980s, UK banks have significantly increased their lending to domestic mortgages relative to GDP. Domestic mortgage lending has expanded from 20% of GDP in the early 1980s to over 60% now, while lending to non-financial firms has stayed between 20% and 30% of GDP.

But even this does not properly capture the degree to which the UK banking sector has turned towards land-related credit creation. Within non-financial corporation lending (light-grey line), lending against commercial real estate has grown much faster than other forms of business lending. Figure 5.4 shows the share of different types of sectoral lending by UK resident only banks over time (Figure

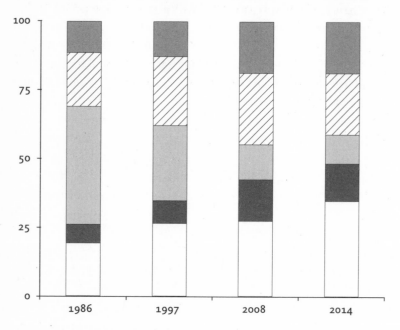

Figure 5.4 Share of bank lending by industry sector, 1986–2014 (UK resident banks only) (%) (*source*: Bank of England)

5.3 includes foreign bank sterling lending). In 1986, commercial real estate made up just 14% of total of non-financial business lending. By 2014, this figure had risen to almost 60% and the relative share of non-financial, non-real estate lending out of total lending in the UK had fallen to just 10%.

In addition, estate agents and other real estate intermediaries (a constituent of non-financial corporations) have seen their borrowing grow from 1.5% of GDP in the mid-1980s to over 11% by 2009 and 7% today. Including these additional categories, land-related lending (excluding construction) made up 80% of GDP at the height of the financial crisis. It has since reduced to 70% of GDP; in 1986, it was just 30%.

The UK is not alone in having its banks turn into real estate lenders. In most advanced economies, banks' main activity is now mortgage lending. A recent historical study of credit in seventeen advanced economies found that the share of mortgage loans in banks' total lending portfolios has roughly doubled over the course of the past century, from about 30% in 1900 to about 60% today (Jordà et al., 2016, p. 110). Again, the most notable increases have been in the last few decades, with mortgage lending increasing from 40% of total lending to 60% since 1990.

What then are the dynamics that are driving the financialisation (Box 5.2) of land?

The house price–credit feedback cycle

The history of the UK and many other advanced economies over the past thirty years suggests the existence of a positive feedback cycle between house and land prices and mortgage credit, as illustrated in Figure 5.5.

The cycle works as follows: if mortgage (and commercial real estate) lending outpaces the supply of new domestic and commercial dwellings, this will cause a rise in land prices. As land prices rise, households and firms are forced to take out larger loans to get on the property ladder, boosting banks' profits and capital (the money banks must hold to cover defaults). This enables banks to issue more loans, which further pushes up prices until such a point that property prices are many times people's incomes (or firm's revenues in the case of real estate lending). As noted, in the UK average house prices are now ten times disposable income, a similar level to that which they reached before the financial crisis (see Figure 5.2). As former Chair of the Financial Services Authority Adair Turner (2015a, p. 71) has

---

Box 5.2 What is financialisation?

Financialisation is a term used to describe the penetration and increasing influence of financial markets, motives, institutions and elites into new areas of the state, economy and society (see for example Epstein, 2005; Krippner, 2005; Palley, 2007).

Financialisation involves the transformation of work, services, land or other forms of exchange into financial instruments, for example debt instruments like bonds, that can traded on financial markets. With regard to land and housing, for example, one might argue that these become 'financialised' when households or firms hold and trade property primarily for the purpose of generating capital gains rather than as a place to live or work. Relatedly, it has been argued that financialisation involves a transfer of risk to individuals from the state, with households expected to provide for their own welfare through the building up of financial assets, with the home being a primary example (Watson, 2009).

Businesses become financialised as their investment strategies become focused on their short-term share price above long-term profit and growth generation and they begin themselves to engage in financial rather than real economy activities, for example by engaging in share buy-backs to boost share prices.

Relatedly, financialisation can refer to the increased scale and therefore power of the finance sector over national and international economies. The growth of this industry is characterised by the explosion in financial trading fuelled by the creation of new financial instruments, as well as increased economic transactions between countries. This increase in the scale and mobility of financial activities may require state support to cover the inflated risks posed to the rest of the economy.

Some have criticised the term 'financialisation' as there are few established metrics as to when an economy or sector becomes 'financialised'.

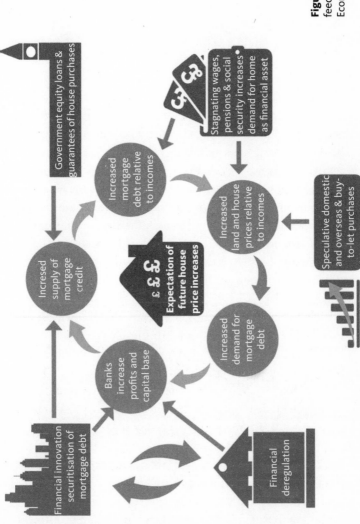

Figure 5.5 The house price-credit feedback cycle (*source:* New Economics Foundation, 2016)

argued: 'Lending against real estate generates self-reinforcing cycles of credit supply, credit demand and asset prices.'

Increases in land and house prices may have a 'crowding out' effect on bank lending to non-financial firms in favour of mortgage lending. A study of bank lending in the US found that increases in house prices led banks to substitute away from commercial lending towards mortgage lending (Chakraborty et al., 2014). The authors found that this resulted in a decrease in the investments of firms that had a relationship with the affected banks. In other words, increasing land prices negatively affected business investment via reduced lending (as well as potentially via increased rents, as discussed in Chapter 3). On the other hand, increases in house prices might also enable small businesses to access more credit via equity withdrawal as collateral values rise – see section 5.5 below.

In the UK the house price–credit cycle has been supported a combination of factors. In certain parts of the country, in particular London and the South East, housing (and land) have become the object of speculative investment by both domestic and foreign (non-bank) investors. The buy-to-let market in the UK has expanded hugely since the introduction of BTL mortgages in 1996 (see section 5.4). The annual amount of overseas investment in the UK housing market has risen from around £6 billion per year a decade ago to £32 billion by 2014 (Armstrong, 2016, p. 2) making up 17% of all foreign direct investment in the country. Given the favourable legal and tax environment in the UK (Chapter 4) and globally low interest rates and central bank quantitative easing policies pushing down returns on shares and government debt, this is not entirely surprising.

In addition, government policy in the UK in recent years has further supported the housing–credit cycle by heavily subsidising the cost of home purchase via the various help-to-buy schemes, which have included equity investment, mortgage guarantees and most recently a 'Help-to-Buy ISA' offering further tax relief.

It is not just in urban areas where speculative finance has flowed or just government subsidies that are responsible for rising land prices. The lucrative nature of the Common Agricultural Policy subsidies (see Chapter 2) has also played a role in the growing perception of farmland as a profitable financial investment. In recent years an influx of investment from wealthy private individuals and institutional investors, such as pension funds and hedge funds, has caused a boom in farmland prices (Fairbairn, 2014). In 2015 Knight Frank reported that the price of English investment-grade farmland had doubled over the previous five years, offering a better return than prime London property, the FTSE 100 or gold (Knight Frank, 2015).

The housing–credit cycle can continue for some time in a benign environment with low interest rates and steady levels of growth and employment. Such conditions allow households and firms to maintain the repayments on their debts even as their total debt to income rises (their 'debt-servicing ratio' remains manageable). As house prices rise, so does their 'net wealth' – that is, the paper value of homes and the land beneath them, once mortgage debt has been subtracted. This can make households feel that they are in position to continue spending, even if their debts are increasing in ratio to their incomes.

However, if there is a serious economic shock to the economy or a rise in interest rates, households may struggle to keep up with the repayments. This may lead to both a fall in consumption and negative equity and defaults. The latter will most likely lead to a fall in domestic and commercial property prices, bank lending contracting, recession and, potentially, a financial crisis as the feedback cycle goes into reverse. Just as house prices can rise more quickly than the rest of the economy, so they can fall, particularly where more speculative investors engage in firesales of property with distressed debt (Shleifer and Vishny, 2011). This happened in the UK in the 1973–74 period and the early 1990s, in Japan in the early 1990s and in many advanced economies after the financial crisis of 2007–8 (as shown in Figure 5.1). The 'correction' was very large in all these cases, resulting in long-term economic damage to the wider economy.

And even if there is not a shock, there is strong evidence that an economic model based upon increasing asset-based wealth as a means of stimulating consumption is highly inefficient. Large increases in net wealth (and debt) are required to generate small increases in consumption via wealth or collateral channels, as we explore further in section 5.6. Such a model also leads to rising and unsustainable levels of wealth inequality, as we explore further in Chapter 6, that eventually weighs down on consumption (Piketty, 2014).

As we explore in section 5.6, there is evidence that modern economies are driven less by the traditional and quite short-term 'business cycle' that most economists have focused their attention on (typically a couple of years) and more by a longer-term 'credit' or 'financial' cycle (over 16–18 years) that is mainly driven by land and property values (Aikman et al., 2014; Anderson, 2009; Borio, 2014; Minsky, 1992).

The reasons for the emergence of this housing–credit cycle are related to deregulation and liberalisation of the mortgage credit market, which we discuss below in sections 5.4 and 5.5 in more depth. But before moving on to the history, it is first worth asking why policy makers and most economists did not, at least until the crisis of 2007–8, pay more attention to the divergence between mortgage debt, land and property prices and incomes.

5.3 Mortgage finance, the 'lifecycle' model and the role of collateral

Since the 1960s up until the crisis of 2007–8, the dominant conception of the role of house purchase and mortgage debt in economic theory was the 'lifecycle model'.[5] Also described as the 'permanent income' hypothesis (Friedman, 1957), the theory suggests that individuals spread or smooth their consumption and savings behaviour over the entire course of their lives. For example, households save more than they spend when they are earning most, building up assets and 'dis-save' when they are retired by running down their accumulated assets to support themselves. The need to accumulate assets for retirement is the main incentive to save in the lifecycle model.

Under the lifecycle hypothesis, mortgage borrowing is theorised as a natural extension of households adapting their spending to meet their lifetime incomes. They are prepared to take out a large

---

5 Seminal contributions to the theory include Franco Modigliani and Richard Brumberg (1954), Milton Friedman (1957), whose 'permanent-income hypothesis' proved to be highly influential, and James Tobin (1967).

loan to increase their housing consumption beyond the level of their income at an early stage in their lifecycle by acquiring a home in the expectation that they will increase their earnings in the future as they become more productive. It is assumed there is no constraints on such borrowing. As the household ages, its income increases relative to the mortgage debt, enabling it to pay off its early life debts and also save for retirement.

If house prices do temporarily increase under this lifecycle model, this may encourage homeowners to increase their consumption as they feel wealthier and their net wealth (their assets minus their liabilities) has increased. However, it is often argued that this effect will be cancelled out in the aggregate because rents will also rise and thus non-property owners will need to save more for a deposit and thus reduce their consumption if they wish to buy a home. Thus changes to house *prices* (as opposed to investment in homes or the building of new homes) affect the *distribution* of household sector wealth rather than the total amount of household sector wealth (Goodhart and Hofmann, 2008, pp. 181–182).

According to the lifecycle theory, there should be a reasonably strong relationship between house prices, the supply of mortgage finance, savings and incomes in the economy. And, relatedly, mortgage finance should not, in theory, lead to long-term house price inflation. There may be some bumpiness over time, reflecting demographic changes or business cycles, but overall, as mortgages are repaid over people's lifecycles, the amount of money in the economy being used for house purchase should even out.

Since, as described in section 5.1, mainstream economic theory also neglected a causal role for money and credit in the economy, house prices and mortgage debt generally were not viewed as important determinants of the long-run dynamics of the economy.[6]

---

6 'New Keynesian' economists have attempted to build credit and asset price effects into general equilibrium models with representative agents as 'frictions' that may amplify or accelerate economic shocks, making them last longer (Bernanke et al., 1999). However, these models still envisage economies eventually returning to an equilibrium state with shocks still emanating from the real economy rather than emerging from bank lending or the 'non-rational' expectations of households or firms – they are unable to generate crises that originate in the 'monetary economy'.

As a result, modern macroeconomics came to neglect both the role of house prices and mortgage credit (Leung, 2004; Goodhart and Hofmann, 2008).

This neglect was to prove fateful. Few mainstream or central bank economists forecast the financial crisis of 2007–8 because few of the mainstream macroeconomic models included an active role for house prices or debt stocks in their models (Bezemer, 2009; Muellbauer 2016). As a result, they were not unduly concerned about the very large increases relative to income in both mortgage credit and house prices that occurred.

Problems with the lifecycle model

In reality, house and land prices and mortgage credit can and do have long-term impacts on the economy, depending on how they interact with credit markets and the banking sector. The neutral 'lifecycle' hypothesis is based upon unrealistic assumptions about household and financial sector behaviour that are needed in order to construct the equilibrium models used by mainstream economists.

These include that households have unlimited ability to borrow and banks have unlimited ability to lend; that, relatedly, there is no risk of default associated with the holding of mortgage debt; that the cost of borrowing does not vary with the amount borrowed; that household earnings do not fluctuate significantly and that households themselves know such earnings will not fluctuate (in other words they have perfect foresight).

Aside from a common-sense scepticism about the above assumptions, empirical evidence casts doubt on upon them. For example, if the lifecycle hypothesis was accurate, we would expect economies with ageing populations – that is most advanced economies – to see lower levels of household debt over time as a higher proportion of these populations would have accumulated assets compared to the past. In fact, quite the opposite has occurred. Household debt, and mortgage debt in particular, has massively increased in nearly all advanced economies as a percentage of GDP (Jordà et al., 2016). In the US case, a recent study found that the bulk of US debt balances has shifted *towards* older households since 2003 and away from younger cohorts (with the exception of student debt) (Brown et al.,

2016). Evidence from the UK and Australia suggests that rather than spending their accumulated wealth in later life, households have been passing it on to their children as inheritance, while younger cohorts have increasingly been making use of mortgage equity withdrawal (see section 5.5) to fund large, one-off expenditures (Parkinson et al., 2009).

Unrealistic assumptions are also made about the financial sector and banks in the lifecycle model. Banks are assumed to willingly lend at the market rate of interest where the supply of mortgage credit meets demand (where the market 'clears'). This is based on the assumption that both households and financial intermediaries (banks) have very high – if not perfect – levels of information and are able to make accurate judgements about the future based upon a range of knowable probabilities (the 'rational expectations' hypothesis).

In reality, empirical research shows that there are, again, asymmetries of information between lenders and borrowers; generally a borrower always has more information about their future ability to repay a loan than a bank (Stiglitz and Weiss, 1981). Under such circumstances, it becomes difficult for the bank to estimate an interest rate that comfortably reflects the (unknowable) risk associated with the loan. An interest rate that covers this type of risk is likely to be very high and may lead to many reliable borrowers being priced out and only people with very high risk tolerance – 'gamblers' – choosing to take out loans. This problem is known as 'adverse selection' in the economics literature (Akerlof, 1970).

Instead of using interest rates to determine borrowing decisions, the evidence suggests banks simply ration their lending quantitatively according to other criteria (Werner, 2005, pp. 194–196). The decision to extend a loan for house purchase then becomes subject to a number of more idiosyncratic variables not related to the price of credit but often related to the borrower's circumstances. A common request is that the bank requires *collateral*: that is, a borrower's pledge of an asset to a lender to secure repayment of a loan. If the borrower fails, the bank covers its losses by repossessing the underlying asset the loan was raised against.

The most desirable form of collateral will be something that cannot be easily hidden or moved and will hold its value over time. If you've read this far you can probably guess what that preferred asset might be: land. It is this 'collateral channel' and the role that it plays in enabling increases in debt and consumption that appears much more significant in driving modern macroeconomic dynamics than any lifecycle 'wealth affects' (Muellbauer and Murphy, 2008).

The collateral channel came to be increasingly important in those advanced economies – not least the UK and the US – that liberalised their credit markets and allowed banks to issue mortgage debt. In fact, mortgage lending by the *banking* sector (as opposed to building societies) is a relatively recent phenomenon in the UK, only really emerging in the 1980s. In the next section, we examine in more detail the history of UK domestic and commercial real estate finance and show how the theoretical arguments against the benign lifecycle model played themselves out in reality. Then in section 5.5 we examine the effects of this collateral channel on the macroeconomy, in particular household consumption and business investment.

5.4 The history of mortgage and real estate finance in the UK

Building societies and mutual home loans

You might have wondered where the term 'building society' comes from. The clue is in the name. Building societies used to finance the building of new homes for their members. Building societies first emerged in the UK in the Midlands in the late eighteenth century, an area that was undergoing rapid economic expansion driven by small metalworking firms whose highly skilled and reasonably wealthy owners wished to invest in property Members of a society would pay a monthly subscription to a central pool of funds which was used to finance the building of houses for members. These homes would, in turn, act as collateral to attract further funding to the society, enabling further construction (Clark, 2001).

Building societies are 'mutuals' – financial institutions that are owned by their members and run in the interests of their members rather than private owners or shareholders. Most of the original societies were self-terminating. When every member of the society had a home, their job was done and they closed themselves down.[7] Their sole purpose was the provision of physical shelter to their members. Under such an arrangement, there was a fairly stable relationship between incomes and the price of homes – after all, it was the cooperative pooling of such incomes which provided most of the money to build the homes.

In the 1840s building societies began to accept savings from members who were not necessarily potential homeowners and permanent building societies emerged which would continue to take in savings and offer loans on a rolling basis, taking on new members as earlier ones completed purchases. By 1860 there were over 750 building societies in existence in London and 2,000 in the provinces and by 1910 over 1,723 societies with 626,000 members and total assets of £76 million (BSA, 2015). Virtually every town in the country had a society named after it.

Over time, many building societies merged, enabling the pooling of liquidity that allowed for larger home building schemes and mortgage financing that was not dependent on local savings (see Box 5.3). Building societies began to pay interest on savings. Building society loans carried risk since they were lending at longer maturity than their deposits – they were creating credit and money in just the same way as banks (see Box 5.1 above). For example, mortgage loans would last five, ten or fifteen years but customers could withdraw their savings more rapidly (see Box 5.3).

However, with the odd exception related to fraudulent activity, there were few examples of building societies failing on 'runs on the bank'. There were a number of reasons for this. The building societies business model was about attracting savers with whom they would have a long-term relationship and a need for a regular but secure income from these savings. The model aligned the needs of younger savers who wished to secure a deposit on a home and older retired people who were looking for a secure income for their savings. Because of the long-term nature of the savings building societies attracted, the chances of a rapid withdrawal of funds were very low.

---

7 The last of the self-terminating building societies, First Salisbury and District Perfect Thrift Building Society, was wound up in March 1980 (BSA, 2015).

Secondly, building societies were conservative organisations in general. They would only lend to those with secure incomes, a savings history and a significant deposit, many times higher than present-day levels (Scanlon and Whitehead, 2011, p. 278). Thus, mortgage finance was not easily accessible to the majority of the population.

Thirdly, as the sector became more organised, it put in place practices to limit potential instability. In 1939, the recently formed Building Societies Association (BSA) created an interest rate cartel for the entire sector. This existed to limit reckless lending and kept the interest rate on savings and loans below market clearing rates. Building societies were able to smooth out market volatility by adjusting the terms of loans or adjusting the interest rate if borrowers ran into trouble, meaning that mortgage lending was very low risk (Scanlon and Whitehead, 2011, p. 278).

Right up until the 1980s in the UK, domestic mortgage financing was essentially restricted to the building society sector, which was separately regulated from the rest of the financial system, including the banking system. A Joint Advisory Committee (JAC) made up of industry and government representatives decided how much mortgage lending should be allowed across the whole country.

During the 1960s and 1970s, so-called 'secondary banks', including US banks, began to enter the London banking sector and lend heavily to commercial property companies, encouraged by rapidly rising land prices in the capital. Excessive commercial property lending was the most significant contributor to the 'secondary banking' crisis of 1973–74 (Reid, 1982). In response to competition from these secondary banks and other financial institutions outside the Bank of England's regulatory remit, the 1971 Competition, Credit and Control (CCC) Act was designed to level the playing field, bringing a wide range of new financial institutions under the Bank's remit (although not building societies) but also allowing the large UK clearing banks to borrow from the fast growing wholesale markets sector (see Box 5.3).[8]

---

8   See Ryan-Collins et al. (2012, pp. 48–52) for a full account of the deregulation of the banking sector.

Box 5.3 How banks and building societies 'fund' mortgages

Banks must ensure that their assets (the loans they make) match the sum of their liabilities (money they owe to customers) and their equity (money owed to the bank's owners). Since a bank's assets will be loans of varying maturities (e.g. a consumer loan of six months versus a mortgage loan that matures over twenty-five years), a bank's liabilities (what it owes to others) also need to have a matching variable maturity structure. In banking-speak, 'funding' refers to the matching liabilities a bank holds against its assets.

Deposits, which as described in Box 5.1 are created by banks when they make loans, are seen as reasonably safe liabilities because even though they are short term (any individual can withdraw all of their deposits at any time) in aggregate it is very unlikely that all of a banks' depositors will want to withdraw their money from a bank at the same time (a so-called 'run' on a bank). Depositors tend to be information-poor – they generally do not spend their time studying the health of their bank and market movements.

Depending on the makeup of their assets, banks will hold deposits along with other types of liabilities, including savings products such as two-year fixed rate bonds or debt borrowed on financial markets of varying maturities.

As well as borrowing from depositors, banks also borrow on 'wholesale money markets'. The term 'money market' covers the vast network of deals involving the lending and borrowing of liquid assets in a range of currencies, generally between financial institutions such as banks, as well as non-financial companies and the government. These assets include tradable securities, such as government securities, Treasury bills or corporate IOUs (commercial paper, or CPs), bank debt (certificates of deposit, CDs) usually maturing within a year or less.

'Wholesale' means funds borrowed or lent by those financial institutions in large quantities, rather than the smaller amounts dealt in by private individuals. Short-term wholesale funding can be a more risky form of funding than deposits since the institutions that issue the loans are more sensitive to market movements.

In the face of a huge property price inflation in the early 1970s, however, credit controls were re-imposed by the Bank of England in 1973. Between 1973 and 1979, the Bank attempted to control credit via a number of quantitative measures. These included stringent liquidity ratios on banks (the amount of cash they need to hold relative to their loans), forcing banks to hold a minimum level of deposits and special deposits (the 'corset') as well as directives and 'moral suasion' (informal verbal guidance) (Muellbauer, 2002, p. 11). These placed limits on the growth of the banking sector's interest-bearing liabilities and marginalised the banks' position in the personal savings and mortgage markets (Stephens, 2007, p. 203). In addition, building societies also enjoyed a much more favourable tax regime than the banks. These privileges meant there was little competition for mortgage products and little pressure on the interest rate cartel.

The result was that the building societies' share of the domestic mortgage market still averaged 83% through the 1970s (Stephens, 1993). Consequently, the availability of mortgage finance was very much dependent on the availability of funds (i.e. people's accumulated savings) and there was considerable rationing of mortgage credit, with restrictive lending criteria compared to today's standards. Mortgage finance was essentially restricted to the better-off or those willing to save patiently for a deposit. As the tax incentives for homeownership were increased after the 1963 abolition of imputed rent charges (see Chapter 4), popular pressure grew for wider homeownership.

The deregulation of mortgage finance

The Thatcher government which came to power in 1979 embarked on a major liberalisation of the financial sector. Foreign exchange controls were removed immediately, which opened the banking sector to greater foreign competition and gave UK banks access to overseas funding, in particular the fast developing Eurodollar markets. To allow UK banks to compete more effectively with foreign banks, further steps were taken including the removal of the 'corset'. This enabled banks to compete effectively with building societies for mortgages for the first time. Quantitative restrictions on building societies were also removed and eventually the interest rate cartel was abandoned in 1983 along with the building societies' tax advantages being removed.

'Centralised' lenders – often the subsidiaries of foreign banks – entered the market and had the advantage of not having to fund the costs of the large branch networks the building societies had built up as well as being able to access cheaper wholesale funding than the retail deposits building societies were dependent on.

The building societies now found themselves at a disadvantage as they were unable to access wholesale markets like the banks. The 1986 Building Societies Act partially levelled the playing field, allowing building societies to borrow a proportion of their funding from wholesale markets and provide mainstream banking services and convert themselves in to banks should they so wish. With both banks and building societies now in a much more liberally regulated regime, the late 1980s saw a flood of credit into property that stimulated a huge housing boom (Chrystal, 1992). In the four years after 1984 the building societies doubled their annual mortgage lending while loans made by the larger banks for house purchase trebled between 1984 and 1989, rising from £15.4 billion to £43.1 billion (Davies, 2002, p. 438).

The increased borrowing was attractive to households for three reasons. Firstly, liberalisation of credit in the early 1980s allowed households to engage in 'equity withdrawal', taking money out of the rising price of their homes to spend on consumer goods, cars or holidays. Secondly, interest rates were progressively lowered by the government during the period. Thirdly, the cost of interest was being subsidised as tax relief on mortgage interest was granted at the borrower's marginal, i.e. highest, rate up to a £30,000 limit. Between the late 1970s and the mid-1980s, the tax relief per mortgagor in real terms rose by 50% (Davies, 2002, p. 438).

The bubble eventually burst in the house price crash of 1990. This left many borrowers in 'negative equity' – around 20% at its peak according to a recent estimate (Aron and Muellbauer, 2016) – where the price of their houses was below what they owed on their mortgage. This amplified and prolonged the severe recession of the following three years, which involved many more job losses than the 2007–8 crisis. The collapse in the housing market in the early 1990s led to a large number of repossessions and a collapse in business lending.

In 1996, a new buy-to-let mortgage, providing landlords with a bespoke financial product to invest in housing for the first time, was introduced by the banks in cooperation with the Association of Residential Letting Agents (ARLA). The banks agreed to reduce the 2% risk premium placed on mortgages attached to rental properties in return for ARLA affiliated agents managing the properties. It proved enormously popular. BTL mortgages expanded from zero to 16.5% of all mortgage advances by 2015 (CML, 2015), with a recent estimate putting the worth of the market at £1 trillion (Dyson, 2014). These products helped drive a large increase in the proportion of homes owned by landlords. Private landlords now own almost one out of five homes in Britain. A study by the National Housing and Planning Association found that the introduction of BTL led to a 7% increase in house prices between 1996 and 2007 (NHPAU, 2008)

Under the Labour government of 1997, further differences between the regulation of building societies and banks were removed (although some do remain today) and a single regulatory body was established for the mortgage industry for both (the Financial Services Authority). Despite the ability to demutualise, only one building society – the Abbey National – did so up to the mid-1990s. However, from the mid-1990s onwards, a wave of demutualisations took place, with the building societies sector going from holding two-thirds of all mortgage assets in 1995 to just one-quarter in 1997 (Stephens, 2007, p. 210). By 2006, once dominant building societies were approving just one-fifth of new mortgages for house purchase, the majority of them through the last remaining larger society, Nationwide (Ball, 2009, p. 127).

There are a range of explanations for the demutualisation. These include the desire of many smaller building societies to merge out of fear of hostile takeover, a switch towards profit maximisation and efficiency savings as building societies became national rather than local institutions focused on their members and the potential windfall profits that members and managers would receive upon demutualisation given the high value of bank shares on the stock exchange at the time. By the mid-1990s house and land prices were rising again and mortgage credit was expanding again. The boom lasted until the financial crisis of 2008.

Not all the blame for the growth of excessive and risky mortgage lending can be blamed on UK policy decisions however. Banking itself was becoming more internationalised in the last quarter of the twentieth century and international regulations inevitably followed.

The Basel Committee on Bank Supervision (BCBS) was founded in 1974 in reaction to the collapse of Herstatt Bank in Germany. The committee served as a forum to discuss international harmonisation of international banking regulation. Its work led to the 1988 Basel Accord (Basel I) that introduced minimum capital requirements and, importantly, different risk weights for assets (including loans) on banks' balance sheets. Loans secured by mortgages on residential properties only carried half the risk weight of loans to non-financial firms (50%), while securitised mortgages, which were viewed as more liquid, only carried a 20% risk weight. This allowed banks to earn fees and net interest margins on holding 2.5 times more credit risk in real estate than they had before without any increase in their capital requirements (Persaud, 2016, p. 5). A significant share of the global growth of mortgage lending and bank leverage occurred in the 1990s following the first Basel accord (Jordà et al., 2016, p. 122).

The securitisation and internationalisation of home mortgage finance and the financial crisis of 2007–8

In the standard textbook model of banking, banks hold loans to maturity and generate profits on the difference between the interest charged on these loans and the interest the bank pays to depositors: the 'interest-rate spread'. Since the 2000s, however, many banks, in particular in the UK and even more so in the United States, began to adopt a new business model. This involves originating (issuing) loans but then packing these up together into securities (debt instruments) and generating profits from selling them on to third-party investors, such as pensions funds, insurance companies or other forms of asset management funds. Often such loans are temporarily held in special purpose vehicles (SPVs) sponsored by banks and held off their

Box 5.4 The parable of Northern Rock

In November 2015 the UK government agreed to sell a £13 billion collection of former Northern Rock mortgages – transferred to public ownership after the bank collapsed during the financial crisis to a US private equity group, Cerberus Capital Management. The loans covered about 125,000 customers owing an average of £100,000. It was the biggest ever sale of financial assets by a European government.

How did a US investment fund specialising in distressed debt come to buy £13 billion worth of nationalised UK mortgages? The story is a remarkable insight into the way in which property and land in the UK has become financialised over the past century.

Northern Rock was a bank when, at the height of the financial crisis in February 2008, it was nationalised by the government. Six months earlier, customers were queuing outside its doors to withdraw their cash in the first genuine bank run in the UK since the nineteenth century. But only seven years before Northern Rock was a quite different kind of institution: it was a building society.

Over time, many building societies merged, enabling the pooling of liquidity that allowed for larger home building schemes and mortgage financing. In 1965, two North East societies the Northern Counties Permanent Building Societies (established in 1850) and the Rock Building Societies (established in 1865) – merged and Northern Rock Building Societies was born.

Following the deregulation of the 1970s and 1980s, increasing competition for mortgage finance from banks, including international banks, led building societies to expand via mergers and acquisitions. Northern Rock acquired 53 smaller building societies, most notably the North of England Building Society in 1994. Finally, in 1997, Northern Rock chose to demutualise and become a shareholder-owned bank. Its assets, patiently built up by its members since the 1860s, were floated on the stock exchange, with existing savers and mortgage borrowers receiving a cash windfall.

Looking for aggressive growth to compete with much larger British banks, Northern Rock formulated a business strategy that involved borrowing heavily in the UK and international money markets rather than depending on traditional retail deposits. It then extended mortgages to customers based on this funding, and re-sold these mortgages on international capital markets. This was achieved via 'securitising' the loans – packaging loans of different riskiness together to form mortgage-backed securities attractive to a range of different investors.

In 2001, Northern Rock set up 'Granite', a securitisation vehicle, to hold and sell these mortgage securities to investors. Unlike deposits, however, this money-market funding was more short-termist and flighty. When the US subprime mortgage crisis struck in 2007, this source of money-market funding suddenly dried up. Banks and other providers of liquidity were suddenly no longer prepared to roll over existing wholesale funding as trust between financial institutions collapsed. Because of its heavy money-market exposure, Northern Rock swiftly ran in to a liquidity crisis. By 14 September 2007, queues were forming outside its doors as people sought to withdraw their deposits: a full-on bank run. The bank was swiftly nationalised. The bank's shareholders lost all of their money.

On 1 January 2010 the government split the bank in to two parts: 'assets' and 'banking'. The bad 'assets' part, called UK Asset Resolution (Ukar), was made up of the Granite assets as well as the bad loans from another collapsed demutualised building society, the Bradford and Bingley.

On 13 November 2015, the Northern Rock mortgages attached to Granite, along with a further £1 billion of Northern Rock loans, was sold to US private equity firm Cerberus Capital Management. Cerberus, named after the mythical multi-headed dog that guarded Hades and prevented the dead from leaving, specialises in distressed debt and has purchased books of loans from RBS, Lloyds and National Australia bank, betting on a recovery in European property markets.

balance sheets (see Box 5.5). By shifting these loans off the balance sheet, banks were able to reduce the amount of capital they had to hold against their assets, meaning they could make more loans.

In theory, any kind of loan could be securitised, but domestic mortgage loans – residential mortgage-backed securities or RMBS

– have proven to be by far the most attractive type of asset for securitisation because they are seen as relatively safe, being backed by secure collateral: land.

Between 2000 and 2007, the funding of residential mortgages through UK outstanding RMBS and covered bonds grew from

---

Box 5.5 What is securitisation?

Securitisation is the practice of pooling together and repackaging a number of illiquid loans – loans that cannot easily be sold or exchanged for cash – and issuing tradable debt securities sold to investors that will be repaid as the underlying loans are repaid.

. There are different types of securitisation, as the process has evolved to become more complex over time. In its most basic form, the process involves two steps. In the first step, a company (usually a bank) with loans or other income-generating assets – termed the 'originator' – identifies the loans it wants to offload from its balance sheet and pools them in to what is called the 'reference portfolio'. It then sells this asset pool to an 'issuer' special purpose vehicle – an entity set up, usually by a financial institution, for the specific purpose of purchasing the assets and realising their off-balance-sheet treatment for legal and accounting purposes.

In the second step, the SPV issues tradable debt securities and sells them to capital market investors, and the money raised through this issuance enables the SPV to buy the pooled loans from the originator bank. The ultimate debtors, the people who took out the loans, are usually not aware of the sale as in most cases the originator bank remains responsible for processing payments and interacting with borrowers. They continue making payments on their loans, but these payments now flow to the SPV (less a servicing fee) and then ultimately on to the new investors.

As the loans have been sold, the risk of loans not being repaid (the 'credit risk') has been transferred from the originator bank to investors. This type of 'pass-through' securitisation thus provides the issuing bank with risk reduction and lower regulatory minimum capital requirements, enabling it to issue more new loans.

£13 billion to £257 billion, moving their share of funding from 2.5% of mortgage funding to 21.5% (CML, 2010, p. 6) As a proportion of GDP, RMBS increased from 2% in 1999 to nearly 27% of GDP at the start of the crisis in 2007 (Milne and Wood, 2014, p. 26) and mainly explains the similarly sized increase in residential mortgage lending over the same period. UK lenders were responsible for over half of the total European issuance of RMBS in the seven years leading up the crisis (Ball, 2009, p. 127).

Securitisation enabled mortgage issuers to offer a wider range of mortgage products, to offer mortgages at much lower rates of interest and offer them at higher loan-to-value (LTV) ratios. This in turn enabled larger numbers of people to access homeownership at higher price-to-income and mortgage debt-to-income ratios. The UK's house price–income ratio doubled between 1997 and the peak of the boom in summer 2007 (see Figure 5.2).

Such a large expansion in mortgage credit would not have been possible if banks were solely dependent on retail deposits for their funding (see Box 5.3). Instead banks accessed large amounts of short-term 'wholesale funding' (Box 5.3) from financial markets – Northern Rock (Box 5.5) being a prime example. The top ten mortgage lenders reduced their combined funding from retail deposits from 72% to 55% in the lead-up to the crisis, while overall mortgage lending tripled to £346 billion (Ball, 2009, p. 127). When the market for RMBS collapsed with the subprime crisis, many UK banks suddenly found their short-term wholesale funding also dried up. Of the top ten mortgage lenders in 2007 (which represented 78% of the market), those with the highest reliance on RMBS (and representing a third of the market) had all been bankrupted, nationalised or taken over by autumn 2008 (Ball, 2009, p. 128).

This was seen spectacularly in the announcement of the sale of Halifax Bank of Scotland (HBOS) – by far the country's largest mortgage lender with a fifth of the market prior to the credit crunch – to Lloyds TSB in September 2008. Around the same time, the Bradford and Bingley was broken up between Banco Santander of Spain and the UK government. Santander also took over Alliance and Leicester, while over the course of the previous year several specialist lenders had ceased to provide new mortgages (Ball, 2009, p. 121).

Mortgage financing collapsed. There were 24,300 loans for house purchase in February 2009, 47% down on a year earlier, according to the Council of Mortgage Lenders (Lambert, 2009). Mortgage lenders tightened their lending criteria, preventing most first-time buyers entering the market – in February 2009, a deposit of 25% was typical.

When the bubble burst, house prices fell by a record 20% in just sixteen months. At the end of the first quarter 2009, Financial Services Authority data showed that almost 400,000 mortgage loan accounts were in arrears and 14,825 new cases of repossession were recorded (HM Treasury Select Committee, 2009, p. 10). The Bank of England acted swiftly to shore up the RMBS sector by offering substantial repurchase agreement (or 'repo') finance against RMBS collateral, meaning banks no longer needed to lend to their own SPVs (Milne and Wood, 2014, p. 28). Together with a combination of a rapid lowering of interest rates and a raft of other interventions, such as the mortgage pre-action protocol, more generous income support for people with mortgage payment difficulties and bank forbearance, this prevented foreclosures and repossessions on the scale of the late 1980s crisis (Aron and Muellbauer, 2016)

Non-performing mortgage debt was as a result not the main problem facing the banking system in the crisis period. In 2009 £984 million of bad mortgage debt was written off in the UK, compared to write-offs of £8.4 billion for unsecured consumer credit and £5.9 billion for non-financial corporate debt (Aron and Muellbauer, 2016), much of which was linked to commercial real estate credit (further discussed in section 5.5).

Reforms to securitisation

Following the US subprime crisis in 2007–8, European authorities took a number of steps to make securitisation transactions safer and simpler, and to ensure that appropriate incentives were put in place to manage risk. This included higher capital requirements and mandatory risk retention for the originator bank to address the problem of banks not caring to whom they lent because they knew they would sell the loans on to investors (under the so-called 'originate and distribute model'). Since the financial crisis, European securitisation markets have remained subdued; in 2015 Europe's securitisation market stood at a third of its pre-crisis size. This is in contrast to markets in the US which have largely recovered.9

In response to this, in 2015 the European Commission identified the development of a simple, transparent and standardised (STS) securitisation market as a key building block of its Capital Markets Union (CMU). The CMU is a collection of European Union initiatives aimed at developing non-bank lending (so-called 'shadow banking') and capital market financing in Europe, with a particular focus on infrastructure and SME financing. The CMU is one of the Commission's priorities to ensure that the financial system supports jobs and growth and helps with the demographic challenges that Europe faces.

Under the proposed legislation, securitisations that meet certain criteria will be eligible for STS classification, which will allow for softer prudential treatment via lower capital charges, thus making securitisation more attractive for financial institutions once again.

One of the key justifications for the revival of European securitisation markets is that the problems caused by securitisation in the financial crisis were mainly concentrated in the United States and that European markets were much more resilient. This is often attributed to more prudent practice and less risky behaviour in the EU compared with the US, and has been used as a key argument by proponents of securitisation who maintain that the stigma attached to securitisation and the post-crisis tightening of the regulatory treatment of securitised products has been excessive.

It is certainly true that in certain countries, e.g. Germany and Denmark, covered bonds were well regulated and relatively safe during the crisis and that in general default rates were lower in Europe. However, it should also be borne in mind that there are legal differences relating to mortgage loans between the US and the EU. In the EU all mortgage loans are 'full recourse' loans, which means that, following a default, the lender can foreclose the secured asset and also has recourse to the borrower, meaning that the lender can

---

9   This is at least in part due to the role of public sponsorship. Almost 80% of securitisation instruments in the US benefit from public guarantees from the US Government Sponsored Enterprises (e.g. Fannie Mae and Freddy Mac). Private label RMBS have recovered less well.

also collect the debt from the borrower's unsecured personal assets and from their future income. In contrast, in many US states mortgage loans are 'non-recourse' loans, which means that, following a default, the lender can foreclose and sell the property, but has no recourse to the borrower's personal assets or future income. If the property is in negative equity at the point of default, the shortfall between the mortgage and the property value is borne by the lender (Harris and Meir, 2015). This difference has a crucial impact on the incentives facing borrowers who are struggling to make repayments. As Harvard economist Martin Feldstein points out:

> The 'no recourse' mortgage is virtually unique to the United States. That's why falling house prices in Europe do not trigger defaults, since the creditors' potential to go beyond the house to other assets or to a portion of payroll earnings is enough to deter defaults. (Feldstein, 2008)

The lower rate of defaults of securitised products in Europe compared with the US may be a reflection of underlying legal differences in mortgage loans between the two countries, as well as differences in securitisation practice.

5.5 Macroeconomic effects of the liberalisation of mortgage credit

The above historical review has shown how, since the 1970s, land has become 'financialised', as the deregulation of the financial system and financial innovation allowed for the emergence of repeated property credit booms and busts. In this section we turn to some of the important effects of mortgage credit liberalisation on the wider economy.

The liberalisation of mortgage credit has revolutionised the relationship between land values, house prices and the wider economy in the UK. It has led, as we discussed, to a huge increase in the value of land and property relative to the rest of the economy and a huge increase in property assets on banks' balance sheets relative to non-property assets (such as business loans). Property is now by far the largest single source of wealth in the UK, making up almost half of total household assets and net wealth. Conversely, mortgage debt makes up by far the largest part of banks' lending and household liabilities.

Wealth comes in different forms. Pension wealth cannot be drawn down to support spending in the economy until people retire.[10] Investments in shares provide regular dividends depending on the profitability of companies. But land and housing wealth is different. Because of the deregulation of mortgage credit that we discussed in section 5.4, housing wealth allows households to borrow significant amounts of new money for consumption *today*. Since consumption makes up around two-thirds of national income in most advanced economies, changes to housing equity have important macroeconomic impacts.

Figure 5.6 illustrates the relationship between housing wealth, credit and consumption in the UK from 1970 until 2010. The graph shows the level of the consumption-to-income ratio (solid line), an index of credit conditions (or ease of credit availability) and the level of the housing wealth-to-income ratio (dashed line) interacted with the credit conditions index, which shows the effect of credit and house price developments on consumption relative to income. This credit conditions index is derived from ten mortgage and other consumer credit indicators, controlling for standard economic and demographic variables, such as incomes, asset prices, interest rates, risk indicators and age.[11]

Prior to the liberalisation of credit in the early 1980s, we can see there is little evidence of a relationship between consumption

---

10 Although it should be noted that reforms by the UK coalition government in 2014 mean that people can now withdraw their pension pots as a lump sum at any age from fifty-five onwards, even if they are still working. The requirement to purchase an annuity has been removed.

11 'Income' refers to all non-property-related income. Consumption is shown in the log form. From 1976 to 2001, the credit conditions index is based on the data published in Fernandez-Corugedo and Muellbauer (2006) in a Bank of England working paper – see the data appendix from page 39 for sources. Before then, it is based upon unpublished work by John Muellbauer and uses regional loan-to-value mortgage rates for first-time buyers. After 2001, the estimates are based on dummy variables that help explain consumption, given all the other factors. Thanks to Professor John Muellbauer for making available the data.

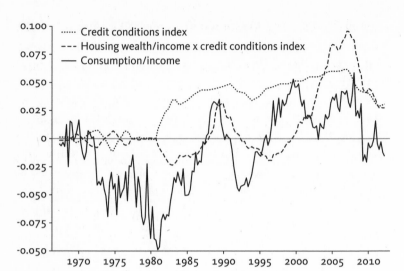

Figure 5.6 The role of mortgage credit conditions in affecting consumption in the UK (*source*: Aron et al., 2012, p. 410, with additional data provided by John Muellbauer)

and housing wealth when we take into account people's incomes – the dashed line moves gently around zero. Consumption was highly volatile during the 1970s due to multiple economic shocks to oil prices, exchange rates, share prices and unemployment and was little affected by housing wealth.

Following credit liberalisation in the early 1980s (reflected in the rising dotted line from 1980), consumption becomes more correlated with housing wealth. After the initial credit liberalisation of the early 1980s, borrowing against property continued to become progressively easier, with a brief dip in the early 1990s after the housing crash, right up until the crisis.

What this chart tells us is that it was changes in the financial sector – i.e. banking and credit market deregulation and related innovations in lending – that created a link between housing wealth and consumption: fundamental changes in the structure of the UK economy. Two main mortgage-credit channels have been identified (Goodhart and Hoffman, 2008; Aron et al., 2012).

Two mortgage-credit channels

Firstly, there is a 'mortgage down payment' channel. Households must save for a deposit to access a mortgage. If banks raise the loan-to-value and loan-to-income ratios on mortgages this will mean households require a relatively smaller deposit. This will allow them to save less and hence increase their consumption levels. Between 1980 and 1988, the UK household saving ratio fell from over 12% to around 5%, while the ratio of consumer expenditure to income rose correspondingly – see Figure 5.6 (a shift of 0.05 is equivalent to 5%) (Muellbauer, 2009, p. 9). A similar phenomenon has been occurring since the last financial crisis: the household savings ratio has fallen from almost 12% in 2010 to just 5% today as ultra-low nominal interest rates have encouraged first-time buyers to take on more consumer debt and kept consumer spending at a healthy level (Chu, 2016).

Secondly, there is a 'collateral channel' which enables households to increase debt or refinance debt at lower interest rates than would be available on normal consumer credit loans via home equity withdrawal (HEW) (Aron et al., 2012, p. 402). There are two main types of HEW: remortgaging an existing property (where the proceeds are not spent on improving the property) and equity release. Across the economy, home equity withdrawal occurs whenever households increase their secured borrowing without spending the proceeds on improving or enlarging the housing stock (Hellebrandt et al., 2009). For example, if I take out a loan against the value of my home in order to buy a car or buy a flat to rent, I am reducing my own share of the equity of my home (and net wealth) – more of it can be thought of as being owned by the bank. This effect will be more significant in countries, such as the UK, with flexible mortgage markets and variable interest rates and in countries, such as the US and Denmark, where the cost of refinancing a fixed rate mortgage is low.

Since the credit deregulation of the 1970s HEW has made important contributions to consumer demand in the UK but only in certain periods when house prices have been rising (Figure 5.7). Both Margaret Thatcher (1979–92) and Tony Blair (1997–2007) enjoyed major consumption booms partially driven by HEW, with equity

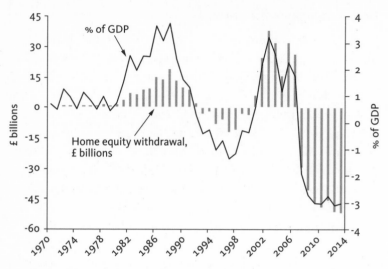

Figure 5.7 Home equity withdrawal in the UK, 1970–2015 (*sources*: ONS, Bank of England)

withdrawal contributing significantly to GDP (see Figure 5.7) in both their tenures. The decade before the financial crisis saw unprecedented levels of home equity withdrawal as homeowners used rising house prices to increase their borrowing to fund consumption. The sociologist Colin Crouch (2009) has described this as a form of 'privatised Keynesianism', with the large injections of mortgage debt via equity withdrawal propping up consumer demand in the face of declining median wages, in contrast to the state supporting demand via fiscal expansion as in the 1950–70 period.

Since the crisis of 2007–8, home equity withdrawal has collapsed. Despite record low interest rates, and increases in house prices in some parts of the country, households overall have remained reluctant to borrow against their homes to fund additional consumption. The negative impact on the economy has been ameliorated by rapid increases in consumer debt – unsecured, short-term lending, often at very high interest rates – in recent years (Inman, 2016).

Home equity withdrawal also has asymmetric effects on consumption across socioeconomic groups, further undermining the lifecycle hypothesis outlined in section 5.3. A fall in house prices will reduce the credit-collateral channel and related consumption of home- and landowners. However, it will make no difference to the borrowing ability of non-homeowners who will remain quantity rationed because of their lack of viable collateral.

The opposite will also apply: a rise in house prices is likely to boost the consumption of homeowners to a greater degree than is offset by the increased savings or rent that a non-homeowner now requires. These asymmetries will be higher in economies with higher levels of homeownership and with more flexible credit markets: both features of the UK.

Increases in house prices and homeownership can thus be seen to have increased overall consumption and supported demand for extended periods of time in the UK since the 1980s. The UK's dereg-ulated mortgage market has enabled people to extract additional purchasing power from the increase in value of their properties – as house prices have risen, so consumption has followed.

The converse also applies. No government wishes to see the damaging effects of a fall in house prices, especially when almost two-thirds of voters own a property. This will reduce people's wealth and expectations of future wealth. Falling values of housing equity also reduce the resources that homeowners have available to draw on to sustain their spending in the event of an unexpected loss of income (e.g. due to redundancy). It will thus reduce home equity withdrawal. These effects will suppress consumption and falls in rent or other costs more applicable to non-property owners are unlikely to balance this effect out.

It should not therefore be surprising that successive govern-ments have sought to increase or at least maintain both house prices and homeownership levels. But as prices rise, an inevitable tension arises between these two objectives. The fact that home-ownership levels are falling rapidly, particularly amongst those under the age of thirty-five, suggests this consumption channel may have a limited lifespan. Indeed, the 'recovery' in the economy in recent years has coincided with a sharp pick-up in consumer debt – often at higher interest rates than home equity withdrawal – rather than housing debt.

Land, business investment and commercial real estate lending

Just as land and property plays a key economic role as collateral for households wishing to borrow money for consumption, so land and property plays a role as collateral in enabling businesses to borrow for investment, developers to build new homes and households to invest in their own homes.

In particular, small and medium sized enterprises (SMEs) often require collateral because their loans are viewed as more risky than other forms of loans (partially due to international Basel regulations). The Bank of England estimates that 75% of all bank lending to UK SMEs is currently secured against commercial real estate (CRE) (Bank of England, 2016b, p. 9). SMEs are a vital source of jobs and innovation – they provide around two-thirds of all jobs in the UK – but are highly dependent on bank finance since they cannot access capital markets as larger businesses can by issuing shares. In addition, many small business directors also collateralise their own homes as a way of raising funding for their firms (Bahaj et al., 2016).

There is a positive link between land prices and business investment. In an upswing, when prices are rising, companies should be able to secure more, or cheaper, credit against their commercial property. In a downswing, companies may be unable either to refinance existing debt or borrow to invest in new productive activity. Research by the Bank of England suggests that every 10% fall in UK commercial real estate prices is associated with a 1% decline in economy-wide investment (Bahaj et al., 2016).

The value of commercially owned land has proven to be even more volatile and pro-cyclical than residential land in the UK and other advanced economies. In all three of the UK's post-war major property-related banking crises – in the early 1970s, the late 1980s and the crisis of 2007–8 – bank losses and defaults have been linked more to CRE lending and large swings in the prices of CRE assets than domestic mortgage lending (Benford and Burrows, 2013; Milne and Wood, 2014).

From one perspective, this is understandable. A feature of a healthy capitalist economy would be that it features risk-taking businesses with insolvencies and hence defaults on commercially owned real estate mortgages being an expected component of the 'creative destruction' needed for innovation and productivity growth (Schumpeter, 1975, pp. 82–85). This view has been enshrined in law in the form of the limited liability business owners enjoy. This means that if a firm fails, their own personal wealth and assets cannot be repossessed by creditors, unlike in the case of domestic mortgages (with the US being an exception as noted in the discussion of securitisation above).

On the other hand, the history of repeated UK commercial real estate crises does call into question whether regulators could do more to prevent the enormous bubbles in CRE lending that have repeatedly damaged the UK economy. In the run-up to the most recent financial crisis, for example, CRE debt increased from £50 billion to £255 billion in the space of just eight years and has since fallen back to £165 billion (DeMontfort University, 2015). It increased again for the first time since the financial crisis in 2015 (DeMontfort University, 2015).

After the crisis, UK banks and building societies significantly reduced their exposure to real estate. But recent decades have seen a huge rise in non-bank CRE lending, including by international investors, by both wealthy individuals and institutional investors. In the UK foreign investors have accounted for around 45% of the value of total CRE transactions since 2009 (Bank of England, 2016b, p. 7) while insurance companies and non-bank lenders made up 22% of the market share (DeMontfort University, 2015)

The recovery in CRE may be partially related to post-crisis monetary policy, with central banks' quantitative easing policies pushing down the returns investors can receive on safer investments such as government bonds and making commercial real estate more attractive. A recent report found that globally CRE generated average returns of 10% in 2014 thanks to rapid capital appreciation, the fifth consecutive year of increasing returns (Allen and Nicolaou, 2015).

The global CRE investment market appears to be changing in two important respects. Firstly, it is losing its traditional 'home bias', with investors increasingly seeking international portfolios rather than concentrating on their home countries (Hobbes, 2014).

Secondly, returns are increasingly coming more from capital gains – that is, appreciation in land values – rather than rental returns. Indeed yields on real estate – rental revenue as a proportion of a property's value – are currently close to historic lows. That huge amount of international investment are flowing into CRE with rental returns so low suggests the emergence of a global bubble. The UK, and London in particular, may lie at the heart of this bubble. Returns on UK real estate were 17.9% in 2014 compared to the global average of 10% (Allen and Nicolaou, 2015).

However, investment volumes in UK CRE slowed in the run-up to the UK's referendum on its membership of the European Union, and following the UK's vote to leave the European Union on 23 March 2016 the market suffered a sharp contraction. Whether this is a temporary downturn or a lasting correction in the market remains to be seen.

5.6 The property–credit nexus and financial fragility

As discussed, for the last few decades of the twentieth century, mainstream economic theory largely neglected a causal role for credit in the economy. The general assumption has been that increases in private sector credit are a good thing, with such 'financial deepening' increasing the efficiency of economies by accelerating improvements in technology and productivity (King and Levine, 1993). Mortgage credit, and household debt more generally, was not the focus of empirical work. All this has now been thrown into doubt as it has become clear that rapid household debt and house price growth can have dangerous and long-lasting impacts on financial fragility and economic growth.

A key development has been to distinguish the type of credit and its economic effects. A number of academic studies show a stronger correlation between credit to the non-financial firms and output growth than credit to the household sector, the majority of which is mortgage credit (Beck et al., 2008; Bezemer et al., 2016; Buyukkarabacak and Valev, 2006). For example, a study of forty-six economies over 1990–2011 found a negative relationship between the stock of bank lending to domestic real estate and economic growth but positive growth effects of credit flows to non-financial business (Bezemer et al., 2016). Similar results have been found in studies of single countries, including Japan (Werner, 1997), the United Kingdom (Ryan-Collins et al., 2016) and the United States (Bezemer, 2014). Another study of thirty countries in the period 1960–2012 found that an increase in the household debt-to-GDP ratio over three years predicts lower subsequent GDP growth and higher unemployment, features that IMF and OECD forecasters failed to predict (Mian et al., 2015).

Mortgage credit may be useful as a form of spreading the cost of a large durable consumer good over a longer period. However, mortgage credit will not support increased growth in the economy unless it enables residential investment, home building or consumption. The vast majority of mortgage credit in the UK and most advanced economies goes towards the transfer of existing homes between households (Bank of England, 2016c). As new credit and money is created and flows into existing homes and land, the inevitable result is house price inflation and rising household debt-to-income ratios: the classic house price or real estate bubble.

When an economic shock hits or interest rates rise, the economy is then faced with a situation where all sectors of the economy (apart from the government), led by households, seek to deleverage and reduce their debts – 'rebuilding their balance sheets' (Koo, 2011). Households reduce their spending and increase their savings, this reduces firms' profits, leading them to pull back from investment and pay off their debts, and banks contract their lending and rebuild their capital base. A range of studies show that such balance sheet recessions tend to last longer and be deeper than crises that do not involve credit bubbles (e.g. stock market bubbles); and within the universe of recessions caused by credit bubbles, land-related credit bubbles are consistently deeper and last longer (Buyukkarabacak and Valev, 2006; Schularick and Taylor, 2009; Borio et al., 2011; Bezemer and Zhang, 2014; Jordà et al., 2015).

The clearest example of the long-term damage a land price credit bubble can do to an economy is Japan. In the lead-up the to the crash in 1991, there was excessive credit creation for real estate purchase, particularly in Japan's fast growing cities, driving a

Box 5.6 Hyman Minsky: stability is destabilising

Hyman Minsky was an American economist whose research focused on the origins of financial cycles and crises in capitalist economies.[12] Minsky disagreed with neoclassical economics' assumption that the economy was best understood as being in a state of long-run equilibrium, buffeted by short-term 'shocks' created by business cycles, with finance, credit and asset prices playing a largely insignificant role.

Instead, the key characteristic of advanced capitalist economies was the role of finance and debt in supporting business investment and profits and uncertainty about the future. Minsky, developing arguments made by Keynes and Irving Fisher, argued that rather than moving around an equilibrium, the need for firms to borrow based upon the expected future realisation of profits meant capitalist economies moved repeatedly through phases of stability and instability. When economies were stable, firms' and banks' confidence would increase, leading to an increase in speculative forms of investment and related borrowing. This would lead to a build-up of debt which eventually would exceed what borrowers could pay off from their incoming revenues, forcing them to borrow to fund interest payments – what Minsky called 'Ponzi financing'.

Under such a scenario, economies become highly fragile and even small economic shocks could lead to firm defaults. The process would then go into reverse, with business investment falling, banks defaulting and unwilling to lend and debt-deflation ensuing.

Minsky's writings were mainly focused on the role of firms and their interaction with the banking system rather than households and mortgage credit. However, his theories were highly applicable to the financial crisis of 2007–8, when a long period of apparent stability (the 'Great Moderation') and rising asset prices led to increasingly risky behaviour by households and banks in borrowing and lending against land and housing. Indeed, the crisis was termed a 'Minsky moment' because his work seemed to

---

12 See Minsky (1992) for a short and accessible summary of his 'financial instability hypothesis' and Minsky (1986) for a comprehensive account.

describe so well pre- and post-crisis dynamics (Minsky was largely ignored prior to the crisis). Economists increasingly now make use of his theories in relation to housing markets, for example describing 'Minskyian households' (Stockhammer and Wildauer, 2016, p. 2) as those which take confidence from increasing house prices to leverage up against their real estate assets to boost their consumption, resulting in increases in household debt-to-income ratios and financial fragility (see for example Dymski, 2010; Ryoo, 2015).

self-reinforcing stock-market boom. A key cause was the relaxation of credit controls on real estate lending by the banking sector – known as 'window guidance' – by the Japanese central bank (Kindleberger and Aliber, 2005, p. 151; Werner, 2002, 2003). The Bank of Japan maintained double-digit year-on-year credit growth quotas for banks to meet even as demand from the real economy subsided, fuelling an asset price spiral with investors eventually borrowing to meet the interest payments on outstanding loans – so-called 'Ponzi financing' (see Box 5.5).

Concerned about excessive real estate growth, the bank implemented a new regulation instructing Japanese banks to limit the rate of the growth of their real estate loans so it would be no greater than the rate of growth of their total loans (Kindleberger and Aliber, 2005). No longer able to borrow to fund their existing loan repayments, investors began to rapidly sell off properties loaded with debt, leading to a rapid decline in real estate values, followed by a collapse in stock prices. Banks, firms and households deleveraged and demand was depressed (Koo, 2011). The crash appears to have permanently lowered real GDP growth per capita. This averaged 3.7% in the twenty years leading up to 1991 but has been under 1% since, with inflation negative in the majority of years that have followed.

Other Asian economies experienced similar real estate related bubbles in the early 1990s, with a noticeable feature being that increases in real estate prices pushed up stock prices which further boosted confidence and fed back into increases in land values (Kindleberger and Aliber, 2005, pp. 29–30).

Today, a number of economists claim that high levels of debt across the globe, with its origins in excessive bank lending against real estate in the build-up to the financial crisis, is depressing demand and preventing a return to pre-crisis levels of growth (Jordà et al., 2015; Mian et al., 2015; Turner, 2015a). Excessive land-related debt appears to be a key cause of the 'secular stagnation' (Summers, 2015) that has plagued the global economy since the crisis.

Regulating property-related credit

Despite the evidence of a powerful link between house prices, credit growth and crises prior to the financial crisis, central banks did not use monetary policy to prevent asset booms. The consensus was that it was better to wait for the bust and 'clean up afterwards' than attempt to contain/prevent the boom altogether. Firstly, it was thought difficult to ascertain when asset prices had risen 'beyond fundamentals'. Secondly, monetary policy approaches had become limited to the use of short-term interest rates rather than adjustments to credit quantities and this was felt to be too blunt a tool to target a narrow part of the market such as property prices (Bernanke and Gertler, 2000; Dell'Ariccia et al., 2012).

In addition, as noted in section 5.5, mortgage lending and home equity withdrawal can support consumption and demand over long periods. This can help give the appearance that the economy is healthy even as productivity or wages are stagnating. Many advanced economies enjoyed an unprecedented period of steady growth coupled with low inflation from the 1990s and up to the crisis – described as the 'Great Moderation' – that may have reassured central banks that policy was working (Bezemer and Grydaki, 2014). Mervyn King described the 1990s as the 'NICE' decade – a period of 'non-inflationary, consistent expansion' (King, 2003, p. 3).

In the 2000s, financial innovations, including RMBS, were seen as spreading risk rather than amplifying it. The build-up of mortgage debt smoothed the business cycle but encouraged excessive leverage in both the banking and household sector which eventually resulted in fragilities that led to financial collapse (Barwell and Burrows, 2011). The smoothing of the cycle enabled by mortgage lending was simply disguising the build-up of much larger, longer

and more dangerous 'credit' or 'financial cycles' that macroeconomics had neglected for much of the post-war period (Borio,
2014). Such developments fit perfectly the ideas of the late American economist Hyman Minsky (1986), who argued that 'stability
is destabilizing' in capitalist, finance-driven markets. Economic
models which incorporated asset prices, stocks of debt and flows of
credit and household and bank balance sheets successfully predicted
the crisis (Keen, 1995, 2013; Bezemer, 2009); standard neoclassical
models that ignored such attributes did not.

In the aftermath of the 2008 financial crisis, however, many
central banks have begun targeting the growth, or restriction, of
credit to particular economic uses in the economy. These policies
were previously unthinkable, as such state intervention was not
supported by conventional macroeconomic equilibrium theory as
discussed in Chapter 3, the lifecycle hypothesis and faith in efficient
market allocation.

Most notably, central banks have developed 'macroprudential'
policies aimed at dampening credit cycles, with a specific focus
on mortgage credit. In the UK, the newly created Financial Policy
Committee (FPC) has powers to impose loan-to-value or loan-to-income ratios for mortgages in the UK . This is the first time a public
body has been given such powers since Margaret Thatcher abolished
the 'corset' controls on credit in 1980 (see section 5.4). However, the
bank has been reluctant to make full use of these tools, setting limits
that will only have effect if there is a major boom in house prices.[13]

Institutional factors

Although the general pattern of increasing mortgage debt and house
prices is common across many advanced economies, there are some

---

13 In 2014 the FPC put a limit on the proportion of mortgages a bank can issue at
   loan-to-income multiples above 4.5 to no more than 15% of a bank's new lending
   for residential home purchases. At present, no bank exceeds this limit and the
   average level of lending above a 4.5 loan-to-income ratio is only 10%, so it is not
   binding on any lending. In addition, the policy will only bite if house price growth
   rises in excess of the bank's central forecast of a 20% rise in house prices between
   2014 and 2017, considerably more than income growth projections (see http://
   www.ft.com/cms/s/0/ef06b7fc-fd13-11e3-8ca9-00144feab7de.html#axzz41Bw8
   VDVi – paywall).

important exceptions. Many empirical studies find that institutional variation both between countries and over time account for major differences in linkages between credit, house prices and economic activity (Aron et al., 2012; Calza, Monacelli, and Stracca, 2013; Duca et al., 2010; Muellbauer and Murphy, 2008). Of particular importance seems to be the structure of the mortgage market, including whether interest rates are floating or fixed, the regulation of home equity withdrawal, average loan-to-value ratios, whether loans are securitised and the degree of owner-occupation. There is considerable variation across countries in this regard (see Table 5.1 for a summary of ten OECD countries).

While different countries will have different supply-side constraints that will also affect house prices, the evidence suggests that countries with more flexible mortgage markets, securitisation, variable

Table 5.1 Mortgage market structure across sample of ten economies (2013 data)

	(1) Interest rate adjustment	(2) Equity withdrawal	(3) Average LTV ratio on new loans (%)	(4) Mortgage debt-to-GDP ratio (%)	(6) Mortgage-backed securitisation	(7) Owner occupation share (%)
Australia	Variable	Yes	80	74	Yes	70
Belgium	Fixed	No	83	28	No	72
Canada	Fixed	Yes	75	43	Yes	66
France	Fixed	No	75	26	Limited	56
Germany	Fixed	No	70	43	Limited	42
Italy	Variable	No	50	15	No	82
Japan	Fixed	No	70-80	36	No	61
Spain	Variable	Limited	70	40	Yes	85
Switzerland	Variable	No	66	116	Limited	36
UK	Variable	Yes	80-90	74	Yes	70
US	Fixed	Yes	80%	69%	Yes	69

Source: adapted from Assenmacher-Wesche and Gerlach (2008, p. 27) and Calza et al. (2013, p. 104) and the sources therein.

interest rates and high levels of equity withdrawal tend to have more volatility and/or pro-cyclicality in house prices, credit and consumption.[14] In other words, the more liberalised the financial system, the stronger the relationship between house prices, consumption and the wider economy.

Tenure patterns will also play an important role in mediating the impact of deregulation and innovation in the financial sector. The higher the levels of homeownership in an economy, the greater the impacts of such developments are likely to be. This is because renters are not in a position to leverage against their property. In many advanced economies, the general pattern in homeownership has been an increase from around 40% homeownership in the 1940s to closer to 60% by the 2000s (Jordà et al., 2016, p. 121). But there are some interesting exceptions. Not all countries implemented changes in policies to boost private homeownership and mortgages. Germany and Switzerland, where homeownership rates are below 50%, provide good counterexamples.

In Germany, loan-to-value ratios at savings and mortgage banks (the main providers of home loans) were often capped at 60%. At the same time, the comparatively high levels of rent protection that were put in place in the immediate post-war years were upheld in the following decades. In addition, the German tax code provided only limited incentives to take on debt and low inflation meant property was a less attractive asset to hedge against increases in consumer prices. In Switzerland, the government levied taxes on the imputed rents of house owners. As a consequence, the homeownership rate in Germany stood at 43% in 2013 and was hence only marginally higher than the 39% ratio reached in 1950. In a similar fashion, homeownership in Switzerland stagnated around 35% in the past half century. And, also like Germany, Switzerland

---

14 For example, Aron et al. (2012) find that credit availability for UK and US but not Japanese households has undergone large shifts since 1980 with the result that the average consumption-to-income ratio rose in the UK and the USA as mortgage down-payment constraints eased and as the collateral role of housing wealth was enhanced by financial innovations, such as home equity loans (see also Muellbauer and Murphy, 2008; Crowe et al., 2013; Calza et al., 2013; Barrell et al., 2015).

has a more devolved fiscal, planning and banking system, with the cantons having considerable autonomy over these issues.

The evidence suggests that house price inflation relative to incomes is thus not an inevitable feature of advanced capitalist systems. Individual countries have developed policies to prevent excessive household mortgage debt building up and to provide attractive alternative tenure options to ownership. These policies do not appear to have weakened economic growth or innovation; both Germany and Switzerland are well known for the innovative and entrepreneurial industrial sectors.

5.7 Conclusion

In this chapter we have examined the important relationship between land, property and the financial system, specifically focusing on the role of banks in creating and allocating new money and credit.

For the majority of the twentieth century in the UK, mortgage lending was limited to building societies. These mutual institutions were run in the interests of their members rather than shareholders and operated a conservative business model whereby long-term property purchase loans could only be issued to those with a strong history of saving and mortgages were funded by relatively safe retail deposits. Such arrangements maintained a link between property-related credit and the wider economy and limited rapid growth and volatility in mortgage credit and property prices. Banks focused the majority of their lending to firms.

In the 1980s, the mortgage credit sector was deregulated and liberalised as public pressure for wider homeownership grew and Conservative administrations sought to free up the UK banking sector in the face of international competition. This led to a major expansion in mortgage credit and house prices and the development of important new links between housing wealth and consumption. No longer was the ownership of property and land simply a means to provide shelter, bring up a family and provide access to work. It was the key to both growing existing wealth and gaining access to new purchasing power from a banking system increasingly attracted to land as collateral. Both have proved important as median incomes have stagnated over the past thirty years. 'Getting on the housing ladder' may sound like an innocuous phrase, but what it means in countries such as the UK is gaining access to the most desirable asset, historically capable of increasing our paper wealth many times more than moving jobs or investing in the stock market or government bonds.

As land prices rise well beyond average incomes, mortgage debt-to-income ratios have increased. In order to access landownership, many households have had to increase their debt to the banking system relative to their income with the result that the financial sector can be seen to have capitalised an increasing proportion of the economic rent from land in the form of interest payments on mortgage debts (Hudson, 2010). As homeownership levels have fallen in the UK in the last decade, rents have become more concentrated in the hands of property owners and indirectly in the banking sector. As we discuss in the next chapter, this has driven up inequality.

These developments were neglected by policy makers and mainstream economists. The 'lifecycle' model viewed mortgage lending as welfare-enhancing as it enabled households to bring forward the consumption of a long-lived durable consumer good and spread the costs over the course of their lifetime. Rises in mortgage debt relative to income were not seen as problematic given household wealth was also increasing; one cancelled out the other. If banks chose to lend against assets rather than future flows of income to companies, so be it – the private sector knew best how to allocate capital.

Little causal significance was attributed to the build-up of household debt-to-income ratios that bank credit creation enabled or how this could lead to a self-reinforcing cycle of ever higher property prices creating increasing demand for ever more mortgage credit. Banks were viewed as intermediaries, not as money creators. Central banks focused on consumer price inflation, not house price inflation.

Despite increasing volatility in property prices through the last forty years, it was not until the financial crisis of 2008 that more than a minority of economists and policy makers began to question their benign model of the relationship between house prices, the financial sector and the wider economy. At the heart of the crisis was a change in banks' business model. In the US, it was a shift away from generating profit via the charging of interest over the course of a loan to generating profits from the origination and distribution of mortgage loans via residential mortgage-backed securitisation. In the UK, which also engaged in securitisation, it was more related to banks funding a huge expansion in mortgage lending via risky short-term borrowing rather than more stable customer deposits. The fact that mortgages were collateralised against land – the most secure of assets – made them the perfect vehicle for the creation of financial instruments that appeared to spread risk and broaden access to homeownership.

Post-crisis, central banks have woken up to the need to re-impose controls on mortgage credit and banks are being forced to hold more of the risk from securitisation and hold more capital generally. However, the banking sector itself remains largely orientated towards property-backed loans over other types of lending.

In the real world of uncertainty about the future, legally identifiable property and land offer the most attractive form of collateral for banks' seeking to de-risk their lending. As a result, the wider economy remains intimately linked to the value of land and property, both through the provision of liquidity to SMEs via commercial real estate as well as the collateral and the wealth channels that play a key role in supporting consumption.

UK land and property remains 'financialised', a fact that is made clear by the floods of foreign money that poured into the South East of the country in the last decade even as the government and central bank have taken steps to limit the economic rent that can be extracted from landownership via limits on tax relief on second homes and buy-to-let mortgages. Even the uncertainty created by Britain's decision to leave the EU does not appear to have put off such investors (Sheffield, 2016).

To break the land–finance positive feedback cycle, steps need to be taken to encourage bank credit creation and investors' savings back to productive activity and away from property. The alternative is ever increasing and unsustainable levels of household debt, repeated booms and busts and, as we shall see in the next chapter, damaging levels of inequality.

CHAPTER 6

· ·

Land, wealth and inequality

Much of the growth in inequality and the increase
in the wealth–income ratio are related to an
increase in rents and land values.
JOSEPH STIGLITZ (2015B, P. 439)

Civil government, so far as it is instituted for the security
of property, is, in reality, instituted for the defence of
the rich against the poor, or of those who have
property against those who have none at all.
ADAM SMITH (1776, P. 167)

6.1 Introduction

In the last two chapters we have seen how a combination of
ill-thought-out housing policy, changes in welfare and taxation
and financial deregulation have resulted in land and housing in
the UK becoming 'financialised'. In this chapter we explore how
this has interacted with two other key economic developments: the
increasing role of housing as a source of wealth and the pattern of
increasing economic inequality in most advanced economies.

Recent decades have seen housing wealth increase at a faster rate
than other types of wealth, and considerably faster than national
income. At the same time, there has been growing public concern
over the causes and consequences of the widening gap between rich
and poor, and the impact it has on our societies. Curiously, there
has been little attempt among mainstream economists to examine
the links between these two trends. As discussed in Chapter 3, land
was largely excluded from the models used by economists in the

middle of the last century, and as a result the role of land in shaping macroeconomic outcomes such as inequality has been overlooked. Moreover, as discussed in the previous chapter, the failure of mainstream economic theory to properly conceptualise the role of the banking system in the economy and the process of money creation has further contributed towards this oversight.

In this chapter we attempt to fill this void by showing how the financialisation of land has played a central role in driving the recent increase in inequalities of wealth, income and living standards. We show that the increase in the wealth-to-income ratio observed in recent decades which has underpinned the rise in inequality has been driven not by productive activity, but rather by increasing residential land values. As well as exacerbating inequalities in wealth, we also show how this dynamic, amplified through the processes of leverage and inheritance, has also contributed towards increasing gaps in living standards and growing regional imbalances. Ultimately, this has led to a position whereby today the key dividing line in many advanced economies is not earnings, but ownership of property.

Firstly, however, we give an overview of recent empirical trends and examine competing and more traditional explanations for this growing inequality.

6.2 Trends in economic inequality

Income inequality

Income inequality refers to the extent to which income is distributed in an uneven manner among a population. Over the past three decades income inequality has risen across much of the developed world, reaching record highs in some countries.

One way of describing the distribution of income is to compare the ratio of the average income of the richest 10% to the average income of the poorest 10%. Today in OECD countries the richest 10% of the population now earns 9.6 times the income of the poorest 10%. This ratio has grown from 7:1 in the 1980s to 8:1 in the 1990s and then to 9:1 in the 2000s (OECD, 2015). These trends have been driven by a surge in incomes among high earners alongside much more modest income growth elsewhere.

Another common way to measure income inequality is the Gini coefficient. The Gini coefficient is a measure of statistical dispersion intended to represent the income distribution of a nation's residents. It is represented as a number between 0 and 1, where 0 corresponds with perfect equality (where everyone has the same income) and 1 corresponds with perfect inequality (where one person has all the income and everyone else has zero income). On this measure the UK is currently the fifth most unequal country in the OECD (2016).

However, because the Gini coefficient indicates the spread of the income distribution or deviation from the mean, it is particularly sensitive to income changes in the middle of the income distribution and less sensitive to changes at the very top and the very bottom of the income distribution. As a result, much of the research into inequality in recent years has drawn attention to the disproportionate share of overall income growth going to those at the top end of the income distribution, and in particular the top 1% of earners.

Over the past three decades the share of the richest 1% in total pre-tax income has increased in most OECD countries, albeit from very different starting points. This has been particularly acute in the UK, where the income share of the top 1% doubled from around 7% in 1985 to 14% in 2012, meaning that the income share of the top 1% in the UK is now larger than anywhere outside the US (OECD, 2014).

There are also significant disparities within the top 1% of incomes. Between 1993 and 2011 the average income of the top 1% increased from £154,243 to £248,480, a rise of 61%. However, over the same period the average income of the top 0.1% increased from £460,050 to £922,433, more than doubling. Meanwhile, the average income of the entire bottom 90% increased from just £10,200 to £12,993 (New Economics Foundation, 2014).

Wealth inequality

Whereas income is the flow of money earned through work, transfers or rents, wealth is the stock of money that can accumulate over time in assets such as property and shares and in bank accounts. How wealth is distributed is important for equity and intergenerational mobility, but also for the stability of the economic system and for its resilience to shocks. Household wealth is influenced by various factors, including asset prices and household savings rates. Inequalities of wealth can have a significant feedback effect on income inequality as accumulated wealth can be invested to generate capital income in the form of interest payments and dividends.

There is less comparable historic data on wealth than there is on income, which partly explains why wealth inequalities have been largely neglected until recently. However, the available data indicates that the distribution of wealth is typically much more concentrated than the distribution of income among advanced economies. In OECD countries the richest 10% of households account for about 50% of total household wealth on average, and the wealthiest 1% account for 18% (OECD, 2015).

In the UK the combined net wealth of all private households is estimated at £11.1 trillion. Figure 6.1 shows the distribution of this wealth across all households in the UK by percentile. The wealth held by the top 10% of households is around five times greater than the wealth of the bottom half of all households combined and over 875 times greater than that of the least wealthy 10% of households. Median household wealth is £225,100, and being in the wealthiest 1% in the UK requires personal wealth of at least £2.8 million (ONS, 2015b).

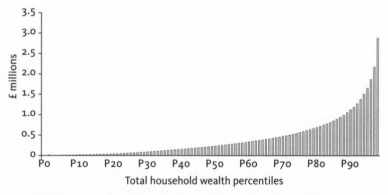

Figure 6.1 Distribution of total UK household wealth, percentile points: July 2012 to June 2014 (*source*: Wealth and Assets Survey – ONS, 2015c)

Note: Includes net property wealth, net financial wealth, physical wealth and private pension wealth.

Spatial inequality

The analysis so far has concentrated on levels of inequality at the national level, but this level of analysis hides important regional and local dynamics. The average household income for a country as a whole can hide vast differences between incomes in different parts of the country.

Today the gap between the richest and poorest region in the UK is wider than the gap between the richest and poorest region in any other EU country. Inner London is the richest space in the EU; but the Welsh valleys are among the poorest places in Europe (Eurostat, 2016). London itself is the most unequal city in the OECD.

There are also stark differences in wealth across different parts of the UK. The South East is the wealthiest region with median household wealth at £342,400, followed by the South West and the East of England with median household total wealth of £308,100 and £267,200 respectively. The North East has the lowest median household total wealth with a value of £150,000 (ONS, 2015b).

6.3 Traditional explanations for increasing inequality

The widespread rise in inequality has been accompanied by a growing debate among economists about the causes and consequences of the widening gap between rich and poor, and the impact it has on our societies. Below are some of the more traditional explanations for this growing inequality.

Marginal productivity theory

As explained in Chapter 3, neoclassical economic theory states that incomes are determined according to contribution to production (the 'marginal productivity theory'). Under this theory, wages reflect the amount of additional output an extra worker would produce – the 'marginal product' of labour. The rationale for this is that if wages were below productivity, firms would find it profitable to hire more workers. This would put upward pressure on wages. Conversely, if wages were above productivity, firms would find it profitable to shed labour, putting downward pressure on wages. In a competitive market an equilibrium is reached whereby wages equal what each worker can produce, resulting in a Pareto efficient outcome.[1]

Under this framework differences in individuals' incomes are therefore said to be related to differences in productivity, skills and effort. Highly paid workers deserve the high wages they receive compared to the less highly paid because they are more productive than members of the latter. Changes in the distribution of income are attributed to changes in technology and to investments in human and physical capital, which have the effect of increasing the skills and productivity of certain individuals. Inequalities are explained because people with skills in high demand in sectors such as IT and finance have seen their earnings rise, reflecting their superior productivity, while low skilled workers have fallen behind.

Under marginal productivity theory the solution to inequality is to increase education and job training opportunities for workers in order to increase skills and productivity across the population. This 'supply-side' approach has dominated economic policy making in recent decades, despite the marginal productivity theory being subject to a number of theoretical and empirical flaws. As with other aspects of neoclassical economics, it is premised on the existence of perfectly competitive markets with complete and full information, and abstracts from important real-world phenomena such as irrational human behaviour, asymmetries of bargaining power and externalities.[2] It also assumes that increasing returns to scale are not a feature of the production process, or in other words that there are diminishing returns to scale in every production technology.

With marginal productivity theory, average wages should rise in line with labour productivity. However, as Figure 6.2 shows, in many advanced countries there has been a 'decoupling' between wages and productivity in recent decades, with wages failing to

---

1 In economics, Pareto efficiency, or Pareto optimality, is a state of allocation of resources in which it is impossible to make any one individual better off without making at least one individual worse off. Pareto efficiency is the state where resources are allocated in the most efficient manner.

2 For further discussion on the flaws of marginal productivity theory see Keen (2011) and Stiglitz (2012).

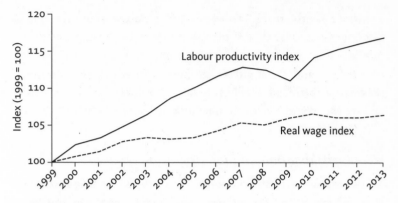

Figure 6.2 Trends in growth in average wages and labour productivity in developed economies (index), 1999–2013 (*source*: ILO, 2015)

Note: Wage growth is calculated as a weighted average of year-on-year growth in average monthly real wages in 36 economies. Index is based to 1999 because of data availability)

keep up with increases in productivity (International Labour Organization, 2015).

Due to this, many economists have increasingly sought to look beyond the textbook description of the marginal productivity theory to try and explain the rapid increase in income and wealth inequality seen in recent decades.

Globalisation and the 'superstar' effect

Some economists have pointed to the polarising effects globalisation has had on labour markets. Under this theory, integration of the world economy through the progressive globalisation of trade and finance has expanded the size of the market that can be served by a single person or firm, therefore creating 'a winner takes all' environment (Frank and Cook, 2010). This often means that small differences in performance can give rise to enormous differences in reward, leading to what has been described as a 'superstar effect' (Rosen, 1981). Although this has long been observed in fields such as sports and entertainment, proponents state that this phenomenon is becoming increasingly common in other fields such as law, finance, fashion and publishing.

More recently, there has been growing debate about the role of technological advance and digitalisation in amplifying this effect. Brynjolfsson and McAfee (2014) argue that increased network externalities and brand effects resulting from advances in computer processing, artificial intelligence and networked communication will see the 'winner takes all' phenomenon become more prominent over time.

Deindustrialisation and the rise of the service sector

Across many advanced economies the process of deindustrialisation and the rise of the services sector have resulted in significant changes to the shape of the labour market. Between 1979 and 2009 the percentage of the UK workforce in manufacturing experienced a 60% decline, and this was matched with a rapid increase in the service industry and high-end technological occupations (Shaheen et al., 2011). While the new technological occupations demanded a highly skilled workforce, many of the new service-orientated roles have been low skilled and more likely to be part time, temporary and low paid (Westwood, 2006). Moreover, the traditional stepping stones that enabled poorly qualified individuals to progress during their career in manufacturing and industry have become increasingly scarce.

As a result, the UK, and in particular London, has experienced a hollowing out of job creation in the medium-skilled occupations, therefore contributing to an increasing divide between those at the top and those at the bottom of the income distribution.

Changes to taxation

Changes in tax policies are also likely to have contributed to the rise in inequality. Top marginal tax rates in most OECD countries, including in Europe, have declined considerably in recent decades. Average top statutory personal income tax rate declined from 66% in 1981 to 43% in 2013 (OECD, 2014). Similarly, the statutory corporate income tax rate declined from 47% in 1981 to 25% in 2012 and taxes on dividend income for distributions of domestic source profits fell from 75% to 42%. Research has found that this not only increases the post-tax shares of top incomes but that lowering top tax rates actually increases the pre-tax share of top incomes. Taxes on net wealth and inheritance tax have also been abolished or reduced in several countries (Förster et al., 2014).

The fall in the wage share and the decline of trade unions

One of the key trends associated with the increase in inequality has been the declining share of wages to total income measured by GDP. Conversely, there has been a growing profit share received by private business owners, shareholders and financial investors (New Economics Foundation, 2014). While most countries have experienced a declining share of wages in national income over the last four decades, the decline in the wage share in the UK is particularly high by international standards. Data from the Office for National Statistics show that between 1977 and 2008 the wage share in the UK fell from 59% of national income to 53%, while the share of profits in national income rose from 25% to 29%.

One study estimated that over the past fifty years the variation in the wage share can explain about 70% of the variation in income inequality in the UK (Reed and Himmelweit, 2012). The reasons behind the fall in the wage share are still subject to ongoing debate; however the principal factors in the literature focus on the effects of technological change, globalisation and financialisation. While all of these are likely to play some role, evidence also suggests that the decline in labour market institutions such as trade unions and collective bargaining has been a major factor. In the UK this is illustrated by the fall in trade union membership and the abandonment of the Fair Wage Resolution wage councils in the 1980s and the 1990s (New Economics Foundation, 2014).

6.4 The role of land and economic rent in increasing inequality

All the above factors have, to varying degrees, contributed to the pattern of increasing economic inequality across advanced economies. However, these explanations alone fail to fully capture why modern capitalist economies have seen a widening of the gap between rich and poor. As discussed in Chapter 3, land was largely excluded from the models used by economists in the middle of the last century. This has meant that the role of land in shaping macroeconomic outcomes such as inequality has been overlooked by mainstream economists. In this section we show how land has played a central role in exacerbating inequalities of wealth, income and living standards in recent decades.

Housing as a growing component of wealth

In the UK, housing is by far the largest single source of wealth. In 2014 the value of households' and non-profit institutions' dwellings was £4.43 trillion – 58% of the entire net wealth of the UK (Armstrong, 2016, p. 2). Housing wealth has increased at a faster rate than financial wealth (e.g. pensions, shares, savings) and non-financial wealth (e.g. ownership of physical assets). It has also increased considerably faster than national income in the UK, in particular since the 1990s, as discussed in Chapter 5. Indeed, in advanced economies generally, it is the increase in housing wealth that has been driving the trends that have been observed in the recent work of French economist Thomas Piketty (2014).

Piketty's book *Capital in the Twenty-first Century* contains data on what he calls the 'capital to income ratio' for the UK since the year 1700. In the book Piketty uses the terms capital and wealth interchangeably, as if they were perfectly synonymous, and does not attempt to separate capital from land and natural resources. However, this ignores key differences between the characteristics of wealth, capital and land.

Wealth is the stock of all assets, regardless of whether they are used as an input to the production process or not. This includes machinery, land, real estate, intellectual property rights, art and jewellery. As explained in Chapter 3, capital is a subset of wealth and relates to the man-made part of wealth which is used in the production process to produce more wealth. Therefore all capital is wealth, but not all wealth is capital. Therefore, every type of wealth other than land which is used in the production process to produce more wealth is called capital.

This has been the source of some confusion, as it is possible for the same asset to be defined as capital under some circumstances and not capital in others. Whether an asset is capital or not depends whether it is being used as an input to production. A car is not defined as capital if it is being used for leisure; however it is capital if it is used to aid logistics in the operation of a business. Land, on the other hand, comprises all non-produced naturally occurring resources. Whereas the supply of capital can be increased, it is not possible to produce more land.

Given that Piketty's measure of capital includes the stock of all assets regardless of characteristics or use, we refer to Piketty's measure as the 'wealth to income ratio'. Piketty's data shows that following a significant decline in the wealth-to-income ratio in the first part of the twentieth century, the ratio began to rise the 1950s and saw a marked increase after 1970. In the UK total wealth amounted to around three times national income in 1970; however by 2010 this had grown to between five and six times (see Figure 6.3).

Piketty's central thesis is that during the twentieth century in nearly all advanced economies the returns to wealth (or capital) were returning to 'normal' levels after a brief blip in the early part of the century. According to Piketty, the rising inequality observed in recent decades is explained by a tendency for the rate of return to wealth to exceed the economic growth rate, causing a growing accumulation of wealth among those who already have wealth (a relationship he describes as $r > g$ in notational form). When the return on wealth significantly exceeds the growth rate of the

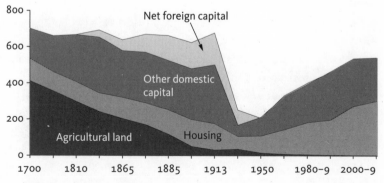

Figure 6.3 National wealth to national income ratio 1700–2010 (Great Britain) (*source*: Piketty and Zucman, 2013)

economy (as it did through much of history until the nineteenth century), Piketty states that inherited wealth grows faster than output and income.

However, Piketty's synthesis of capital and wealth and his omission of land means that his analysis overlooks some key dynamics underlying the rise in the wealth-to-income ratio. As can be seen in Figure 6.3, much of the rise in the wealth-to-income ratio in the UK since the 1950s has come from housing. Since 1970 housing has accounted for 87% of the increase in the wealth-to-income ratio, and included in the measure of housing is the land that sits beneath the buildings. As explained in Chapter 3, because land is fixed in supply and does not depreciate, its relative price tends to increase as output and demand grows. In contrast, capital depreciates over time, meaning that maintaining or increasing the capital stock requires saving for investment in future production.

Indeed, Piketty's dataset shows that much of the increase in the wealth-to-income ratio observed since 1970 has little to do with savings; rather it is the result of rising asset prices (capital gains), mainly relating to increases in the value of residential land (Rognlie, 2014). Once the effects of capital gains are removed, the underlying wealth-to-income ratio has actually fallen significantly in the UK since 1970 (see Figure 6.4). This indicates a decline in the UK's productive capital stock over the past four decades relative to national income.

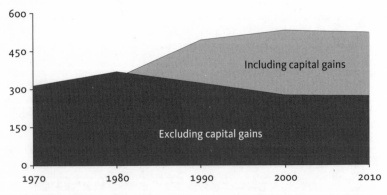

Figure 6.4 National wealth to national income ratio 1970–2010, excluding capital gains (Great Britain) (%) (*source*: Piketty and Zucman, 2013)

The implications of this analysis are vital for understanding the dynamics of growing inequality in recent decades. Firstly, it means that the increase in the wealth-to-income ratio observed in Piketty's data, which has underpinned the rise in inequality, has been driven not by productive activity, but rather by increasing residential land values which have manifested themselves through rising house prices. Put another way, this wealth has originated from windfalls resulting from exclusive control of a scarce natural resource in the face of rising demand from economic development, population growth and financial deregulation. As discussed in Chapter 3, the classical economists would have viewed this as an accumulation of unearned economic rent; a transfer of wealth from the rest of society towards land and property owners (George, [1879] 1979).

Secondly, the decoupling of wealth from the productive capacity of the economy points to asymmetries in the way that wealth is measured under modern national accounting frameworks. When the value of land under a house goes up, the total productive capacity of the economy is unchanged or diminished because nothing new has been produced, it merely constitutes an increase in the value of an asset. While this increases the wealth of the land-owner, it also has a corresponding cost. This is because housing serves a dual role as both an investment good and a consumption good. Whoever rents or buys the land in future will have to pay more and as a result will have to save more and consume – or, in the case of firms, invest – less. As we explained in Chapter 5, these effects can be asymmetric, often affecting owners and non-owners in an unequal manner. Overall, it is not clear that increases in house prices leave the household sector as a whole better off over the longer term (Barker, 2004).

However, under current national accounting frameworks only the increase in the wealth of the landowners gets recorded in measures of wealth; the present discounted value of the decreased flow of resources to the rest of the economy is ignored (Stiglitz, 2015c). Thus, while increases in house prices (as opposed to investment in homes or the building of new homes) will lead to an increase in wealth in the national accounts, the corresponding cost to the rest of the economy is not captured. This has contributed towards the divergence between measures of wealth and the productive capacity of the economy.

Housing and wealth inequality

The impact that housing has on wealth inequality depends on a number of factors, including the initial distribution of housing wealth, the change in the rate of owner-occupancy and regional disparities in house price inflation. For example, if previously public housing switches into private ownership on a large scale, and most of these newly private assets are held by households in the lower and middle parts of the distribution, then this may serve to narrow the distribution of wealth, even if house prices do not change. On the other hand, if the private housing stock becomes more concentrated in fewer hands and a higher proportion of people become private renters, this will increase wealth inequality even if house prices do not change. Similarly, if areas with more affluent or older households who already possess initial housing equity experience above average house price inflation, then a widening of the distribution of wealth may occur (Henley, 1998).

In the UK housing represents a significant component of total household wealth. As of 2014 the aggregate household gross property wealth in the UK was £4,984 billion. There was also £1,057 billion of mortgage debt, leaving £3,927 billion of net property

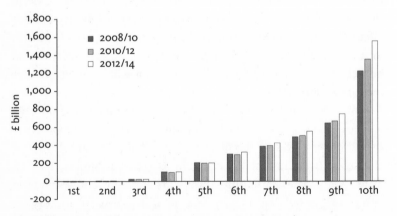

Figure 6.5 Breakdown of net property wealth, by deciles: Great Britain, 2008/10–2012/14 (*source*: Wealth and Assets Survey, 2015c)

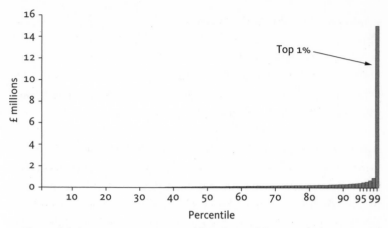

Figure 6.6 Average net property wealth in the UK, by percentile (upper bound) (*source*: ONS)

Note: Upper bound estimates

wealth. Property wealth is currently distributed very unevenly across the population. Figure 6.5 shows the distribution of total net property wealth across all households in the UK by decile. Those in the first decile of households have negative wealth, reflecting net debts or negative equity, whereas the property wealth of the top 10% of households is nearly five times greater than the wealth of the bottom half of all households combined (ONS, 2015d).

Data on the distribution of property wealth within the top 10% is limited; however, the preliminary data that does exist suggests that much of the wealth is concentrated within the top 1%. While Figure 6.5 shows the *total* net property wealth across all households in the UK, Figure 6.6 shows the *average* property wealth by percentile, provided by the Office for National Statistics. It shows that the average net property of the top 1% of households is £15 million.

Studies examining changes in the distribution of housing wealth over extended periods of time are limited. One study which examined changes in the distribution of net housing wealth in Great Britain between 1985 and 1991 found that the largest gains in absolute terms went to the wealthiest group (P90) of households, but in percentage terms the most dramatic increase was experienced by middle wealth households (P50). This reflects the sizeable capital gains that accrued to owner-occupiers, particularly those who were already owner-occupiers at the start of the period, and the growth in owner-occupancy and increase in the proportion of housing assets held by households in the middle part of the distribution. The lowest 10% of wealth (P10) saw no increase in net housing wealth over the period (Henley, 1998).

A similar pattern is found in a study by Bastagli and Hills (2012) which examined changes in net housing wealth between 1995 and 2005, a period which saw the most rapid increase in house prices in UK history. As above, the largest gains in absolute terms went to the wealthiest group (P90) of households, but in percentage terms the most dramatic increase was experienced by middle wealth households (P50). Again, the lowest 10% of households (P10) saw no increase in net housing wealth over the period. Similar results are found in Karagiannaki (2011b) which examined changes in net housing wealth over the same time period.

Table 6.1 Change in net property wealth between 1985 and 1991, selected percentiles (Great Britain)

Percentile	1985	1991	Change	Change (%)
P10	0	0	0	0%
P50	£8,594	£21,318	£12,724	148%
P90	£70,220	£98,104	£27,884	40%

Source: Henley (1998)
Note: Figures in 1991 prices.

Table 6.2 Net property wealth between 1995 and 2005, selected percentiles (Great Britain)

Percentile	1995	2000	2005	Change	Change (%)
P10	0	0	0	0	0
P50	£27,000	£44,000	£102,000	£75,000	178%
P90	£121,000	£197,000	£306,000	£185,000	53%

Source: Bastagli and Hills (2012)
Note: Figures in 2005 prices.

In all of these studies housing wealth inequality as measured by the Gini coefficient is found to have declined slightly over the relevant time periods, largely driven by the increase in the proportion of housing assets held by households in the middle part of the distribution.[3] However, measuring the effect of these trends on inequality using conventional measures of inequality such as the Gini coefficient is problematic. As noted previously, the Gini coefficient indicates the spread of the wealth distribution or deviation from the mean, and is therefore very sensitive to changes in the middle of the distribution and less sensitive to changes at the very top and the very bottom of the distribution. Measures of inequality such as the Gini coefficient are therefore not well suited to describe the distribution of housing wealth due to the large proportion of households whose wealth is zero or negative (Durand and Murtin, 2015).

An alternative approach is to present the effect of these trends on inequality by referring to the concentration of housing wealth in higher wealth percentiles. However, this is also somewhat misleading as it does not provide any indication of the disparity between the middle and the bottom of the distribution and again masks the fact that for a large fraction of households wealth remains zero or negative.

As a result, conventional measures of inequality do not fully capture the dynamics of inequalities in housing wealth. The key trend underpinning the changes in the distribution of housing wealth in recent decades has been the widening gap between *those who own property and those who do not*. For those who own property, rising house prices represent untaxed capital gains which increases net wealth and, as a secondary effect, boosts consumption. For those who do not own property, rising house prices mean facing higher rents in the rental market and having to save more to be able to afford a deposit for a mortgage.

Thus, recent rises in house prices have contributed towards growing inequalities between two classes separated not by their contribution to production, but by access to property and exclusive

---

3 These studies may underestimate the increase in net wealth, particularly at the higher end of the distribution, as they do not consider the effect of equity withdrawal.

control of a scarce natural resource (land). As house prices continue to rise, this divide between the 'housing haves and the housing have-nots' will continue to get wider as the wealth of those at the bottom remains zero or negative (Appleyard and Rowlingson, 2010).

The past decade has seen this dynamic become even more pronounced . As discussed in Chapter 4, following the surge in home-ownership in the second half of the twentieth century, the number of people who own their homes is now declining. Owner-occupancy with a mortgage has been falling since 1999, and total homeowner-ship has been falling since 2003 (DCLG, 2015). This is particularly pronounced among those in the 25–44 age groups. As house prices have continued to increase and the gap between house prices and earnings has grown larger, the cost of homeownership has become increasingly prohibitive. Although easier access to mortgage credit and Right to Buy discounts covered this widening gap for a while, eventually this started to have a negative effect as rising house prices rendered homeownership increasingly unaffordable for much of the population. As Stephens (2007) notes:

> In one sense the liberalisation of mortgage finance was socially progressive and helped to widen access to housing finance … [but] has been undermined by its impact on house prices, which in turn have narrowed access to home-ownership, while housing market instability has sharpened the risks associated with home-ownership by making future price trends uncertain.

The result has been that inequality of net property wealth has increased in recent years, even on the basis of the flawed measure of the Gini coefficient.[4] As can be seen in Figure 6.5 above, wealth in the top deciles increased dramatically between 2008 and 2014, while wealth in the other deciles remained relatively stable or decreased. Without intervention, the likelihood is that these trends will get worse in the coming decades, as more and more people find them-selves renting from a small, wealthy minority of property owners.

---

4 According to the ONS Wealth and Assets Survey, the Gini coefficient of net prop-erty wealth increased from 0.62 to 0.66 between 2006–8 and 2012–14.

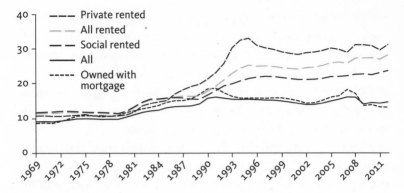

Figure 6.7 Percentage of income spent on housing costs by tenure type (Great Britain) (*source*: Belfield et al., 2014)

Note: Figures in 2012–13 prices. Income is measured before housing costs are deducted and both income and housing costs are unequivalised. Housing costs are gross of housing benefit.

Housing and income inequality

In addition to affecting the distribution of wealth, there are also a number of ways in which rising house prices impact on incomes and living standards. Firstly, in recent decades a substantial gap has opened up between the cost of housing under different forms of tenure (Figure 6.7). Until the 1980s the cost of housing was broadly similar across all forms of tenure, as measured by percentage of income spent on housing costs. However, in the late 1980s the cost of renting increased sharply relative to incomes, whereas the cost of owning with a mortgage remained broadly stable (Belfield et al., 2014). As a result, the cost of housing has increased disproportionately for those in rented accommodation, which tend to be households on lower incomes.[5]

This has had the effect of exacerbating inequalities in ultimate spending power and living standards. Figure 6.8 shows the Gini

---

[5] The National Equality Panel found that the median wages of those who own their property (whether bought outright or with a loan or mortgage) are significantly higher than the earnings of people who rent (whether privately or in social housing). For example, the median wage for women living in social housing is £6.58, whereas the median hourly wage for men with a mortgage is £12.64 (Hills, 2010).

coefficient for income inequality both before and after housing costs. It shows that income inequality was largely unaffected by housing costs during the 1960s and 1970s, but from 1979 onwards there has been a growing divergence between the two measures. This indicates that over the past thirty years housing costs have become a significant contributor towards widening gaps in ultimate spending power and, therefore, living standards.

Research from the Resolution Foundation has shown that between 2002 and 2015 rising housing costs more than outweighed the modest income gains made for the bottom 56% of working age households (Clarke et al., 2016). Housing costs have therefore wiped out any possible improvements in living standards generated through income growth for low and middle income households.

In addition, the ability to convert housing equity into income (home equity withdrawal) has blurred the relationship between wealth and income. As explained in Chapter 5, home equity withdrawal is a way of getting cash from the value of a home without having to move out. The decade before the financial crisis saw unprecedented levels of home equity withdrawal as homeowners used rising house prices to increase their borrowing to fund consumption. By converting a stock of wealth into a flow of income, equity release provides a direct link between houses prices and individual spending power, and therefore living standards.

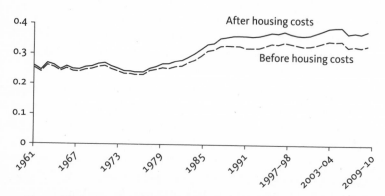

Figure 6.8 Income inequality (Gini coefficient) from 1961 to 2013–14 before and after housing costs (Great Britain) (*source*: Institute of Fiscal Studies, 2015)

Intergenerational dynamics

Housing also plays an important role in shaping the distribution of wealth between age groups. Table 6.3 shows the distribution of housing wealth among individuals by age in Great Britain.

Older owners generally have more housing wealth than younger owners because they have had more time to earn money and pay off their mortgage, and as a result have a much higher level of equity in their home (Hamnett and Seavers, 1996). This has enabled many older homeowners to purchase additional properties either as second homes for themselves, accommodation for their children or as buy-to-let. Younger people, on the other hand, are likely to be earning less than older people, and will have had less time to save for a deposit on a house and enter the property market. Those who have managed to enter the housing market for the first time tend to have high levels of debt and little equity.

Table 6.3 Household net property wealth, individuals by age (Great Britain, 2012 to 2014)

	Do not own property	Less than £50,000	£50,000 but < £125,000	£125,000 but < £250,000	£250,000 but < £375,000	£375,000 but < £500,000	£500,000 or more	All house-holds
	% of individuals							
16–24	41	8	15	19	8	4	6	100
25–34	39	24	17	11	4	2	2	100
35–44	29	17	25	17	6	2	4	100
45–54	24	8	20	25	11	5	7	100
55–64	19	4	14	30	15	7	11	100
65+	22	1	13	31	18	6	9	100
All persons	30	11	18	21	10	4	6	100

Source: Wealth and Assets Survey, Office for National Statistics
Notes: Includes all households, including those who rent their main accommodation. The figures for those aged 16 to 24 are likely to be skewed by the high percentage of individuals aged between 16 and 24 who still live in their parental home.

This picture has changed dramatically over time, however. Today young adults have significantly less wealth on average than previous generations did at the same age. According to the Institute for Fiscal Studies, the average household wealth of adults in their early thirties who were born in the early 1980s is £27,000, while those born in the 1970s had nearly double this – £53,000 – at around the same age. This wealth differential between these two groups is driven by the lower net property wealth of today's younger generation, as the rate of homeownership of those born in the early 1980s is substantially lower than any other post-war cohort at the same age (Cribb et al., 2016).

These dynamics are further reinforced by the process of inheritance. In a study examining the evolution of the annual flow of inheritances in the UK in the period 1984–2005, Karagiannaki (2011a) finds that most of the increase in the flows of inheritance (which grew from £22 billion in 1984 to £56 billion in 2005, in constant prices) was driven by increases in house prices. In addition, the proportion of inheritances including housing assets rose from 58% in 1984–85 to 65% in 2005–6, reflecting the increase in homeownership in the second half of the twentieth century.

There is a strong consensus in the academic literature that the inheritance of bequests is an important contributor to wealth inequality. Given the unequal distribution of housing wealth and the fact that a large proportion of the population has zero or negative wealth, the inheritance of housing contributes significantly towards this (Appleyard and Rowlingson, 2010). This further exacerbates the gap between those who own property and those who do not, and it can reasonably be expected that this will become more pronounced in future. This is because, at present, owner-occupation is highest among those in their forties, fifties and early sixties, and the large cohort of people who became homeowners in the 1980s are not yet old enough to pass on their wealth to future generations but will do at some time in the future.

Spatial dynamics

One of the feedback loops in this trend is increasing socioeconomic sorting into neighbourhoods, or 'ghettoisation', and an increased polarisation of house prices between areas (New Economics Foundation, 2014). Houses in more attractive neighbourhoods come to be treated as luxury goods as people are willing to pay excessively high prices to access them. Inequality levels are in turn exacerbated by the land value appreciation of homeowners in these increasingly affluent areas.

The promise of capital gains has enticed new buyers into these areas, most noticeably overseas investors who are usually able to buy outright and gain from speculation. Estate agency Knight Frank estimated that overseas buyers spent £2.2 billion on new-build central London property in 2012, accounting for 73% of all transactions (Knight Frank, 2013).

In terms of house prices to earnings ratios, there is a significant division between the South of England and the rest of the country. Recently, London in particular can be seen as something of outlier, with average house price-to-income ratios considerably higher than the rest of the country and reaching record highs in the last few years, partially driven by speculative domestic and overseas purchases (see Figure 6.9).

Figure 6.9 Change in average house price to earnings across UK regions, 1983–2014 (*source*: Halifax, 2015)

Note: The left-hand side of each bar represents the average house price to earnings ratio in 1983; the right-hand side of each bar represents the average house price to earnings ratio in 2014.

The role of leverage

A key factor underpinning the growing disparities in income and wealth is the role of leverage. Leverage is the process whereby assets are used as collateral against which money is borrowed and then invested further. By buying assets using borrowed funds, leverage means that gains (and losses) can be amplified. So long as the income from the asset or the asset price appreciation is higher than the cost of borrowing, leverage provides those who are deemed creditworthy a means of accumulating further wealth.

Leverage allows those who already have asset wealth to utilise it to increase their wealth further. An extreme example of this can be seen with today's Russian oligarchs, many of whom achieved significant wealth by borrowing against their modest wealth in the mid-1990s in order to buy natural resources cheaply, enabling them to accumulate large fortunes through the capturing of economic rents (Turner, 2015a). A more recent example of how leverage can be used to amplify disparities in wealth can be seen with the boom in the buy-to-let property market in the UK, whereby thousands of homeowners have purchased additional properties for the purposes of letting out and generating rental income. Throughout 2014 around 15% of total mortgage lending was for buy-to-let purposes.

As discussed in Chapter 5, a consequence of the growing role of leverage has been an increasing share of economic rents flowing to the financial sector in the form of interest payments. Commercial banks do not need to have existing assets to leverage as they create money, in the form of bank deposits, by extending credit. The ability of banks to create new money in the form of loans, which has been greatly enhanced following successive waves of financial deregulation, plays a key role in facilitating leverage in the economy.

This may in part explain why the profitability of the financial sector has expanded so much in recent decades. The share of total profits absorbed by financial corporations, having been very low at around 1% through the 1950s and 1960s, grew substantially from the early 1980s to the present day, reaching 15% after the financial crisis (Reed and Himmelweit, 2012).

6.5 Why inequality matters

Health and social problems

In recent years an increasing amount of research has sought to explore the relationship between economic inequality and health and social problems. Wilkinson and Pickett (2010) find a significant correlation between income inequality and many different factors of health and social malaise among twenty-three developed countries and among US states.[6] They conclude that inequality and social stratification lead to higher levels of psychosocial stress and status anxiety, which in turn can lead to depression, dependency, less community life, parenting problems and stress-related diseases. These negative impacts do not just accrue to those on low incomes, they show that inequality has negative consequences for everyone.

Although Wilkinson and Pickett's empirical work has been subject to some criticism (see Snowdon, 2010; Saunders, 2011), there is a strong consensus in the broader academic literature in support of a correlation between income inequality and health and social problems. Research suggests that inequality is particularly harmful after it reaches a certain threshold, which Britain was below in the 1960s, 1970s and early 1980s, but then breached in 1986–87. It has settled well above that threshold since 1998–99 (Rowlingson, 2011).

In the words of Jencks (2002), 'The social consequences of economic inequality are sometimes negative, sometimes neutral but seldom – as far as I can discover – positive'.

Weak demand and financial instability

Rising inequality has also been shown to contribute to problems of weak demand and financial instability. In a society with high levels of inequality more money flows to wealthy people who tend to save more (they have a low *marginal propensity to consume*). In contrast, less money flows to lower income households who tend

---

6 The index includes measures of the following health and social problems: life expectancy and infant mortality, mental illness (including drug and alcohol addiction), children's education performance, imprisonment rates, obesity, social mobility, level of trust, homicides, teenage births and child well-being.

to spend most of their income on essential goods and services (they have a higher *marginal propensity to consume*).

If inequality rises beyond a certain point then middle and low earners may be forced to rely on credit in order to maintain consumption either in absolute or relative terms. If this gets to a point where unsustainable credit growth is essential to maintain demand then this can pose risks to financial stability. Increasing asset-market credit creation is itself also likely to be a driver of wealth inequality, particularly given an inelastic supply of locationally desirable land in many advanced economies, if it drives up property prices.

The effect may be to substantially increase the wealth-to-income ratio of those with only small initial endowments while increasing the debt-to-income ratio of those without such endowments (Stiglitz, 2015a; Turner, 2015a). Increasing inequality and stagnating median wages in advanced economies may thus provide an important demand-side explanation for increases in mortgage and consumer credit as households seek to maintain their consumption levels; conversely, increasing household debt-to-GDP ratios may repress consumption demand and lead to less demand from firms for borrowing for capital investment (Kumhof et al., 2015; Perugini et al., 2015; Stockhammer, 2004)

Empirical research has found that this phenomenon played a key role in causing the Great Depression and the 2008 financial crisis (Kumhof et al., 2015). The period 1920–29 witnessed a large increase in the income share of high-income households as well as a large increase in low and middle income households' indebtedness. Marriner Eccles, chair of the US Federal Reserve from 1934 to 1948, described the following:

> a giant suction pump had by 1929–30 drawn into a few hands an increasing portion of currently produced wealth. This served them as capital accumulations. But by taking purchasing power out of the hands of mass consumers, the savers denied to themselves the kind of effective demand for their products that would justify a reinvestment of their capital accumulations in new plants. In consequence, as in a poker game where the chips were concentrated in fewer and fewer hands, the other fellows

could stay in the game only by borrowing. When their credit ran out, the game stopped.

As discussed in Chapter 5, in the run-up to 2008 a similar phenomenon occurred; however this time consumption was often financed with mortgage credit secured against rising housing and land values, which appeared for a time to make borrowing affordable. Mortgage equity withdrawal and remortgaging effectively disguised stagnating median incomes by enabling households to maintain consumer spending via the build-up of debt. This occurred both in the United States (Grydaki and Bezemer, 2013) and in the UK (Engelen et al., 2011; Turner, 2015a)

6.6 Conclusion

In this chapter we have shown the fundamental role of changes in land and property prices in driving wealth, income and living standards inequalities in the UK and other advanced economies. Increasingly, the key dividing line in many advanced economies is not earnings but ownership of property, which will enable more rapid growth in the value of existing wealth and access to additional purchasing power through leverage. This has contributed to the growth of regional and intergenerational imbalances.

In a capitalist system where credit is most easily obtained by those already in possession of property and where the majority of new credit is extended against real estate rather than productive activity, these inequalities are likely to get worse over the coming decades. Such a system is not only highly inequitable, it is also economically very inefficient and financially fragile. The concentration of land wealth in the hands of an increasingly small percentage of the population sucks purchasing power and demand out of the economy, as those with the highest marginal propensity to consume find themselves needing to borrow ever higher quantities of debt to maintain consumption. Without such demand, firms will draw back from investment in production and banks further decrease their productive lending, instead recycling their profits or loans into even more consumer or mortgage debt where demand is greater. Ultimately, these dynamics may be a key explanation of the 'secular stagnation' and 'productivity puzzle' that has cast a shadow over advanced economies in the last few decades. In the next and final chapter, we propose some solutions that could help reverse the damaging role land has come to play in modern economies.

CHAPTER 7

. . . .

Putting land back into economics and policy

> It is quite true that land monopoly is not the only
> monopoly which exists, but it is by far the greatest of
> monopolies – it is a perpetual monopoly, and it is
> the mother of all other forms of monopoly.
>
> WINSTON CHURCHILL (1909B)

7.1 Introduction

The premise of this book is that many of the key challenges facing modern economies are tied to our understanding and use of land, defined as locational space. In the chapters above we have attempted to identify how both economic theory and public policy have failed to properly address the problems of land and what the consequences have been. These include a housing affordability crisis, rising household debt, financial instability and growing inequality. In this concluding chapter we summarise these challenges and then propose a number of policy alternatives that recognise the key role of land in our economy.

One problem of land is the tension created once land is turned into individual private property, recognised in law. Landed property can empower people, by providing physical and economic security (including collateral to leverage credit) and thus be a driver of economic growth; but at the same time private ownership naturally excludes others both in an absolute physical sense and economically, by monopolising the proceeds of collective development through the capture of economic rent. Property in land is thus both 'freedom' and 'theft'. By failing to recognise land's distinctive properties – in particular its natural scarcity – economic theory and the policy interventions that have followed it have neglected this tension.

A second major problem is the fact that land can be used for multiple but not necessarily complementary economic functions at the same time. Through the course of this book we have shown how land's role has changed as modern economies developed. Land's primary economic function evolved from being the site of food production to being the site of capitalist industrial production following the industrial revolution, to becoming the site of a near-universally entitled consumption good – the family home – in the twentieth century and increasingly the source of speculative investment. During all these periods, land has also served as a source of wealth, power and status, and so the control of land, and the laws governing its ownership, transfer and use, have always been a central focus of political contestation.

Ever since land became private, personal property it has been intimately bound up with the evolution of finance, acting as an asset upon which to secure lending and generate credit and wealth. In the last few decades, land's function as a financial asset upon which it is possible to secure credit and enjoy unearned 'capital' gains has grown, and in some places overtaken its role as a source of shelter or production. This tension between land's role as a site of a consumption good (such as housing) and a financial asset makes it particularly challenging to fit neatly into any economic theory that reduces people and firms' decision making in regard to land to simple utility-maximising criteria.

Perhaps the key challenge facing economists and policy makers today is how to break the positive feedback cycle between the financial system, land values and the wider economy. This land–credit cycle (often referred to as 'the financial cycle') poses a risk to economic sustainability and financial stability. The evidence suggests that rising land values have been *the* major contributor to the rise in general economic inequality of recent decades, and the growing wealth gap between those who own landed property and those who must rent it.

In the UK, the US and many other advanced economies, economic growth – consumption and investment – appears now to be increasingly dependent on land values, largely embodied in house prices. With hindsight, the 'Great Moderation' of the early 1990s up to the mid-2000s, when economies enjoyed low consumer price inflation and steady growth, might be renamed the 'Great Asset-Price Inflation'. Consumption growth during this period was propped up by mortgage equity withdrawal from rapidly increasing house and land prices, itself driven by a huge expansion in land-related lending by the banking sector. This helped to cover up for declining investment, productivity and wage growth but it could not last; household debt cannot rise relative to incomes forever.

The fact that in most Western democracies the majority of the population are now property owners makes it more challenging for regulators and politicians to pop the land–credit balloon. The fact that such a high proportion of people's paper wealth is concentrated in the form of ordinary family homes rather than more standard financial assets, with all of the psychological implications that entails, only makes it harder to address these economic imbalances. But this model of 'residential capitalism' is not economically sustainable, even if is politically difficult to change. Policy responses to the financial crisis may have prevented the property bubble from bursting completely, but much of the Western world is now facing up to the reality of a Japanese-style 'lost decade', with high private debt weighing down on consumption growth. Even if it may be possible, via permanently low interest rates, to prevent economies from crashing under such arrangements, the prospects for a continuance of a 'secular stagnation' (Summers, 2015) appear high.

To summarise, the factors which have contributed toward this eventual outcome, particularly in Anglo-Saxon economies such as the UK, are a confluence of:

- The emergence of the concept of tradable, privately owned property in land and the enclosure of previously common land into private ownership, beginning in the fifteenth century (Chapter 2).
- The marginalisation of land and economic rent from economic theory due to (1) the rise of neoclassical economics in the early twentieth century and the development of universal scientific rules determining the distribution of income across all factors of

production, and (2) the shift away from agriculture and towards industrial production and services which obfuscated the role of land in the production process (Chapter 3).

- Partially as a result of this shift in economic theory, an increasing preference among governments to abandon the taxation of land and property in favour of taxing flows of income and expenditure, a settlement enshrined in European social democratic models (Chapters 3 and 4).
- The emergence of a model of 'residential capitalism', whereby access to mortgage credit and homeownership was widened in the late twentieth century. This was accompanied by the withdrawal of the state from the supply of housing and a shift towards subsidising individuals' ability to pay rent or buy a home in the market, and the political prioritisation of private homeownership over other forms of tenure (Chapters 4 and 5).
- Further deregulation of and innovations in the financial sector leading banks to develop a preference for lending against landed property rather than investing in productive activity (Chapter 5).
- As a consequence, the housing market and wider land economy have now become a major driver of economic inequality (Chapter 6).

How then to deal with these challenges? We hope that the arguments presented thus far will be enough to convince readers that a libertarian, free-market-orientated approach to the land problem makes little sense. Because legal frameworks are essential for land to become property at all, any analysis of the land problem that starts from the premise of minimising state involvement cannot succeed. There can never be an entirely free market in landed property. The complex drivers, time lags and information asymmetries inherent in the property market strongly suggest that there can be no self-correcting equilibrium in landownership or land values, as envisaged in neoclassical economic theory. This is supported by the historical record, which is one of consistent booms and busts, or financial cycles (Anderson, 2009; Borio, 2014; Kindleberger and Aliber, 2005).

For the same reasons, we do not think the 'land problem' is one that can be addressed by any one 'big bang' solution on its own. Most of the policy levers open to governments have long time lags, and interact with each other and the property market they seek to influence in unpredictable fashions. It is common for coexisting policy measures to pull in opposite directions, such as the UK government's moves both to increase homeownership in the face of acute affordability pressures while simultaneously seeking to preserve the asset wealth of existing homeowners which underlies those very affordability pressures (Lloyd, 2009).

Thus, the proposals that follow are not intended to be a comprehensive set of policy solutions – each is complex enough to deserve a book of its own – but rather to identify those areas that perhaps offer the greatest promise for further exploration in the current context. It should also be borne in mind that many of the proposals below have been experimented with at different points of time in some form or other. The fact that they may or may not have flourished in different contexts in different places does not mean they should be disregarded, or assumed to be the solution to all the problems of land. Since every plot of land is unique in time and space, controlled experiments are challenging. The concept of private property in land took centuries to take root: new interventions in the land economy may also require considerable time and scale to gain real traction. Feudal serfdom proved to be a highly successful and enduring system, but few would argue for its reintroduction today.

History suggests that multiple models of ownership, and multiple means of addressing the problems of land and economic rent, can and should coexist. If the workings of the land economy are causing economic and social problems, the question facing policy makers is therefore which types of response are currently underrepresented? In what direction should interventions lean?

7.2 Ownership

Public ownership of land

At its simplest, public ownership serves to remove land from the market in perpetuity and socialise rents in the process; this was the reason underpinning the inclusion of land nationalisation in the Labour Party Manifesto in 1900. As discussed in Chapter 2, public landownership today is widespread, and takes many forms: from municipal parks and public highways, to social housing and heritage buildings. Holding land under permanent public ownership can ensure that such socially desirable uses are preserved in particular locations when market forces would dictate that they make way for more profitable uses.

In Singapore, about 90% of the land is owned by the state. Much of the land that is provided to the private sector for development is leased long-term from the government, rather than purchased outright and then returned to the government at the end of the lease. There are four major government bodies involved in land transactions and development: the Singapore Land Authority, the JTC Corporation which developed industrial estates,[1] the Housing and Development Board and the Urban Redevelopment Authority. These bodies interact to optimise Singapore's land resources for economic and social development by coordinating and leasing government-owned land for residential, commercial, retail, industrial, educational and other uses (Kaganova, 2011). This system provides the Singapore government with a handsome source of public revenues: in 2012 alone government receipts from land sales totalled the equivalent of £9.1 billion (Purves, 2015).

Alternatively, public ownership and leasing of land can be used to generate profits much as commercial landowners do, and to deploy these for other public benefits. This approach works most readily where public sector entities are willing and able to purchase sufficient land for entire new settlements: at this scale, the public body can easily capture all of the land value created by the development of the new town, as New Town Development Corporations did so successfully in the UK (DCLG, 2006).

A similar approach can be used to capture the land value uplift created by the provision of infrastructure. As discussed in Chapter 3, such infrastructure investment often brings about a large increase in the value of adjacent land. For example, it has been estimated that the extension of the Jubilee Line of the London Underground which opened in 1999 increased local residential land values within 1,000

---

1 Formerly known as the Jurong Town Corporation.

yards of each of the stations by £13 billion (Riley, 2001). As a result, such publicly funded infrastructure projects almost always involve a substantial transfer of wealth from a large number of taxpayers to a small number of landowners – a classic case of economic rent.

To counter this, if a public body acquires land at pre-development prices, it can then sell or lease the land at development prices upon completion of the new infrastructure, thereby capturing the rent itself. This form of land value capture has been perhaps most effectively used to finance Hong Kong's Mass Transit Railway (Box 7.1).

Box 7.1 Hong Kong's Mass Transit Railway

Hong Kong's Mass Transit Railway (MTR) is recognised as one of the world's leading railway operators. First opened in 1979, it is operated by the Mass Transit Railway Corporation (MTRC), a government-owned statutory corporation. The MTR's innovative and efficient funding model has been widely praised across the world.

Initially, the Hong Kong government lent the MTRC HK$800 million and granted it the development rights for the land above the stations. The MTRC bought the undeveloped land from the government at greenfield value and then sought commercial partners to develop the stations, offices, flats or shops above them. Once the railway was built the land was leased for rent to shops, banks and restaurants at greatly increased values due to the presence of the railway and adjacent developments. This model is known as the Railway + Property model (R+P model) and has continued to be used by the MTRC to build all subsequent lines in Hong Kong (Purves, 2015).

Today it is one of the most profitable railway systems in the world, while ticket prices are low by world standards. Rather than requiring public subsidy, as is common with many railway systems, the MTR contributes significantly to the public purse. In 2015 MTRC reported profits of HK$13,138 million, of which HK$2,891 came from property development and HK$3,668 million came from property rental income. As the majority shareholder, most of these profits returned to the Hong Kong government.

In South Korea, around half of all residential land development and almost all industrial land development is carried out by the Korean Land Corporation (KLC).[2] Since being formed in 1975, the KLC has played a key role in transforming the economy of South Korea by efficiently managing land and promoting economic development. The KLC's functions include developing and selling land for residential use, acquiring idle and vacant land for resale, and developing new towns (Kaganova, 2011). This has helped ensure that land and housing have remained affordable in South Korea – between 1995 and 2013 the ratio of house prices to income declined from a base of 100 at the beginning of 1995 to 62.3 at the end of 2013, while the UK's shot up from 100 to 167.7 (Muellbauer, 2014b).

In the UK, similar benefits could be achieved by establishing a national Land Bank, responsible for purchasing, developing and selling land for residential and commercial use, acquiring idle and vacant land for resale, and developing new towns. A 'Land Bank of Britain' could use public money to buy land without planning permission and then lease or sell land to private developers at development prices following the grant of planning permission. As well as being a source of land release for housing and other development, the increase in land values could provide significant sources of revenue for the government, as in South Korea and Singapore.

Compulsory purchase

Many of the public ownership models above rely on the state being able to purchase land at low enough costs for development to generate significant land value uplift (Woetzel et al., 2014). While states can and do buy land on the open market, they are often hesitant to do so, for political and practical reasons. Once government announces itself as a potential buyer, sellers can expect that substantial investment in infrastructure will follow, allowing them to hold out for inflated sale prices and capture the economic rent. For these reasons, compulsory purchase is a critical tool for enabling infrastructure provision across multiple landholdings.

---

2 In 2009 the KLC merged with the Korean National Housing Corporation to the Korean Land and Housing Corporation.

As the example of the UK New Towns shows, compulsory purchase can also enable the state to capture land value uplift for reinvestment in infrastructure and services. But even without being deployed, the very existence of strong compulsory purchase powers can also help shift landowner incentives in favour of long-term investment models that deliver better public benefits. As with nuclear deterrence, the existence of strong compulsory purchase powers should mean that such powers would rarely have to be used. Improving the ability of the state to buy land at closer to existing use value, so as to enable much greater land value capture, can therefore be a powerful tool for reducing landowners' ability to extract economic rent, even if the state does not actually use its powers to capture all of the economic rent directly.

Private land investment and 'land pooling'

Direct public acquisition of land can be expensive and is often politically controversial. The same objective – namely, the diversion of economic rent from private profit to public benefit – can be achieved if landowners are prepared to invest in their land for the long term, rather than seeking maximum sale prices at the start of the development process (see Chapter 4).

Often, landowners have little choice: if they do not sell their sites to a developer capable of raising the finance and pushing the scheme through the planning process, their land will never be profitably developed. Those landowners that do have a choice are those that have sufficient access to finance to lead development themselves, and/or those that are more concerned with building high-quality places than maximising short-term asset prices. 'Legacy land-owners', as they are known, include philanthropic bodies, public institutions, housing associations, universities, churches and some wealthy families (especially those with a strong local connection to particular place). What these landowners can share is an interest in the quality of new developments over the long run, whether for reasons of social responsibility, civic pride or simply the desire to maximise long-term income from their investments.

But in most large-scale developments, multiple landowners compete to ensure that their site is the location of the more profitable parts of the scheme (usually the private homes), while their rivals' sites host the amenities. Land pooling arrangements can overcome these barriers, but these require careful coordination and can easily fall apart if one landowner refuses to participate.

Incentivising landowners to pool their land assets into partnerships, as is commonplace in the Netherlands, can be effective at aligning interests and maximising the total value of multiple sites (Needham, 2014). This lowers the economic rent that can be extracted from any one piece of land that happens to be in a more advantageous location. Encouraging landowners to cooperate like this can also reduce the upfront land costs by demonstrating to its owners that they stand to gain more from the long-term investment of their assets than from sale to a speculative developer.

Community landownership, and other non-market models

State landownership or acquisition may not be an attractive or politically feasible proposition in many advanced democracies, and in any case, states have proved themselves perfectly capable of selling off land and property at full market prices in pursuit of short-term financial or political gain. But land rents can also be captured by municipalities, trusts and other non-market or not-for-profit bodies.

Community land trusts (CLTs) are non-profit, community-based organisations that develop housing or other assets at permanently affordable levels for long-term community benefit. A CLT typically does this by separating the value of the building from the land that it stands on; the land is owned by the CLT and then leased to households who purchase the homes that sit on the CLT land. Because the household needs to purchase only the building and not the land, a CLT home is more affordable than a conventional home (Conaty and Large, 2013).

Typically, the CLT will be democratically controlled by its members, and its assets can only be sold or developed in a manner which benefits the local community. If the CLT decides to sell a home, the cash realised is protected by an 'asset lock' and is reinvested into something else that the trust's members think will benefit the local community – no dividends are paid to members, ensuring that the economic rent is invested back into the community that helped to create it.

CLTs range in size, can be rural or urban and provide a variety of housing tenures as well as other community facilities, including energy generation, community food and farming. They have proven to be effective at helping to meet local housing need, bringing forward land that might not otherwise be available and achieving wider social and economic benefits for the community involved. One challenge they face is the difficulty of identifying and then purchasing land in more urban areas with high prices, as is common in the UK. Community groups typically lack the funds to make land purchases or are dependent on the land being gifted. To scale up and play a part in addressing some of the broader macroeconomic problems we have outlined in this book, CLTs need greater support from government. Support could take the form of stronger legal rights for communities to acquire land (as has been pioneered in Scotland) (Bryden and Geisler, 2007) and revolving loan funds backed by guarantees (Community Land Trust Network, 2015).

7.3 Tax reform

In Chapter 3, we noted how land value taxation was the approach to the problem of economic rent preferred by many of the classical liberal political economists – Ricardo, Smith, Mill and later Henry George. These thinkers were keen to maintain the institution of private property, which they saw as important for economic development. A pure land value tax on the market value of unimproved land would appear to be the most economically efficient way of raising taxes, not distorting but rather supporting investment and productive activity. LVT also has a strong moral basis: capturing the unearned windfalls from collective development for the state and wider community. In the UK, the Mirrlees Review, the most comprehensive review of the UK tax system ever undertaken, notes:

> The economic case for taxing land itself is very strong and there is a long history of arguments in favour of it. Its supply is fixed and cannot be affected by the introduction of a tax.

> With the same amount of land available, people would not be willing to pay any more for it than before, so (the present value of) a land value tax (LVT) would be reflected one-for-one in a lower price of land: the classic example of tax capitalization. Owners of land on the day such a tax is announced would suffer a windfall loss as the value of their asset was reduced. But this windfall loss is the only effect of the tax: the incentive to buy, develop, or use land would not change. Economic activity that was previously worthwhile remains worthwhile. (Mirrlees and Adam, 2011, p. 371)

By attaching a cost to owning land, LVT diminishes the incentive to buy land for speculative purposes – i.e. to realise capital gains – rather than productive purposes, as the tax imposes a holding cost on land, and a good part of any increase in land values would be shared with the public purse. Instead a land tax encourages efficient land use, creating less incentive for developers to hoard undeveloped land. Property taxes that include the value of buildings on land are less efficient, since they are, in effect, a tax on the investment in that property. Even so, they are less likely to affect people's behaviour than income or employment taxes.

Additionally, since land cannot be hidden or moved to a tax haven, land value taxation is difficult to avoid or evade – which contrasts well with many other forms of tax in a globalised world, in particular corporation taxes. Empirical studies support the theory, finding that taxes on immoveable property are the least damaging to economic growth, with income and corporation taxes the most damaging (Arnold, 2008; Arnold et al., 2011). There is also evidence that land taxes reduce house price volatility (Blöchliger, 2015, pp. 15–16; Muellbauer, 2005; Oxley and Haffner, 2010, pp. 15–16).

Yet, despite the compelling economic and ethical case for land value taxation, it has struggled to gain widespread political support in the UK and most other advanced economies. Indeed, taxes on property generally have been falling as a share of total taxation in advanced economies. Today immovable property taxes make up around 1% of GDP and 2.5% of total tax revenues on average across the OECD economies, and their share is declining (Blöchliger, 2015, p. 6), while only three countries feature a pure land tax: Australia, Denmark and Estonia. The UK actually has one of the highest level of property taxes across advanced economies at 3.4% but, as discussed in Chapter 4, residential property tax, which comes mainly via council tax, is highly regressive and ineffective at capturing land rents.

As noted in Chapter 3, there are a range of historical reasons why land taxes were resisted, related to the downplaying of land in economic theory, the shift from agricultural to industrial production and the failure of socialist and single-tax progressive movements to unite on the issue, and the political power exerted by the land-owning interest. Property taxes generally tend to be politically unpopular because of their visibility or 'salience' – they are generally administered as annual or monthly demands for payment by local or regional authorities, in contrast to less obtrusive consumption, income or national insurance taxes (Cabral and Hoxby, 2012).[3] So while the economic case for land value tax is essentially uncontested, political and also practical challenges remain.

Practical and political challenges around the implementation of land value tax

The practical issues concern the perceived challenges associated with LVT's implementation. LVT requires land values to be assessed fairly and accurately on a regular basis. There is currently no reliable published data on land values in the UK, and residential property has not been revalued for the purposes of the council tax since April 1991.[4] However, that is not to say that establishing such a regime is impossible. A similar apparatus already exists to record non-domestic land and property values for the purposes of

---

3   The salience of the property tax has been shown to be one factor explaining the unpopularity of property tax, and revolts against property taxes in the US, which has a relatively high rate of property tax compared to most advanced economies (Cabral and Hoxby, 2012).

4   This is the case for England and Scotland only. In Wales the council tax bands were re-set on 1 April 2005 by the National Assembly for Wales, based on 2003 valuations. Unlike the rest of the UK, Northern Ireland does not have council tax and instead still operates a system of domestic rates, but one subject to a ceiling so there is a marginal tax rate of zero on higher values.

business rates. The basis for valuation is a 'rating list' for each local authority, identifying every relevant non-domestic property in the area and estimating its annual rental value based on its location, physical properties and other relevant economic conditions. The rating lists are compiled and maintained by the Valuation Office Agency, which employs the equivalent of just over 4,000 full-time staff. The rating lists are updated continuously to reflect changes in properties, and new lists are compiled every five years (Mirrlees and Adam, 2011). It is not unreasonable to think that this could quite easily be expanded to cover all land in the UK.

Another perceived obstacle to the implementation of a land value tax is the challenge of identifying the site value of land separately from any improvements. The lack of a competitive market in unimproved land (as distinct from buildings) means that establishing the market price of land can be difficult. It may be the case in somewhere like the UK that taxing property (land and structures) would be more straightforward than taxing the site value of land and would yield many of the same benefits. At the very least there seems an overwhelming case for the revaluation of council tax (Muellbauer, 2015) and the gradual abolition of capital gains relief on primary residences and the transferable main residence allowance for inheritance tax.

Having said this, there are internationally recognised techniques for determining land value where the market is thin, and such regimes already operate in countries such as Denmark, Estonia, Barbados and Australia, which use a system of land value taxation (Box 7.2).

A final obstacle is the risk that the imposition of a large land value tax overnight could create undesirable side effects with regard to household wealth and financial stability. As discussed in previous chapters, housing represents a significant component of total household wealth and also underpins a significant part of banks' balance sheets in the form of mortgage loans secured on propertied land. Any major decline in property prices could leave some households in negative equity and some banks at risk of insolvency, posing risks to credit creation and financial stability. At the same time, distribution of land value is unlikely to coincide smoothly with people's income and net wealth – the case every politician fears is the income-poor pensioner sitting in a valuable house who is unable to pay a recurring levy.

There are a number of options for avoiding such an outcome. Land value tax could be introduced as a replacement for other taxes such as council tax, thereby offsetting the burden on households, and phasing it in gradually over an extended period of time would minimise the risk of creating overnight winners and losers as well as giving banks sufficient time to adjust their portfolios to declining real estate prices. There are successful examples of phasing in major tax changes slowly over time, for example the abolition of MIRAS. Poorer owners of valuable land could be allowed to delay payment until they die or at the point of sale. Or they could give up a percentage of their equity in the property each year that wasn't paid to the state or local authority, enabling the community to gain from any capital appreciation (Mayhew and Smith, 2016). Another option would be to hypothecate the proceeds of any large-scale land tax evenly across the population as some kind of universal basic income, as envisaged by Henry George ([1879] 1979), or perhaps hypothecate it to support a widely popular public service such as the National Health Service.

The salience issue – that property taxes are unpopular because of their visibility – is a challenging problem. Visibility is clearly desirable from a decision-making perspective because it makes taxpayers aware of the costs of local public services, which enhances accountability. However, visibility makes property taxes more difficult to sell politically and more difficult to increase or reform than other taxes. Obvious options would be to allow households to pay the tax in monthly instalments (as is now common with council tax in the UK) or, as Ireland has done, reduce the salience of the property tax by allowing taxpayers the option of having the tax withheld from employment or pension income (Slack and Bird, 2014, p. 8).

Ultimately, the biggest challenge facing the implementation of taxes on land and property may be that some of the most powerful groups in society tend to have the most to lose from the introduction of this type of tax. Nevertheless, the stagnation of incomes and ageing demographics that have been a feature of advanced economies

Box 7.2 Examples of LVT and split-rate property taxes
A number of countries and municipalities have introduced LVT or variants upon it. One of the best known examples is Denmark, which has municipal taxes based on land values as well as a 1% tax paid to the state for property worth up to around £340,000 and 3% for any higher values.

Australia has operated a system of applying land value tax that predates the creation of the independent country in 1901. The tax is administered at the state level and today there are two states which operate a universal land value tax, Queensland and New South Wales. The tax is applied to land regardless of whether income is earned from it, though primary residences are generally exempt. This exemption has the effect of removing around 60% of land by value from the tax base (Henry et al., 2009), but in 2015 land value tax still raised a total of AU$7.6 billion across Australia (Australian Bureau of Statistics, 2015).

One study which examined the effects of the land value taxation in Melbourne found evidence of a long-run association between the use of the land value tax and the intensity of development, and that land value taxes stimulate faster development (Lusht, 1992).

In 2008 Australian Prime Minister Kevin Rudd commissioned the 'Australia's Future Tax System Review', informally known as the Henry Tax Review, in order to guide tax system reforms over the next ten to twenty years. The report concluded that 'economic growth would be higher if governments raised more revenue from land and less revenue from other tax bases' but warned that 'this efficiency is harmed if there are significant exemptions from land tax that encourage people to change how they use land' (Henry et al., 2009).

A variant of LVT is a system of split rate taxation where separate taxes are levied on the value of the land and the value of the physical property, and are usually taxed at different rates. The idea behind split rate taxation is that by enabling taxes on land to be higher than on buildings, new development is encouraged while speculation and hoarding of land is penalised. Split rate taxation can be seen as a compromise between pure land value taxation and an ordinary property tax falling on land value plus buildings. The approach allows gradual transformation of the traditional real estate property tax into a pure land value tax.

For over 100 years a form of split rate taxation has been in operation in the US state of Pennsylvania. Originating in 1913 in the cities of Pittsburgh and Scranton, by 2013 there were eighteen cities and school districts in Pennsylvania operating a system of split rate taxation. In 2011, Altoona became the first place to shift the entire burden of property tax onto the land, in effect making it a full land value tax area. Evidence suggests that the split-rate taxation system in Pennsylvania has positively stimulated the construction and refurbishment of residential and commercial buildings, and resulted in a more efficient use of land (Cohen and Coughlin, 2005) and helped to curb urban sprawl (Banzhaf and Lavery, 2010).

over recent decades suggest the policy may become more politically attractive. Recently there have been calls by major international bodies including the OECD (Blöchliger, 2015) and the IMF (Norregaard, 2013) for an increase in property taxation as the tax best placed to boost growth in the post-crisis period. As incomes decline and wealth increases, and financial wealth becomes ever harder to locate and tax, it may become increasingly tempting for politicians to turn to land and property taxation to maintain tax bases.

7.4 Financial reform

We laid out in Chapter 5 the central role of the financial system and its pro-cyclical interaction with land as the key challenge facing modern economies today. In modern economies, not least the UK, new loans collateralised against property have become the main source of the money supply and house prices have become intimately linked to consumption demand and economic growth via the collateral channel. Falls in land and house prices that might come about by separating land values from housing or via a full-fledged land value tax could thus lead to financial instability and economic slowdown. To make such reforms effective, it is thus necessary to make reforms to the banking and wider financial system to wean it off land as its main means of de-risking lending.

This can be achieved through a variety of means: changes to financial regulation to incentivise non-property-related lending by banks; structural changes to the ownership and function of the banking sector to support business lending over property lending; or simply preventing commercial banks from engaging in credit creation via sovereign money reform, accompanied by the promotion of equity-based mortgages to support home purchase.

Financial regulation and credit guidance

As discussed in Chapter 5, a key development in the last thirty years of capitalist economies has been the banking system's shift towards lending against existing property assets over and above business lending, their textbook role. In the UK, the share of domestic resident UK bank lending supporting productive investment has fallen from around 35% of all lending to less than 10% since 1986, while property lending has increased by the equivalent amount – from 25% to almost 50%. This explosion in lending contributed to rising house prices, which in turn encouraged further lending.

Up until the financial crisis, central banks focused almost exclusively on consumer price inflation (CPI) and neglected the large increases in house and land prices that were partially driven by increases in bank credit creation. Post-crisis, while maintaining CPI as their primary target, central banks have begun to take a closer interest in monitoring asset prices and introduced policies aimed at restricting certain forms of credit across entire national economies – so-called 'macroprudential' policy (Galati and Moessner, 2013).[5] For example, in June 2014 the Bank of England provided new powers to the newly formed Financial Policy Committee to restrict the amount that homeowners can borrow relative to their income (Bank of England, 2014). Similar policies have been introduced in New Zealand and Hong Kong.

---

5 Regulation had previously only focused on the stability of individual financial institutions – so-called 'microprudential' policy.

Such policies are welcome but potentially don't go far enough, given the strong incentives banks have to lend against land. A more radical step would be for policy makers to regulate the total quantity of credit creation and the quality of its use (i.e. the allocation of credit for different purposes). During their history almost all central banks, including the Bank of England in the 1960s and 1970s, have employed forms of direct credit regulation which has variously been called credit controls, the direction of credit, credit guidance, the framing of credit, window guidance or moral suasion (Goodhart, 1989, pp. 156–158).

First implemented by the German Reichsbank in 1912, credit controls were copied by the US Federal Reserve in the 1920s and had the greatest impact when adopted by the Japanese, Korean and Taiwanese central banks in the early 1940s during the Second World War and the decades after (World Bank, 1993). Called 'window guidance' in these countries, the central bank determined desired nominal GDP growth, calculated the necessary amount of credit creation to achieve this and then allocated this credit creation both across the various types of banks and across industrial sectors

Credit creation for the purchase of land and property was suppressed under these regimes as it was seen to produce excessive asset price inflation and subsequent banking crises. Most bank credit was allocated to productive use, which meant investment in plant and equipment to produce more goods, investment to offer more services, or other forms of investment that enhanced productivity (such as the implementation of new technologies, processes and know-how), and often a combination of these.[6]

Economic history thus provides evidence that by limiting bank credit for transactions that do not contribute to GDP, asset bubbles and banking crises could be avoided in future. To be sure, such a measure would not stop speculation in land and property; instead, it would not allow speculators to use the public privilege of money creation for their speculative transactions, which might help avoid property market booms and busts.

---

6 For more on the institutional and political economy details of the East Asian credit guidance regime, see Werner (2003).

More generally, national and international regulators in advanced economies – the latter including the Bank of International Settlements and the IMF – need to reverse the strong favouritism shown towards property lending in terms of capital and liquidity requirements. Regulations should support banks that are able to de-risk their loans via methods other than land-based collateral, most obviously via the building up of long-term relationships with non-financial businesses, as discussed in the next section. More generally, there may be a case for saying that highly leveraged banks are not the best types of institution to engage in mortgage lending or indeed that debt contracts are not the best form of finance for land-related purchases, discussed further below.

Structural reforms to the banking sector

A range of studies suggest that bank lending behaviour is strongly influenced by ownership type, size and other institutional factors. As noted in Chapter 5, the deregulation of the financial sector in the UK led to a situation where it is dominated by a small number of large national or international shareholder-owned banks: the largest four banks now control around 80% of retail deposits. These banks operate a 'transaction' banking model (Collins, 2012) characterised by a preference for centralised and automated credit-scoring techniques to make loan decisions, a need for high quarterly returns on equity and a strong preference for collateral. Increasingly, the model favours the generation of profits through the securitisation and selling on of loans, with the most popular type of securitised loan being residential mortgage-backed securities. The imperatives of short-term shareholder value both incentivise excessive risk-taking and mean that lending to SMEs – involving high transaction costs for relatively small loans – does not make business sense for larger banks (Berger and Udell, 2002).

By contrast, in other countries, for example Germany, Switzerland and Austria, there is a much stronger culture of 'relationship banking'. In Germany, two-thirds of bank deposits are controlled by either cooperative or public savings banks, most of which are owned by regional or local people and/or businesses. These 'stakeholder banks' are more focused on business lending, do not have such stringent collateral requirements and devolve decision making to branches. They de-risk their loans not by requiring property as collateral but by building up strong and long-lasting relationships and an understanding of the businesses they lend to (Boot, 2000). Although the general pattern in advanced economies has been a shift towards mortgage lending, in Germany lending to non-financial businesses is significantly higher than mortgage lending at 40% of GDP, while mortgage lending has only increased to around 30% of GDP (Ryan-Collins, 2016).

Empirical studies find that 'stakeholder' banks, including public savings banks and cooperative banks, maintain their lending in the face of financial shocks (e.g. changes in interest rates) in contrast to shareholder banks, which are much more pro-cyclical (Bertay et al., 2015; Ferri et al., 2014). This is unsurprising if their models of lending are based on relationships rather than collateral values; a bank with a long and strong relationship with a firm is much more likely to have the confidence to see it through the bad times.

In the UK, more relationship banking could be achieved by establishing a network of interconnected, mutually supporting local stakeholder banks, modelled on the German banking sector. One option might be to break up any major bank that requires government rescue[7] into a network of regional 'citizen's banks' focused on real economy, localised lending (Prieg and Greenham, 2015).

State housing and investment banks

Changing the structure of the banking industry may take decades, of course, and in countries like the UK the lack of affordable housing has already reached crisis proportions. A more immediate but potentially long-term solution to raise large amounts of finance for the creation of new house building is to establish state housing and investment banks.

Such banks are commonplace in Europe and play a key role in funding both affordable homes and the large-scale infrastructure that is required for new housing developments (Falk, 2014). The

---

7 For example, at the time of writing the UK government owned 73% of the Royal Bank of Scotland.

European Investment Bank (EIB) lent a record £5.6 billion for investment in forty affordable housing projects in Britain last year but future funding may now be under threat following Britain's decision to leave the EU. Britain stands almost alone as an advanced nation in not having any major state investment or infrastructure bank (Skidelsky et al., 2011). The purpose of a housing investment bank would be to make long-term loans for the construction of affordable housing, which are guaranteed by the government, at cheaper rates than affordable housing providers are currently able to access (Jefferys, Lloyd, Argyle, et al., 2014).

A housing investment bank could access funding from several sources. Firstly, the government could capitalise the bank by issuing government bonds. Secondly, the housing investment bank could borrow directly from capital markets. It should be an attractive proposition for institutional investors seeking long-term secure assets to match long-term liabilities (e.g. of pension funds). Thirdly, it could be financed by central bank purchases of bonds it issued via 'quantitative easing' (Ryan-Collins et al., 2013). The Bank of England has bought £445 billion worth of assets since the financial crisis of 2008 and reinvests a good quantity of these periodically. The bank has so far shown a preference for the purchase of government debt over other forms, but in the latest round of QE it also purchased investment grade corporate debt from utilities and large companies.

A final alternative would be to take deposits from households, possibly through a scheme similar to French Livrét A accounts (Chaloner and Pragnell, 2014). Similar to Individual Savings Accounts (ISAs) in the UK, French households are able to save into Livrét A accounts, which are government backed and provide a secure tax-free interest rate. The accounts are held with local commercial banks but the savings are then pooled by a public corporation, the Caisse des Dépôts et Consignations. The short-term deposits are then converted into long-term loans at below market rates to public and non-profit enterprises to fund affordable housing. Nearly all loans are guaranteed by local authorities, with the remainder by a mutual 'guarantee fund' that charges a % fee. The scheme provides 70% of social housing finance in France, delivering 120,000 new homes in 2011.

Alternatives to bank debt financing

Bank debt has advantages over other forms of financing: it offers a return to the lender that is fixed as long as the borrower remains solvent. In contrast, equity-based investment involves the lender sharing risk with the borrower. Debt-based contracts played a key role in mobilising capital in the Industrial Revolution in Britain and in supporting industrialisation in Germany and France in the early twentieth century (Gerschenkron, 1962; Turner, 2015a, p. 54).

But since the 1980s, as banks have increasingly turned towards property-related lending, it is has become less clear that bank debt provides greater economic benefits than harm. Bank-credit-driven house price bubbles and the resulting financial crises have increased in frequency in recent decades, and the resulting recessions have increased in depth (Jordà et al., 2015). Although land-backed collateral gives the appearance of security, in fact land-backed assets are inherently risky for banks since they are generally much more illiquid, with long maturities, than banks' liabilities. As a result, banks have built up a major 'maturity mismatch' and are prone to increasing liquidity crises (Goodhart and Perotti, 2015; Persaud, 2016). In addition, as we have seen, land's natural scarcity and fixed supply mean that land and property prices typically rise and fall more rapidly than other assets as economic conditions change. Holding large quantities of such assets arguably makes banks' balance sheets more pro-cyclical than holding business loans.

Following the crisis of 2007–8, a number of proposals have been put forward suggesting alternatives to debt-based financing for home purchase. It has been argued in particular that mortgage debt should be more 'equity-like', with the lender sharing the risk of the home depreciating. This could involve the use of Islamic finance mortgages where resident households and banks become the joint owners of a property until it is fully repaid by the resident (Buiter and Rahbari, 2015). Similarly, 'shared responsibility mortgages' (Mian and Sufi, 2015) would involve mortgage payments falling in value with the house price, but lenders would gain from any increase in the house price if the home is sold. This would protect poorer households but whether it would be sufficient to prevent fire-sales of property in a rapid downturn or prevent banks contributing to house price increases via excessive mortgage lending in the good times remains to be seen.

A more permanent solution for de-linking land from finance would simply be to ban maturity transformation involving property assets, or all assets, via shifting to a narrow banking (Cochrane, 2014; Kay, 2009) or 'sovereign money' system where only the central bank would have the power to create new money (Benes and Kumhof, 2012; Dyson and Jackson, 2013).[8] Under such a system, the lending and depository functions of banks would be separated and they would be limited to playing a true intermediary role of matching savers and borrowers in the way that peer-to-peer lenders, such as Zopa, do today, without leveraging their balance sheets.

Mortgage finance under such a regime could be provided by institutional investors with long-term liabilities, such as pension funds and insurance companies, to solve the problem of maturity mismatch. Such investors would be in a better position to agree to more equity-like repayment contracts given their long time horizons. Banks could still play a role by potentially issuing covered bonds backed by mortgages: Denmark has employed such a scheme very successfully for many years and its mortgage market, despite being large relative to GDP, came out of the crisis relatively unscathed (Berg and Bentzen, 2014).

7.5 Reforms to tenure

Tenure refers to the legal forms under which land is owned, occupied and used. As discussed at the start of this book, and is illustrated in the case of the UK in Chapter 4, the rules, norms and policies relating to land have varied immensely throughout history, and are a major determinant of the role land plays in the economy. Since the enclosures began in England in the late fifteenth century, private ownership of land has risen to become the dominant form

---

8   The idea has received a lot of attention in the post-crisis period, but has a long heritage. A range of eminent economists, including Irving Fisher (1936), Milton Friedman (1948), Henry Simons (1951) and James Tobin (1986), supported the concept.

of land tenure around the world. However, as with most historical upheavals, there have been other trends running concurrently which have drawn on entirely different economic and cultural roots.

Even among today's advanced economies private landownership is not absolute, and alternative models of ownership have continued to exist. Some have been successful in promoting economic development and reducing, if not eliminating, the problem of economic rent. The laws governing tenure could therefore be reformed to ensure that the interests of private landowners can be better balanced against wider social needs.

Differentiated tenure options

Properly understood, property in land is a complex system of layered rights reflecting individual, collective and social needs. The simplistic perception of property in land as equivalent to the individual ownership of goods can obscure this understanding. By clearly defining the rights and responsibilities of different stakeholders over land, legal systems can allow public interests and private ownership to coexist.

One example that has survived in England and other common law jurisdictions is the leasehold–freehold system. While the origins of the distinction between leaseholder and freeholder lie in the feudal past, this system can allow individuals to own leasehold property with sufficiently secure title to raise finance while preserving the public interest in the land itself in the form of freehold, which can command annual payments of ground rent. Related tenures like 'commonhold' (a new but rarely used tenure in the UK), condominium tenure in the US and strata title in Australia allow residents of apartment blocks to collectively own shared areas like gardens and stairs. These systems allow for the efficient management of common resources while giving individuals exclusive ownership of their homes.

Restricted sale tenures

To reduce the problem of rent extraction in the form of unearned capital gains by homeowners, housing tenures can be designed to give occupiers full ownership, while restricting the value at which they can sell their homes when they choose to do so. Such models are useful for providing subsidised homeownership while ensuring that the subsidy is preserved for future occupiers, rather than being captured by the lucky first beneficiary of the subsidy.

For example, the St Clements Community Land Trust in east London limits the resale price of its homes to a multiple of the original, submarket, purchase price by pegging the maximum uplift in the resale price to the increase in average local wages. Such resale formulae can be set according to the varying needs and priorities of each CLT, and/or by government policy (New Economics Foundation et al., 2013).

Reversionary tenures

While most leaseholds in the housing sector usually last for such long periods as to be effectively permanent (999 years is common in the UK), time-limited leases used to be the norm, and remain so in the commercial property sector. This concept allows for innovative approaches to the financing of rental housing that can match up the investment needs of financial institutions like pension funds with social needs for low-cost rental housing, via sale and lease-back models of social housing provision.

In this model, a pension fund finances social housing construction on land acquired from a local authority; the local authority then leases the homes back from the pension fund for a period of 25–50 years, paying a guaranteed inflation-indexed rent for the duration. Retaining the freehold gives the pension fund sufficient security on its investment, and the lease agreement gives it the long-term income stream it needs. At the end of the lease period the pension fund can gift the land back to the authority, as it has achieved its goal of investing capital to secure long-term income (Jefferys, Lloyd, and Gregory, 2014). Thus both a financial and a specific social need are met for a significant period, but the wider public interest in the land is preserved and the private interest cannot extract economic rent in perpetuity.

Diversified housing tenure

There is little evidence that economies where homeownership dominates as a form of tenure are more productive or efficient. On the contrary, as discussed in Chapters 2, 4 and 5 there is evidence that high levels of homeownership combined can reduce labour mobility and increase unemployment, while easy access to housing credit results in greater financial fragility and growing wealth inequality. Two of Europe's most successful and innovative economies, Germany and Switzerland, have homeownership levels well below 50% and well regulated, secure private rental and cooperative housing sectors. Policy can foster a pluralism of housing models to level the playing field between tenures and ensure enough homes are provided so that people have reasonable choices and are not incentivised to overinvest in homeownership.

There are a number of steps that can be taken to achieve this in a UK context. Firstly, the private rented sector should be made more secure, with longer guaranteed tenancies, limitations on rent rises and stronger tenants' rights (Berry, 2016). Secondly, the government should take steps to boost the stock of non-market housing, including homes with social rents, community-led schemes and cooperatives, to ensure that different housing types and sizes are available in all tenures, and to make housing supply less dependent on the volatile private market in land and homes (Jefferys, Lloyd, Argyle, et al., 2014; Woetzel et al., 2014).

Subsidies and taxation policies that favour homeownership over other forms of tenure need to be scaled back. Finally, decent investment alternatives and secure pensions should be provided so that households are less prone to invest in the housing market to pay for their retirement, or to rely on it to fund their care in old age.

7.6 Planning reform

The neoclassical economics framework places a strong emphasis on reducing barriers to the supply of goods and services that are demanded in market contexts. Reflecting the dominance of this paradigm, much research has emphasised how planning systems stifle a 'free market' in home building, while media stories typically portray planning as an overbearing and unnecessarily bureaucratic regulatory function.

Yet, as discussed throughout this book, land – the product that planners deal in – is not just another good or service. Its special properties – scarcity, permanence, irreproducibility, immobility – mean that it cannot simply increase or expand to meet greater demand. This means that price signals alone cannot efficiently guide decisions over what land should most appropriately be used for – decisions which have huge economic significance (Cheshire, 2013). Even the most market-orientated states implicitly recognise this, and impose non-market regulatory controls on land use.

Planning offers an explicit opportunity for public policy to determine the outcome of land use decisions, and to mediate competing interests in democratically deciding what those uses should be. Many of the accusations levelled at the planning system are motivated by desires to exploit it to extract rents, or to criticise its existence out of an ideological preference for free market principles.

Planning obligations

As mentioned above, the granting of planning permission often brings about a large increase in the value of the land. Many planning systems include mechanisms to capture some of the uplift in land value, often referred to as 'betterment' or 'planning gain'. As discussed in Chapter 4, planning law allows local planning authorities to enter into legally binding agreements with developers to provide certain public benefits as part of the development. Section 106 agreements normally place obligations on developers to ensure that part of the planning gain goes towards benefiting local communities. These contributions may be in the form of affordable housing or financial contributions used to fund community services or infrastructure (Crook et al., 2010).

Plan making

The UK planning system is uniquely discretionary (Monk et al., 2013), and even with the addition of planning obligations, the initiative to propose development remains with developers. Planning powers can be used more proactively than this, in order to determine appropriate land uses and set land values accordingly (Needham, 2014). This requires planning authorities to be given more resources and stronger powers of plan making or zoning: these effectively dictate what land can be used for, providing certainty and preconditions for investment that private markets need – in other words, planning can be a 'market maker' rather than a market stifler (RTPI, 2015). There is evidence from European cities, for example in Germany and the Netherlands, that when planning authorities have been given more legislative power and financial support, better results have been achieved in terms of development quality and more sustainable local economies and built environments (Oxley et al., 2009; Falk, 2014; RTPI, 2015).

7.7 Changes to economics and national accounting

Implementing the above reforms will be made challenging by the fact that mainstream economic theory – still dominated by the neoclassical paradigm – and much of economic policy fails to properly take into account the role of land in the economy.

Economic theory

As discussed in Chapter 3, today's economics textbooks mostly neglect land as a distinct factor of production, conflating it with capital in the still dominant 'two factors of production' models. Meanwhile, 'income' is described as a reward for one's contribution to production, while wealth is understood as 'savings' due to one's productive investment effort. This means windfalls resulting from exclusive ownership of land or other naturally scarce resources – economic rents – are often overlooked.

In addition, many economics textbooks describe commercial banks as simply 'financial intermediaries' which take deposits from savers and lend this money out to borrowers, assumed to be non-financial firms that use these funds to invest in production.[9] As discussed in Chapter 5, this model of banking is deeply flawed. It overlooks the fact that in reality banks create new money and purchasing power in the act of extending credit and that the majority of this credit now flows to supporting the purchase of existing landed assets – in particular via commercial and domestic mortgages – rather than to firms.

---

9   See Ryan-Collins et al. (2012) for a counterexample.

This flawed economic theory has, in turn, led to flawed economic policy. Despite the financial crisis of 2007–8, the ministries of finance and central banks of many advanced economies have yet to fundamentally change the macroeconomic models they use. The UK Treasury and Office of Budget Responsibility models of the economy assume household consumption is driven by income and net worth, again ignoring the role of credit supply and the effects of the build-up of household debt. The Bank of England and the European Central Bank also persist in using equilibrium-based macroeconomic models, although they are at least investigating alternative models that better allow for house prices and the role of credit.[10]

The teaching of economics and related disciplines needs to be reformed to reaffirm the role of land; it should not be left solely to geography, agriculture, environment and urban studies courses. In developing undergraduate economics courses practitioners across the field should seek to highlight land's role as a distinct factor of production separate from capital, and a set of legal rights over the use of economic space. The role of economic rent needs to be placed squarely into theories of distribution and taxation. It is also vital that the economics profession provides a more accurate depiction of the role of banking and money creation in modern economies and how this interacts with land values. It is encouraging to see the emergence of new sources of funding for academic research in the field of macroeconomics that places emphasis on the interaction between money, credit and house prices.[11]

Public data and national accounting

The land market is of critical importance to the economic and social health of the UK. As well as playing a key macroeconomic role, understanding the land market is crucial for assessing important

---

10 See for example the Bank of England's 'One Bank Research Agenda' (Bank of England, 2015, pp. 28–29).

11 See for example the Institute of New Economic Thinking, a new funding body set up to fund alternative macroeconomic research following the financial crisis (http://www.ineteconomics.org); and the recent £4.6 million call by the UK Economic and Social Research Council for a Network Plus in to 'Understanding the Macroeconomy' (see http://www.esrc.ac.uk/funding/funding-opportunities/understanding-the-macroeconomy-network-plus).

policy questions, from the efficiency of planning reform to the economics of housing development. However, as already discussed, there is currently no reliable public dataset on land values in the UK. Moreover, land is not included as a distinct asset class in the National Accounts, despite being one of the largest and most important asset classes in the economy. Instead, the value of the underlying land is included in the value of dwellings and other buildings and structures, which are classed as 'produced non-financial assets'. This makes little sense. Land should be measured separately and classified as a 'non-produced asset', alongside assets such as natural resources and the radio spectra.

At the time of writing, the OECD and Eurostat (2015) are working with national governments to improve land valuation practice and incorporate land into national accounting frameworks. This work is being carried out in the UK by the Office for National Statistics, which has said that it expects this be included in the 'Blue Book' 2017.[12]

While this is a welcome step forward, it is likely that this will only provide aggregate estimations of land values for different sectors of the economy. In order to provide researchers, academics and policy makers with the necessary insight into the land market, a public body (most likely the ONS) should be tasked with assessing, collecting and publishing granular data on land prices in areas across the UK on a regular basis.

Measurement of public sector debt

The UK government's primary measure of government debt, upon which it bases its fiscal targets, is 'public sector net debt'. This is defined as public sector financial liabilities (for loans, deposits, currency and debt securities) less liquid assets (ONS, 2016). Liquid assets are cash and short-term assets which can be released for cash at short notice and without significant loss, and mainly

12 The Blue Book is the United Kingdom National Accounts, which are published annually by the Office for National Statistics. It records and describes economic activity in the United Kingdom and as such is used by government, banks, academics and industries to formulate the economic and social policies and monitor the economic progress of the United Kingdom.

comprise foreign exchange reserves and bank deposits (ONS, 2016). According to the ONS definition, the public sector comprises central government, local government (and any other non-market bodies controlled and mainly financed by them) but also 'public corporations' that may be owned by the state but be at arm's length from it.

The UK government targets total debt across all three sectors but this is not standard practice internationally. Many countries monitor and target a 'general government' measure of debt, which includes central and local government but specifically excludes public corporations. Indeed, general government debt is the focus of the European Union's macroeconomic rules as set out in the 1992 Maastricht Treaty and the subsequent stability and growth pact. Moreover, when analysing public debt across countries, the OECD conducts its comparisons using the measure that excludes public corporations (Chaloner and Pragnell, 2014).

This distinction is particularly relevant to the provision of affordable housing. The housing services activities of local authorities and their 'arm's length management organisations' fall under the definition of public corporations and therefore their financial liabilities are included in the public sector debt measure, but not the general government measure. The current UK government's focus on reducing the deficit as measured by public sector debt has therefore created severe restrictions on the level of investment in affordable housing by public corporations. If instead the UK government were to follow European and international precedent and set its fiscal rules with reference to general government rather than public sector debt, there would be no such restrictions on investment in affordable homes by public corporations, even in times of austerity.

More generally, the treatment of assets in the definition of public sector net debt is problematic since only liquid financial assets are included on the asset side. Governments usually hold many other assets, not least land assets, many of which generate future income which could be used to service the debt or could be sold to pay down debt. For example, social housing assets generate revenue directly from the rental income of future tenants – revenues which cover the cost of the original construction and ongoing property management.

The government should therefore consider developing a more comprehensive definition of government debt to include income-generating physical assets. For example, a better measure of government debt could be gross government debt minus liquid and income-generating assets, relative to national income. Under this measure increasing government gross debt would then not be a concern if it was matched by an increase in assets such as publicly owned land and housing (Muellbauer, 2014). This would no doubt incentivise governments to invest more heavily in land-based infrastructure such as affordable housing and transport.

7.8 Conclusion

The preceding policy proposals provide a menu of options than can, in combination, address the two tensions outlined at the beginning of the chapter: the problem of economic rent, and the fact that land fulfils multiple and sometimes conflicting functions. The consequences of failing to deal with these issues can be seen all too clearly in the dysfunctional state of financialised housing and land markets, which have driven a housing affordability crisis, rising inequality and inefficiency in the allocation of resources.

Some of these interventions are already well-established practices, but are often at too small a scale to significantly impinge on economic rent and the macroeconomy more generally – Community Land Trusts being a good example. In the UK and many other advanced economies, high land prices relative to incomes restrict the organic growth of such innovations. Under such circumstances, more radical structural change is probably needed.

Economic rent from land can be captured via changes to its use, its ownership or the way it is taxed. Planning should be seen as having a key strategic macroeconomic role and as such be controlled by larger scale public entities with the long-term interests of communities and regions in mind rather than left to private developers seeking to maximise short-term gains. Stronger plan making, requiring better resourcing of public planning teams, could go a long way towards setting land values at levels reflecting social needs and priorities. But as the initiative to develop land remains mainly in private hands, plan making needs to be backed up with means to bring land forward for development in line with the plan.

The difficulties involved in getting hold of land to build much-needed transport and energy infrastructure in the UK make clear that mass compulsory purchase of land by the state will be politically challenging. Happily this is not required: evidence from the UK's own past, and from equivalent countries, shows that the very existence of strong compulsory purchase powers can be enough to incentivise landowners to negotiate long-term investment partnerships that align their interests more closely with those of the community at large. Relatively small technical changes to compulsory purchase compensation rules could therefore have a significant impact, at least within defined development areas.

Taxation probably offers a better way forward for capturing economic rent across the board. The obvious strategy for introducing a land value tax – the most efficient form of property tax – would be as part of a wider reform of the entire taxation system away from taxing income and production and towards taxing economic rents. The key would be to make such a reform tax neutral, unobtrusive and demonstrate to the public that the tax would both support the economy and reduce inequalities.

Any fall in land values that such a reform would bring about could cause financial chaos if measures were not also taken to deal with the land–credit feedback cycle that lies at the heart of modern capitalist economies. Banks must be weaned off property loans as their preferred asset and land as their preferred collateral. Whether this can be done solely through regulation remains to be seen. The long-term borrowing required for land purchase should be funded by institutions with equally long time horizons – institutional investors being the obvious choice. Banks should be focused on productive investment and loans de-risked either via a greater role for the state or via the favouring of ownership models and geographical scales that support relationship-banking models.

Such challenges will no doubt take time. In the shorter term in the UK context there is a simple need for large-scale public investment in affordable housing, not just more profit-driven, pro-cyclical private sector development. Changes to public sector accounting can help achieve this; land and housing can provide long-term flows of revenue that mean it should be seen more as an asset than a liability, and also make it attractive to institutional investors seeking higher returns in a low interest environment. Equally, a better tenure balance, which does not discriminate in favour of homeownership in terms of tax or subsidies, and gives renters much greater security, could potentially be achieved in a relatively short timescale.

These changes may seem ambitious. But there are reasons to be hopeful. As house prices keep rising relative to incomes, a tipping point will eventually be reached when the majority of populations in Western democracies will favour policies that reduce the concentration of wealth in property. In London, for example, private renters now outnumber homeowners, and on current trends 60% of households will be renting by 2025 (Morley, 2016). The model of residential capitalism, whereby the home provides an asset upon which to leverage credit to maintain consumption, will gradually become economically and democratically unviable under such a scenario. And as advanced economies enter a 10th year of sluggish growth, negative or near negative real interest rates and rising inequality, the case for shifting the burden of taxation onto unearned capital gains from property will surely rise, not least because of the increasing difficulty of taxing globally mobile corporate profits.

We hope this book has helped readers overcome some of the misunderstandings of the role of land in the economy that have held back such reforms, and pointed the way towards future improvements in the treatment of land in economic policy. If history teaches us anything it is that landed property is a social institution whose nature and economic functions are never fixed, but are constantly changing in response to political pressure and economic forces.

With that in mind, we owe it to ourselves and to future generations to examine the workings of the land economy closely, and challenge misconceptions promoted by vested interests and misguided economic theory. Land is an inherently scarce but vital resource upon which all economic activity is dependent. Until we properly recognise this simple fact and everything that follows from it we will never create a fairer, more efficient and more sustainable economy.

BIBLIOGRAPHY

Ackroyd, Peter. 2001. *London: The Biography*. London: Random House.

Adam, S., Chandler, D., Hood, A., Joyce, R. 2015. *Social Housing in England: A Survey*. London: Institute for Fiscal Studies.

Aikman, David, Andrew G. Haldane, and Benjamin D. Nelson. 2014. 'Curbing the Credit Cycle'. *The Economic Journal* 125 (585). doi:10.1111/ecoj.12113.

Akerlof, George A. 1970. 'The Market for "Lemons": Quality Uncertainty and the Market Mechanism'. *The Quarterly Journal of Economics* 84 (3): 488–500.

Allen, Kate and Anna Nicolaou. 2015. 'Global Property Bubble Fears Mount as Prices and Yields Spike'. *Financial Times*, 16 April. https://next.ft.com/content/7ba6556e-e28d-11e4-ba33-00144feab7de.

Ambaye, Daniel W. 2015. *Land Rights and Expropriation in Ethiopia*, Springer Theses. New York: Springer.

Ambrose, Peter. [1986] 2014. *What Happened to Planning?*, Routledge Revivals. Abingdon: Routledge.

Anderson, Phillip J. 2009. *The Secret Life of Real Estate and Banking*. London: Shepheard-Walwyn.

Andrews, D., Sánchez, A.C., Johansson, Å. 2011. 'Housing Markets and Structural Policies in OECD Countries'. *OECD Economics Department Working Papers*, No. 836. doi: 10.1787/18151973.

Appleyard, Lindsey, and Karen Rowlingson. 2010. *Home-Ownership and the Distribution of Personal Wealth*. York: Joseph Rowntree Foundation.

Armstrong, Angus. 2016. 'Commentary: UK Housing Market: Problems and Policies'. *National Institute Economic Review* 235 (1): F4–8. doi:10.1177/002795011623500103.

Arnold, Jens. 2008. 'Do Tax Structures Affect Aggregate Economic Growth?' *OECD Economics Department Working Papers*, No. 643. doi: 10.1787/18151973

Arnold, Jens, Bert Brys, Christopher Heady, Åsa Johansson, Cyrille Schwellnus, and Laura Vartia. 2011. 'Tax Policy for Economic Recovery and Growth'. *The Economic Journal* 121 (550): F59–80.

Aron, Janine, John V. Duca, John Muellbauer, Keiko Murata, and Anthony Murphy. 2012. 'Credit, Housing, Collateral and Consumption: Evidence from Japan, the U.K. and the U.S.' *Review of Income and Wealth* 58 (3): 397–423. doi:10.1111/j.1475-4991.2011.00466.x

Aron, Janine, and John Muellbauer. 2016. 'Modelling and Forecasting Mortgage Delinquency and Foreclosure in the UK'. *Vox*. 31 August. http://voxeu.org/article/mortgage-delinquency-and-foreclosure-uk.

Assenmacher-Wesche, Katrin, and Stefan Gerlach. 2008. 'Financial Structure and the Impact of Monetary Policy on Asset Prices'. *Swiss National Bank Working Papers* 2008-16.

Aubrey, Thomas. 2016. *Bridging the Infrastructure Gap*. London: Centre for Progressive Capitalism.

Australian Bureau of Statistics. 2015. 'Australian National Accounts: National Income, Expenditure and Product'.

Bahaj, Saleem, Angus Foulis, and Gabor Pinter. 2016. 'The Residential Collateral Channel'. *Bank of England Staff Working Paper.*

Ball, Michael. 2009. *RICS 2009 European Housing Review.* London: Royal Institute of Chartered Surveyors. https://news.kyero.com/2009/03/rics-2009-european-housing-review/1295.

Ballinger, John Kenneth. 1936. *Miami Millions: The Dance of the Dollars in the Great Florida Land Boom of 1925.* Miami: Franklin Press.

Bank of England. 2014. 'Financial Stability Report June 2014'. London: Bank of England. http://www.bankofengland.co.uk/publications/Pages/fsr/2014/fsr35.aspx.

Bank of England. 2015. 'One Bank Research Agenda – Discussion Paper'. London: Bank of England.http://www.bankofengland.co.uk/research/Documents/onebank/discussion.pdf.

Bank of England. 2016a. 'Explanatory Notes – Total Lending to Individuals'. London: Bank of England. http://www.bankofengland.co.uk/statistics/Pages/iadb/notesiadb/ltoi.aspx.

Bank of England. 2016b. 'Financial Stability Report, July 2016'. London: Bank of England. http://www.bankofengland.co.uk/publications/Pages/fsr/2016/jul.aspx.

Bank of England. 2016c. 'Understanding and Measuring Finance for Productive Investment'. Discussion paper. London: Bank of England. http://www.bankofengland.co.uk/financialstability/Pages/fpc/fsdiscussionpapers/080416.aspx.

Bank of England. 2016d. 'Three Centuries of Macroeconomic Data'. London: Bank of England. http://www.bankofengland.co.uk/research/Pages/onebank/threecenturies.aspx.

Banzhaf, H. Spencer, and Nathan Lavery. 2010. 'Can the Land Tax Help Curb Urban Sprawl? Evidence from Growth Patterns in Pennsylvania'. *Journal of Urban Economics* 67 (2): 169–179.

Barker, Kate. 2004. *Review of Housing Supply: Delivering Stability: Securing Our Future Housing Needs: Final Report: Recommendations.* London: HMSO.

Barlow, S. M. 1940. *Report of the Royal Commission on the Distribution of the Industrial Population.* London: HMSO.

Barrell, Ray, Mauro Costantini, and Iris Meco. 2015. 'Housing Wealth, Financial Wealth, and Consumption: New Evidence for Italy and the UK'. *International Review of Financial Analysis* 42 (December): 316–323. doi:10.1016/j.irfa.2015.08.007.

Barwell, Richard, and Oliver Burrows. 2011. 'Growing Fragilities? Balance Sheets in the Great Moderation'. *Bank of England Financial Stability Paper*, no. 10.

Bastagli, Francesca, and John Hills. 2012. 'Wealth Accumulation in Great Britain 1995–2005: The Role of House Prices and the Life Cycle'. *CASEpaper* 166.

Beck, Thorsten, Berrak Büyükkarabacak, Felix Rioja, and Neven Valev. 2008. 'Who Gets the Credit? And Does It Matter?' *CEPR Discussion Papers* 7400, August.

Belfield, Chris, Jonathan Cribb, Andrew Hood, and Robert Joyce. 2014. *Living Standards, Poverty and Inequality in the UK: 2014.* IFS Reports. London: Institute for Fiscal Studies.

Benes, Jaromir, and Michael Kumhof. 2012. 'The Chicago Plan Revisited'. *IMF Working Papers* 12 (102).

Benford, James, and Oliver Burrows. 2013. 'Commercial Property and Financial Stability'. *Bank of England Quarterly Bulletin*, Q1, Winter.

Berg, Jesper, and Christian Sinding Bentzen. 2014. 'Mirror, Mirror, Who Is the Fairest of Them All? Reflections on the Design of and Risk Distribution in the Mortgage Systems of Denmark and the UK'. *National Institute Economic Review* 230 (1): R58–75.

Berger, Allen N., and Gregory F. Udell. 2002. 'Small Business Credit Availability and Relationship Lending: The Importance of Bank Organisational Structure'. *The Economic Journal* 112 (477): F32–53.

Berkes, Fikret. 1987. 'Common-Property Resource Management and Cree Indian Fisheries in Subarctic Canada'. In *The Question of the Commons*. Tucson, AZ: University of Arizona Press.

Bernanke, Ben, and Mark Gertler. 2000. 'Monetary Policy and Asset Price Volatility'. *NBER Working Paper Series*, No. 7559.

Bernanke, Ben, Mark Gertler, and Simon Gilchrist. 1999. 'The Financial Accelerator in a Quantitative Business Cycle Framework'. *Handbook of Macroeconomics* 1: 1341–93.

Berry, Sian. 2016. 'Why a London Renters Union Stands In a Proud Tradition'. *The Huffington Post*. http://www.huffingtonpost.co.uk/sian-berry/london-housing_b_9090016.html.

Bertay, Ata Can, Asli Demirgüç-Kunt, and Harry Huizinga. 2015. 'Bank Ownership and Credit over the Business Cycle: Is Lending by State Banks Less Procyclical?' *Journal of Banking and Finance* 50: 326–39.

Bezemer, Dirk. 2009. 'No One Saw This Coming: Understanding Financial Crisis Through Accounting Models'. *Munich Personal RePEc Archive*, No. 15892. http://mpra.ub.uni-muenchen.de/15892/.

Bezemer, Dirk. 2014. 'Schumpeter Might Be Right Again: The Functional Differentiation of Credit'. *Journal of Evolutionary Economics* 24 (5): 935–50.

Bezemer, Dirk, and Maria Grydaki. 2014. 'Financial Fragility in the Great Moderation'. *Journal of Banking and Finance* 49: 169–77.

Bezemer, Dirk, and Lu Zhang. 2014. 'From Boom to Bust in the Credit Cycle: The Role of Mortgage Credit'. *Research Institute SOM Working Paper Series*, No. 14025–GEM.

Bezemer, Dirk, Lu Zhang, and Maria Grydaki. 2016. 'More Mortgages, Lower Growth?' *Economic Inquiry* 54 (1): 652–74. doi:10.1111/ecin.12254.

Birchall, J. 2014. *Building Communities: The Co-operative Way*, Routledge Revivals. Abingdon: Routledge.

Blanchflower, David G., and Andrew J. Oswald. 2013. 'Does High Home-Ownership Impair the Labor Market?' *NBER Working Paper* No. 19079, May.

Blöchliger, Hansjörg. 2015. 'Reforming the Tax on Immovable Property'. *OECD Economics Department Working Papers* No. 1205.

Bogdanor, Vernon, and Robert J. A. Skidelsky. 1970. *The Age of Affluence, 1951–1964*. Macmillan.

Boot, Arnoud W. A. 2000. 'Relationship Banking: What Do We Know?' *Journal of Financial Intermediation* 9 (1): 7–25.

Booth, Robert. 2014. 'Inside "Billionaires' Row": London's Rotting, Derelict Mansions Worth £350m'. *The Guardian*, 31 January.

Borio, Claudio. 2014. 'The Financial Cycle and Macroeconomics: What Have We Learnt?' *Journal of Banking and Finance* 45: 182–198.

Borio, Claudio, R. McCauley, and P. McGuire. 2011. 'Global Credit and Domestic Credit Booms'. *BIS Quarterly Review*, September.

Bramley, Glen. 2003. 'Planning Regulation and Housing Supply in a Market System'. In *Housing Economics and Public Policy*, ed. T. O'Sullivan and K. Gibb. Oxford: Blackwell Science. doi: 10.1002/9780470690680.ch11

Brooks, Richard. 2005. 'Commentary'. In *Time for Land Value Tax*, ed. Dominic Maxwell and Anthony Vigor. London: Institute for Public Policy Research.

Brown, Meta, Lee Donghoon, Joelle Scally, Katherine Strair, and Wilbert van der Klaaw. 2016. 'The Graying of American Debt'. *Liberty Street Economics*. 24 February. http://libertystreeteconomics.newyorkfed.org/2016/02/the-graying-of-american-debt.html#.V_AHIoWmqUo.

Bryden, John, and Charles Geisler. 2007. 'Community-Based Land Reform: Lessons from Scotland'. *Land Use Policy* 24 (1): 24–34.

Brynjolfsson, Erik, and Andrew McAfee. 2014. *The Second Machine Age: Work, Progress, and Prosperity in a Time of Brilliant Technologies*. New York: W. W. Norton.

BSA (Building Societies Association). 2015. 'The History of Building Societies (BSA Factsheet)'. https://www.bsa.org.uk/information/consumer-factsheets/general/the-history-of-building-societies.

Buiter, Willem H., and Ebrahim Rahbari. 2015. 'Why Economists (and Economies) Should Love Islamic Finance'. *JKAU: Islamic Economics* 28 (1): 139–62.

Buyukkarabacak, Berrak, and Neven Valev. 2006. 'Credit Expansions and Financial Crises: The Roles of Household and Firm Credit'. *Andrew Young School of Public Policy Studies Working Paper*, 06–55.

Cabral, Marika, and Caroline Hoxby. 2012. 'The Hated Property Tax: Salience, Tax Rates, and Tax Revolts'. *NBER Working Paper* No. 18514, November.

Callan, Tim. 1992. 'Taxing Imputed Income from Owner-Occupation: Distributional Implications of Alternative Packages'. *Fiscal Studies* 13 (4): 58–70.

Callcutt, J. 2007. *The Callcutt Review of Housebuilding Delivery*. London: Department for Communities and Local Government.

Calza, Alessandro, Tommaso Monacelli, and Livio Stracca. 2013. 'Housing Finance and Monetary Policy'. *Journal of the European Economic Association* 11 (s1): 101–22.

Chakraborty, Indraneel, Itay Goldstein, and Andrew MacKinlay. 2014. 'Do Asset Price Booms have Negative Real Effects?' (Unpublished working paper).

Chaloner, Justin, and Mark Pragnell. 2014. 'Increasing Investment in Affordable Housing: Towards a Level Playing Field for Affordable Housing'. *Capital Economics*, 3 April.

Chang, Ha-Joon. 2007. *Bad Samaritans: The Myth of Free Trade and the Secret History of Capitalism*. New York: Bloomsbury.

Cheshire, Paul. 2009. 'Urban Containment, Housing Affordability and Price Stability-Irreconcilable Goals'.

Cheshire, Paul. 2011. House of Commons CLG Select Committee, 10 October.

Cheshire, Paul C. 2013. 'Land Market Regulation: Market versus Policy Failures'. *Journal of Property Research* 30 (3): 170–88.

Cheshire, Paul. 2014. 'Turning Houses into Gold: The Failure of British Planning'. *Centre for Economic Performance Working Paper* No. 421.

Cheshire, Paul, and Stephen Sheppard. 1998. 'Estimating the Demand for Housing, Land, and Neighbourhood Characteristics'. *Oxford Bulletin of Economics and Statistics* 60 (3): 357–82.

Cheshire, Paul, and Stephen Sheppard. 2004. 'Land Markets and Land Market Regulation: Progress towards Understanding'. *Regional Science and Urban Economics* 34 (6): 619–37.

Chrystal, Kenneth Alexander. 1992. 'The Fall and Rise of Saving'. *National Westminster Bank Quarterly Review*, February, 24–40.

Chu, Ben. 2016. 'No, It's Not Time for Britain to Be Intensely Relaxed over Household Debt'. *The Independent*, 17 January. http://www.independent.co.uk/voices/no-it-s-not-time-for-britain-to-be-intensely-relaxed-over-household-debt-a6817926.html.

Churchill, W. 1909a. Speech made to the House of Commons on 4 May. http://www.grundskyld.dk/pdf/Winston-Churchill-Land-Monopoly.pdf.

Churchill, W. 1909b. 'Mother of all Monopolies'. Speech Delivered at King's Theatre in Edinburgh on 17 July 1909. http://www.cooperative-individualism.org/churchill-winston_mother-of-all-monopolies-1909.htm.

Clark, John Bates. 1890. 'The Moral Basis of Property in Land'. *Journal of Social Science* 27: 21–6.

Clark, John Bates. 1891a. 'Distribution as Determined by a Law of Rent'. *The Quarterly Journal of Economics* 5 (3): 289–318.

Clark, John Bates. 1891b. 'Marshall's Principles of Economics'. *Political Science Quarterly* 6 (1): 126–51.

Clark, John Bates. 1899. *The Distribution of Wealth*. Macmillan.

Clark, Peter. 2001. *British Clubs and Societies 1580–1800: The Origins of an Associational World*. Oxford: Oxford University Press.

Clarke, Stephen, Adam Corlett, and Lindsay Judge. 2016. *The Housing Headwind: The Impact of Rising Housing Costs on UK Living Standards*. London: Resolution Foundation. http://www.resolutionfoundation.org/publications/the-housing-headwind-the-impact-of-rising-housing-costs-on-uk-living-standards/.

CML (Council of Mortgage Lenders). 2010. *The Outlook for Mortgage Funding Markets in the UK in 2010–2015*. London: Council of Mortgage Lenders. http://www.cml.org.uk.

CML (Council of Mortgage Lenders). 2015. 'Key UK Mortgage Facts'. https://www.cml.org.uk/industry-data/key-uk-mortgage-facts/.

Cochrane, John H. 2014. 'Toward a Run-Free Financial System'. http://faculty.chicagobooth.edu/john.cochrane/research/papers/run_free.pdf.

Cohen, Avi J., and Geoffrey C. Harcourt. 2003. 'Retrospectives: Whatever Happened to the Cambridge Capital Theory Controversies?' *The Journal of Economic Perspectives* 17 (1): 199–214.

Cohen, Jeffrey P., and Cletus C. Coughlin. 2005. 'An Introduction to Two-Rate Taxation of Land and Buildings'. *Review* 87 (3): 359–74.

Collins, Michael. 2012. *Money and Banking in the UK: A History*. Vol. 6. Abingdon: Routledge.

Community Land Trust Network. 2015. 'Housing: It's in Our Hands'. http://www.communitylandtrusts.org.uk/_filecache/99b/546/193-final-post-election-clt-manifesto-housing-its-in-our-hands.pdf.

Conaty, Pat, and Martin Large. 2013. *Commons Sense: Co-Operative Place Making and the Capturing of Land Value for 21st Century Garden Cities*. Manchester: Co-Operatives UK. https://www.uk.coop/sites/default/files/uploads/attachments/commons_sense.pdf

Cribb, Jonathan, Andrew Hood, and Robert Joyce. 2016. 'The Economic Circumstances of Different Generations: The Latest Picture'. *IFS Briefing Note* BN187. https://www.ifs.org.uk/uploads/publications/bns/bn187.pdf.

Crook, A. D. H., G. Burgess, R. Dunning, E. Ferrari, J. Henneberry, F. Lyall Grant, S. Monk, S. Rowley, C. Watkins, and C. Whitehead. 2010. *The Incidence, Value and Delivery of Planning Obligations in England in 2007–08*. London: Department of Communities and Local Government.

Crouch, Colin. 2009. 'Privatised Keynesianism: An Unacknowledged Policy Regime'. *The British Journal of Politics and International Relations* 11 (3): 382–99.

Crowe, Christopher, Giovanni Dell'Ariccia, Deniz Igan, and Pau Rabanal. 2013. 'How to Deal with Real Estate Booms: Lessons from Country Experiences'. *Journal of Financial Stability* 9 (3): 300–19.

Davies, Glyn. 2002. *History of Money: From Ancient Times to the Present Day*. Cardiff: University of Wales Press.

DCLG (Department of Communities and Local Government). 2006. *Transferable Lessons from the New Towns*. London: DCLG.

DCLG (Department of Communities and Local Government). 2010. 'Table 502: house prices from 1930, annual house price inflation, United Kingdom, from 1970'. https://www.gov.uk/government/uploads/system/uploads/attachment_data/file/305683/Table_502_-_ONS.xls.

DCLG (Department of Communities and Local Government). 2015. *English Housing Survey 2013–14*. London: DCLG. https://www.gov.uk/government/uploads/system/uploads/attachment_data/file/461439/EHS_Households_2013-14.pdf.

DCLG (Department of Communities and Local Government). 2016a. *English Housing Survey: Headline Report 2014–15*. London: DCLG. https://www.gov.uk/government/statistics/english-housing-survey-2014-to-2015-headline-report.

DCLG (Department of Communities and Local Government). 2016b. *English Housing Survey: Housing for Older People Report 2014 to 2015*. London: DCLG.

DCLG (Department for Communities and Local Government). 2016c. 'Table 241: permanent dwellings completed, by tenure, United Kingdom, historical calendar year series'. https://www.gov.uk/government/statistical-data-sets/live-tables-on-house-building

DCLG (Department for Communities and Local Government). 2016d. 'Table 102: Dwelling stock: by tenure, Great Britain (historical series)'. https://www.gov.uk/government/statistical-data-sets/live-tables-on-dwelling-stock-including-vacants.

DEFRA (Department for Environment, Food and Rural Affairs). 2015. *Managing Common Land*. London: Natural England and Department for Environment, Food and Rural Affairs. https://www.gov.uk/guidance/managing-common-land.

De Groot, Henri, Gerard Marlet, Coen Teulings, and Wouter Vermeulen. 2015. 'The Revival of Cities and the Urban Land Premium'. *Vox*, June. http://voxeu.org/article/city-revivals-and-urban-land-premiums.

Dell'Ariccia, Giovanni, Deniz Igan, and Luc Laeven. 2012. 'Policies for Macrofinancial Stability: How to Deal with Credit Booms'. *IMF Staff Discussion Note* SDN/12/06, June 7. http://www.imf.org/external/pubs/ft/sdn/2012/sdn1206.pdf

DeMontfort University. 2015. 'The UK Commercial Property Lending Report – 2015'. http://www.dmu.ac.uk/about-dmu/schools-and-departments/leicester-business-school/the-uk-commercial-property-lending-report.aspx.

Department for Work and Pensions. 2016. 'Housing Benefit Caseload Statistics'. https://www.gov.uk/government/statistics/housing-benefit-caseload-statistics.

De Soto, Hernando. 2000. *The Mystery of Capital: Why Capitalism Triumphs in the West and Fails Everywhere Else*. New York: Basic Books.

Dodd, Nigel. 1994. *The Sociology of Money: Economics, Reason and Contemporary Society*. Cambridge: Polity Press.

Doling, John, and Richard Ronald. 2010. 'Home Ownership and Asset-Based Welfare'. *Journal of Housing and the Built Environment* 25, 165–173.

Dolphin, T. 2009. *Time for Another People's Budget*. London: Institute for Public Policy Research.

Dorling, Danny. 2014. *All That Is Solid: How the Great Housing Disaster Defines Our Times, and What We Can Do about It*. London: Penguin.

Dowling, Tim. 2014. 'Deep Concerns: The Trouble with Basement Conversions'. *The Guardian*. 18 August. http://www.theguardian.com/lifeandstyle/2014/aug/18/basement-conversions-disputes-digging-iceberg-homes.

Duca, John V., John Muellbauer, and Anthony Murphy. 2010. 'Housing Markets and the Financial Crisis of 2007–2009: Lessons for the Future'. *Journal of Financial Stability* 6 (4): 203–217.

Durand, Martine, and Fabrice Murtin. 2015. 'The Relationship Between Income and Wealth Inequality: Evidence from the New OECD Wealth Distribution Database'. Paper prepared for the IARIW Sessions at the 2015 World Statistics Conference Sponsored by the International Statistical Institute. Organisation for Economic Co-operation and Development.

Dymski, Gary A. 2010. 'Why the Subprime Crisis Is Different: A Minskyian Approach'. *Cambridge Journal of Economics* 34 (2): 239–255.

Dyson, Ben, and Andrew Jackson. 2013. *Modernising Money*. London: Positive Money.

Dyson, Richard. 2014. 'Buy-to-Let Boom: One in Five Homes Now Owned by Landlords'. *The Telegraph*, 22 October. http://www.telegraph.co.uk/finance/personalfinance/investing/buy-to-let/11179073/Buy-to-let-boom-one-in-five-homes-now-owned-by-landlords.html.

Engelen, Ewald, Ismail Erturk, Julie Froud, Sukhdev Johal, Adam Leaver, Mick Moran, Adriana Nilsson, and Karel Williams. 2011. *After the Great Complacence: Financial Crisis and the Politics of Reform*. Oxford: Oxford University Press.

Engels, Friedrich. 1887. *The Labour Movement in America*. William Reeves.

Epstein, Gerald A. 2005. *Financialization and the World Economy*. Cheltenham: Edward Elgar.

Eurostat. 2016. 'Disposable Income of Private Households by NUTS 2 Regions'. http://ec.europa.eu/eurostat/tgm/table.do?tab=table&init=1&language=en&pcode=tgs00026&plugin=1.

Fairbairn, Madeleine. 2014. '"Like Gold with Yield": Evolving Intersections between Farmland and Finance'. *Journal of Peasant Studies* 41 (5): 777–95.

Falk, Nicholas. 2014. *Funding Housing and Local Growth*. London: The Smith Institute. http://media.urbed.coop.ccc.cdn.faelix.net/sites/default/files/Funding%20Housing%20and%20Local%20Growth%2C%20The%20Smith%20Institute.pdf.

Feldman, Maryann P., and Richard Florida. 1994. 'The Geographic Sources of Innovation: Technological Infrastructure and Product Innovation in the United States'. *Annals of the Association of American Geographers* 84 (2): 210–29.

Feldstein, Martin. 2008. 'How to Help People Whose Home Values Are Underwater'. *The Wall Street Journal*, 18 November, A21.

Fernandez-Corugedo, Emilio, and John Muellbauer. 2006. 'Consumer Credit Conditions in the United Kingdom'. *Bank of England Working Papers* No. 314. http://www.bankofengland.co.uk/research/Pages/workingpapers/2006/wp314.aspx.

Ferri, Giovanni, Panu Kalmi, and Eeva Kerola. 2014. 'Does Bank Ownership Affect Lending Behavior? Evidence from the Euro Area'. *Journal of Banking and Finance* 48: 194–209.

Fisher, Irving. 1936. '100% Money and the Public Debt'. *Economic Forum*, April–June: 406–20.

Florida, Richard. 2004. *The Rise of the Creative Class*. New York: Basic Books.

Forrest, Ray, and Alan Murie. 1986. 'Marginalization and Subsidized Individualism: The Sale of Council Houses in the Restructuring of the British Welfare State'. *International Journal of Urban and Regional Research* 10 (1): 46–66.

Forrest, Ray, Philip Leather, and Patricia Kennett. 1999. *Home Ownership in Crisis? The British Experience of Negative Equity*. Ashgate.

Förster, Michael, Ana Llena-Nozal, and Vahé Nafilyan. 2014. 'Trends in Top Incomes and Their Taxation in OECD Countries'. *OECD Social, Employment and Migration Working Papers* No. 159.

Frank, Robert H., and Philip J. Cook. 2010. *The Winner-Take-All Society: Why the Few at the Top Get so Much More than the Rest of Us*. London: Random House.

Friedman, Milton. 1948. 'A Monetary and Fiscal Framework for Economic Stability'. *The American Economic Review* 38 (3): 245–64.

Friedman, Milton. 1957. 'The Permanent Income Hypothesis'. In *A Theory of the Consumption Function*, 20–37. Princeton, NJ: Princeton University Press.

Friedman, Milton. 1975. *There's No Such Thing as a Free Lunch*. La Salle, IL: Open Court.

Gaffney, Mason. 1994a. 'Land as a Distinctive Factor of Production'. In *Land and Taxation*, ed. Nicholas Tideman, 39–102. Georgist Paradigm Series. London: Shepheard-Walwyn.

Gaffney, Mason. 1994b. 'Neo-Classical Economics as a Stratagem against Henry George'. In *The Corruption of Economics*, ed. Mason Gaffney and Fred Harrison, 29–163. London: Shepheard-Walwyn.

Galati, Gabriele, and Richhild Moessner. 2013. 'Macroprudential Policy – a Literature Review'. *Journal of Economic Surveys* 27 (5): 846–78.

Garvie, Deborah. 2013. *Little Boxes, Fewer Homes*. London: Shelter

George, Henry. [1879] 1979. *Progress and Poverty*. Condensed centenary ed. London: Hogarth Press.

Gerschenkron, Alexander. 1962. *Economic Backwardness in Historical Perspective: A Book of Essays*. Cambridge, MA: Belknap Press of Harvard University Press.

Goodhart, Charles. 1989. *Money, Information and Uncertainty*. 2nd ed. London: Macmillan.

Goodhart, Charles, and Boris Hofmann. 2008. 'House Prices, Money, Credit, and the Macroeconomy'. *Oxford Review of Economic Policy* 24 (1): 180–205.

Goodhart, Charles, and E. Perotti. 2015. 'Maturity Mismatch Stretching: Banking Has Taken a Wrong Turn'. *CEPR Policy Insight* No. 81.

Grant, James. 1880. *Old and New Edinburgh*. London: Cassel.

Gray, Kevin, and Susan Francis Gray. 2011. *Land Law*. Oxford: Oxford University Press.

Griffith, Matt. 2011. *We Must Fix It: Delivering Reform of the Building Sector to Meet the UK's Housing and Economic Challenges*. London: Institute for Public Policy Research.

Grydaki, Maria, and Dirk Bezemer. 2013. 'The Role of Credit in the Great Moderation: A Multivariate GARCH Approach'. *Journal of Banking and Finance* 37 (11): 4615–26.

Halifax. 2015. 'Halifax House Price–Earnings Ratio (All Houses, All Buyers)'. http://www.lloydsbankinggroup.com/globalassets/documents/media/economic-insight/house-price-tools/affordabilityq42014.xls.

Hall, Peter, and Colin Ward. 2014. *Sociable Cities: The 21st-Century Reinvention of the Garden City*. Abingdon: Routledge.

Hamnett, Chris, and J. Seavers. 1996. 'Home Ownership, Housing Wealth and Wealth Distribution in Britain'. In *New Inequalities: The Changing Distribution of Income and Wealth in the United Kingdom*. Cambridge: Cambridge University Press.

Hanley, Lynsey. 2007. *Estates: An Intimate History*. London: Granta.

Harris, Ron, and Asher Meir. 2015. 'Recourse Structure of Mortgages: A Comparison between the US and Europe'. *DICE Report* 13 (4): 15–22.

Harrod, Roy F. 1939. 'An Essay in Dynamic Theory'. *The Economic Journal* 49 (193): 14–33.

Harvey, David. [1982] 2006. *The Limits to Capital*. New updated ed. London: Verso.

Haywood, Russell. 2009. *Railways, Urban Development and Town Planning in Britain: 1948–2008*. Ashgate.

Heath, Sarah. 2014. 'Rent Control in the Private Rented Sector (England)'. House of Commons Library, SN/SP/6760, 11 July.

Heinsohn, Gunnar, and Otto Steiger. 2006. 'Interest and Money: The Property Explanation'. In *A Handbook of Alternative Monetary Economics*, ed. Philip Arestis and Malcolm Sawyer. London: Macmillan.

Hellebrandt, Tomas, Sandhya Kawar, and Matt Waldron. 2009. 'The Economics and Estimation of Negative Equity'. *Bank of England Quarterly Bulletin*, Q2.

Henley, Andrew. 1998. 'Changes in the Distribution of Housing Wealth in Great Britain, 1985–91'. *Economica* 65 (259): 363–80.

Henry, Ken, Jeff Harmer, John Piggott, Heather Ridout, and Greg Smith. 2009. *Australia's Future Tax System*. Canberra: Commonwealth Treasury.

Hill, Rod, and Tony Myatt. 2010. *The Economics Anti-Textbook*. London: Zed Books.

Hills, John. 2007. 'Ends and Means: The Future Roles of Social Housing in England'. *CASEreport* 34, February. http://eprints.lse.ac.uk/5568/1/Ends_and_Means_The_future_roles_of_social_housing_in_England_1.pdf

Hills, John. 2010. 'An Anatomy of Economic Inequality in the UK – Report of the National Equality Panel'. *CASEreport* 60, January.

Hirsch, Fred. 2005. *Social Limits to Growth*. London: Routledge.

HM Treasury Select Committee. 2009. 'Mortgage Arrears and Access to Mortgage Finance, August 2009'.

Hobbes, Peter A. 2014. 'The Erosion of the Real Estate Home Bias'. MSCI. https://www.msci.com/www/research-paper/research-insight-the-erosion-of/0118148353.

Howard, Ebenezer. [1898] 2010. *To-morrow: A Peaceful Path to Real Reform*. Cambridge: Cambridge University Press.

Hsieh, Chang-Tai, and Enrico Moretti. 2015. 'Why Do Cities Matter? Local Growth and Aggregate Growth'. *NBER Working Paper* No. 21154.

Hudson, Michael. 2008. 'Henry George's Political Critics'. *American Journal of Economics and Sociology* 67 (1): 1–45.

Hudson, Michael. 2010. 'The Transition from Industrial Capitalism to a Financialized Bubble Economy'. *Levy Economics Institute Working Paper* No. 627, October, 1–34.

Ingham, Geoffrey K. 2004. *The Nature of Money*. Cambridge: Polity Press. http://www.loc.gov/catdir/toc/ecip047/2003017409.html.

Inman, Phillip. 2016. 'The Credit Boom Is a Ticking Timebomb for UK Plc'. *The Guardian*, 4 January. https://www.theguardian.com/business/economics-blog/2015/jan/04/credit-boom-ticking-timebomb-uk-plc.

Institute of Fiscal Studies. 2015. 'Incomes in the UK'. http://www.ifs.org.uk/tools_and_resources/incomes_in_uk.

International Labour Organization (ILO). 2015. *Global Wage Report 2014/15: Wages and Income Inequality*. Geneva: ILO. http://www.ilo.org/wcmsp5/groups/public/@dgreports/@dcomm/@publ/documents/publication/wcms_324678.pdf.

International Monetary Fund (IMF). 2011. *Durable Financial Stability: Getting There from Here, Global Financial Stability Report, April 2011*. Washington, DC: IMF. https://www.imf.org/external/pubs/ft/gfsr/2011/01/pdf/text.pdf.

Jefferys, Pete, and Toby Lloyd. 2015. 'Why Don't We Build Enough New Homes in England?' *Built Environment* 41: 166–82.

Jefferys, Pete, Toby Lloyd, Andy Argyle, Joe Sarling, Jan Crosby, and John Bibby. 2014. *Building the Homes We Need*. London: KPMG and Shelter.

Jefferys, Pete, Toby Lloyd, and James Gregory. 2014. *Increasing Investment in Affordable Homes*. London: Shelter. http://england.shelter.org.uk/__data/assets/pdf_file/0011/799769/2014_capital_economics_shelter_summary.pdf.

Jencks, Christopher. 2002. 'Does Inequality Matter?' *Daedalus* 131 (1): 49–65.

Jenkins, Blair. 2009. 'Rent Control: Do Economists Agree?' *Econ Journal Watch* 6 (1): 73–112.

Jones, Colin, and Alan Murie. 2008. *The Right to Buy: Analysis and Evaluation of a Housing Policy*. Oxford: Wiley-Blackwell.

Jordà, Òscar, Moritz Schularick, and Alan M. Taylor. 2015. 'Leveraged Bubbles'. *Journal of Monetary Economics* 76: S1–20.

Jordà, Òscar, Moritz Schularick, and Alan M. Taylor. 2016. 'The Great Mortgaging: Housing Finance, Crises and Business Cycles'. *Economic Policy* 31 (85): 107–52.

Kaganova, Olga. 2011. 'International Experiences on Government Land Development Companies: What Can Be Learned?' IDG Working Paper No. 2011-01, February. http://www.urban.org/url.cfm?renderforprint=1&ID=412299&buildstatic=1.

Karagiannaki, Eleni. 2011a. 'Recent Trends in the Size and the Distribution of Inherited Wealth in the UK'. *CASEpaper* 146, June.

Karagiannaki, Eleni. 2011b. 'The Impact of Inheritance on the Distribution of Wealth: Evidence from the UK'. *CASEpaper* 148, June.

Katz, B., M. A. Turner, K. D. Brown, M. Cunningham, and N. Sawyer. 2003. *Rethinking Local Affordable Housing Strategies: Lessons from 70 Years of Policy and Practice*. Washington, DC: Brookings Institution.

Kay, John Anderson. 2009. *Narrow Banking: The Reform of Banking Regulation*. Tonbridge: Centre for the Study of Financial Innovation.

Keen, Steve. 1995. 'Finance and Economic Breakdown: Modeling Minsky's "Financial Instability Hypothesis"'. *Journal of Post Keynesian Economics* 17 (4): 607–35.

Keen, Steve. 2011. *Debunking Economics: The Naked Emperor Dethroned?* 2nd ed. London: Zed Books.

Keen, Steve. 2013. 'A Monetary Minsky Model of the Great Moderation and the Great Recession'. *Journal of Economic Behavior and Organization* 86: 221–35.

Kemp, P. 2002. *Private Renting in Transition*. London: Chartered Institute of Housing.

Keohane, Nigel, and Broughton Nida. 2013. *The Politics of Housing*. London: Social Market Foundation.

Kindleberger, Charles P. 1993. *A Financial History of Western Europe*. 2nd ed. Oxford: Oxford University Press.

Kindleberger, Charles P., and Robert Z. Aliber. 2005. *Manias, Panics and Crashes: A History of Financial Crises*. 5th ed. New York: John Wiley and Sons.

King, Mervyn. 2003. 'The Governor's Speech at the East Midlands Development Agency/Bank of England Dinner'. *Bank of England Quarterly Bulletin*, Winter.

King, Robert G., and Ross Levine. 1993. 'Finance and Growth: Schumpeter Might Be Right'. *Quarterly Journal of Economics* 108 (3): 717–37.

Kingman, David. 2013. *Why BTL Equals 'Big Tax Let-off': How the UK Tax System Hands Buy-to-Let Landlords an Unfair Advantage*. London: Intergenerational Foundation. http://www.if.org.uk/wp-content/uploads/2013/11/Why-BTL-Equals-Big-Tax-Rip-off.pdf.

Knight Frank. 2013. 'International Investors Spent £2.2 Billion on Central London New-Build Property in 2012', January. http://www.knightfrank.co.uk/news/international-investors-spent-%C2%A32.2-billion-on-central-london-new-build-property-in-2012-01526.aspx.

Knight Frank. 2015. 'Agri-Investments: The Pathway to Capital Growth'. http://www.knightfrank.co.uk/resources/residential/publications/uk_farmland.pdf.

Knoll, Katharina, Moritz Schularick, and Thomas Michael Steger. 2014. 'No Price like Home: Global House Prices, 1870–2012'. *CESifo Working Paper* No. 5006, October. http://www.cesifo-group.de/portal/page/portal/DocBase_Content/WP/WP-CESifo_Working_Papers/wp-cesifo-2014/wp-cesifo-2014-10/cesifo1_wp5006.pdf

Koo, Richard C. 2011. *The Holy Grail of Macroeconomics: Lessons from Japan's Great Recession*. Singapore: John Wiley and Sons.

Krippner, Greta R. 2005. 'The Financialization of the American Economy'. *Socio-Economic Review* 3 (2): 173–208.

Kumhof, Michael, Romain Rancière, and Pablo Winant. 2015. 'Inequality, Leverage, and Crises'. *The American Economic Review* 105 (3): 1217–45.

Laamanen, Jani-Petri. 2013. 'Home-Ownership and the Labour Market: Evidence from Rental Housing Market Deregulation'. *Tampere Economic Working Papers Net Series* No. 89. Tampere: University of Tampere.

Lambert, Simon. 2009. 'Mortgages Rise But Warning on False Dawn'. *This Is Money*. http://www.thisismoney.co.uk/money/mortgageshome/article-1672223/Mortgages-rise-but-warning-on-false-dawn.html.

Lansley, Stewart, and Howard Reed. 2016. *A Citizen's Income: A Recipe for Change*. London: Compass.

Lavoie, Marc, and Mario Seccareccia. 2016. 'What Even Famous Mainstream Economists Miss About the Cambridge Capital Controversies'. Blog. Institute for New Economic Thinking. https://www.ineteconomics.org/perspectives/blog/what-even-famous-mainstream-economists-miss-about-the-cambridge-capital-controversies.

Leung, Charles. 2004. 'Macroeconomics and Housing: A Review of the Literature'. *Journal of Housing Economics* 13 (4): 249–67. doi:10.1016/j.jhe.2004.09.002.

Linklater, Andro. 2013. *Owning the Earth: The Transforming History of Land Ownership*. London: Bloomsbury. http://www.bloomsbury.com/us/owning-the-earth-9781620402900/.

Litman, T. 2015. *Analysis of Public Policies That Unintentionally Encourage and Subsidize Urban Sprawl*. Victoria Transport Policy Institute, Supporting paper commissioned by LSE Cities at the London School of Economics and Political Science, on behalf of the Global Commission on the Economy and Climate for the New Climate Economy Cities Program. https://files.lsecities.net/files/2015/03/NCE-Sprawl-Subsidy-Report-021.pdf

Lloyd, Toby. 2009. *Don't Bet the House on It*. London: Compass.

Locke, John. 1690. *Locke: Two Treatises of Government*. Cambridge: Cambridge University Press.

Lord, Chris, James Lloyd, and Matt Barnes. 2013. *Understanding Landlords: A Study of Private Landlords in the UK using the Wealth and Assets Survey*. London: Strategic Society Centre.

Lund, Brian. 2011. *Understanding Housing Policy*. Bristol: Policy Press.

Lusht, Kenneth M. 1992. 'Site Value Tax and Land Development Patterns: Evidence from Melbourne, Australia'. *Working Paper Series in Real Estate*. College of Business Administration, Pennsylvania State University.

Lyons, Michael. 2014. *The Lyons Housing Review. Mobilising across the Nation to Build the Homes Our Children Need*. Labour Party.

Malpass, Peter, and Henry Aughton. 1999. *Housing Finance: A Basic Guide*. London: Shelter.

Malthus, Thomas Robert. 1872. *An Essay on the Principle of Population Or a View of Its Past and Present Effects on Human Happiness, an Inquiry Into Our Prospects Respecting the Future Removal Or Mitigation of the Evils Which It Occasions by Rev. TR Malthus*. Reeves and Turner.

Marshall, J. L. 1969. 'The Pattern of Housebuilding in the Inter-war Period in England and Wales'. *Scottish Journal of Political Economy* 16 (1): 184–205.

Martin, Graham. 2001. *The Future of Low-cost Home-ownership*. York: Joseph Rowntree Foundation.

Marx, Karl. [1847] 1995. *The Poverty of Philosophy*, trans. H. Quelch. Amherst, NY: Prometheus Books.

Marx, Karl. 1867. *Das Kapital: A Critique of Political Economy*. Washington, DC: Regnery Publishing.

Mathias, Peter. 2013. *The First Industrial Nation: The Economic History of Britain 1700–1914*. Abingdon: Routledge.

Matthews, Alan. 2011. 'Post-2013 EU Common Agricultural Policy, Trade and Development: A Review of Legislative Proposals. *International Centre for Programme on Agricultural Trade and Sustainable Development (ICTSD) Issue Paper* no. 39, October.

Mayhew, L., and D. Smith. 2016. *The UK Equity Bank: Towards Income Security in Old Age*. London: International Longevity Centre-UK (ILC-UK), June. http://www.ilcuk.org.uk/images/uploads/publication-pdfs/The_UK_Equity_Bank._web.pdf .

McLeay, Michael, Radia Amar, and Thomas Ryland. 2014. 'Money Creation in the Modern Economy'. *Bank of England Quarterly Bulletin* 54 (1).

Mian, Atif, and Amir Sufi. 2015. *House of Debt: How They (and You) Caused the Great Recession, and How We Can Prevent It from Happening Again.* Chicago: University of Chicago Press.

Mian, Atif, Amir Sufi, and Emil Verner. 2015. 'Household Debt and Business Cycles Worldwide'. National Bureau of Economic Research.

Mill, John Stuart. 1884. *Principles of Political Economy.* D. Appleton.

Milne, Alistair, and Justine A. Wood. 2014. 'An Old Fashioned Banking Crisis: Credit Growth and Loan Losses in the UK 1997–2012'. In *The Causes and Consequences of the Long UK Expansion,* ed. J. S. Chadha, A. Chrystal, J. Pearlman, P. Smith, and S. Wright. Cambridge: Cambridge University Press.

Minsky, Hyman. 1986. *Stabilizing and Unstable Economy.* New Haven, CT: Yale University Press.

Minsky, Hyman P. 1992. 'The Financial Instability Hypothesis'. *The Jerome Levy Economics Institute Working Paper* no. 74, May.

Mirrlees, James, and Stuart Adam. 2011. *Tax by Design: The Mirrlees Review.* Vol. 2. Oxford: Oxford University Press.

Modigliani, Franco, and Richard Brumberg. 1954. 'Utility Analysis and the Consumption Function: An Interpretation of Cross-Section Data'. In *Post-Keynesian Economics,* ed. Kenneth Kurihara. New Brunswick, NJ: Rutgers University Press.

Monk, Sarah, Christine Whitehead, Gemma Burgess, and Connie Tang. 2013. 'International Review of Land Supply and Planning Systems'. York: Joseph Rowntree Foundation.

Morley, Katie. 2016. '"Generation Rent" Dominates London Property Market for the First Time'. *The Telegraph,* 19 February. http://www.telegraph.co.uk/personal-banking/mortgages/generation-rent-dominates-london-property-market-for-the-first-t/.

Muellbauer, John. 2002. 'Mortgage Credit Conditions in the UK'. *Economic Outlook* 26 (3): 11–18.

Muellbauer, John. 2005. 'Property Taxation and the Economy after the Barker Review'. *The Economic Journal* 115 (502): C99–117.

Muellbauer, John. 2009. 'Household Decisions, Credit Markets and the Macroeconomy: Implications for the Design of Central Bank Models'. *BIS Working Papers* no. 306, March. http://www.bis.org/publ/work306.pdf.

Muellbauer, John. 2012. 'When is a Housing Market Overheated Enough to Threaten Stability?' *University of Oxford Department of Economics Discussion Paper Series* no. 623, September.

Muellbauer, John. 2014a. 'House Prices and Their Macro-economic Consequences: Some European Contrasts'. Presentation made at the OeNB workshop, Vienna, October 9–10, 2014. https://www.oenb.at/en

Muellbauer, John. 2014b. 'Six Fiscal Reforms for the UK's "Lost Generation"'. *Vox,* 25 March. http://www.voxeu.org/article/six-fiscal-reforms-uk-s-lost-generation

Muellbauer, John. 2015. 'A Fiscal Fix for a Peculiarly Flawed Property Market'. *The Financial Times,* 7 April.

Muellbauer, John. 2016. 'Macroeconomics and Consumption'. *CEPR Discussion Paper* DP11588.

Muellbauer, John, and Anthony Murphy. 2008. 'Housing Markets and the Economy: The Assessment'. *Oxford Review of Economic Policy* 24 (1): 1–33.

Muellbauer, John, and David Williams. 2011. 'Credit Conditions and the Real Economy: The Elephant in the Room'. *BIS Papers* no. 64. http://www.bis.org/publ/bppdf/bispap64p.pdf

National Audit Office. 2014. *Tax Reliefs*. London: National Audit Office.

National Housing and Planning Advice Unit (NHPAU). 2008. *Buy-to-Let Mortgages and the Impact on UK House Prices: A Technical Report*. Fareham: NHPAU. http://webarchive.nationalarchives.gov.uk/20120919132719/http:/www.communities.gov.uk/documents/507390/pdf/684943.pdf

Neale, Jon. 2009. *Improving Housing Quality: Unlocking the Market*. London: RIBA.

Needham, D. Barrie. 2014. *Dutch Land Use Planning*. Abingdon: Routledge.

New Economics Foundation. 2014. *Inequality and Financialisation: A Dangerous Mix*. London: New Economics Foundation. http://b.3cdn.net/nefoundation/005f-379c2df9c812f1_gqm6ivkyo.pdf.

New Economics Foundation. 2016. *The Financialisation of UK Homes: The Housing Crisis, Land and the Banks*. London: New Economics Foundation. http://neweconomics.org/the-financialisation-of-uk-homes/?lost=true&_sf_s=+publications+++the+financialisation+of+uk+homes.

New Economics Foundation, CDS Co-operatives, Pat Conaty, Johnston Birchall, Steve Bendle, and Rosemary Foggitt. 2013. *Common Ground – for Mutual Home Ownership*. London: New Economics Foundation.

Norregaard, John. 2013. 'Taxing Immovable Property Revenue Potential and Implementation Challenges'. *IMF Working Paper* WP/13/129, May.

Nozick, Robert. 1974. *Anarchy, State and Utopia*. New York: Basic Books.

OECD (Organisation for Economic Co-operation and Development). n.d. 'OECD Analytical House Prices Indicators'. https://stats.oecd.org/Index.aspx?DataSetCode=HOUSE_PRICES.

OECD (Organisation for Economic Co-operation and Development). 2014. 'Focus on Top Incomes and Taxation in OECD Countries: Was the Crisis a Game Changer?' http://www.oecd.org/social/OECD2014-FocusOnTopIncomes.pdf

OECD (Organisation for Economic Co-operation and Development). 2015. *In It Together: Why Less Inequality Benefits All*. Paris: OECD Publishing.

OECD (Organisation for Economic Co-operation and Development). 2016. 'OECD Income Distribution Database (IDD): Gini, Poverty, Income, Methods and Concepts'. http://www.oecd.org/social/income-distribution-database.htm.

OECD (Organisation for Economic Co-operation and Development), and Eurostat. 2015. 'Eurostat–OECD Compilation Guide on Land Estimation'. http://www.oecd-ilibrary.org/docserver/download/3015051e.pdf?expires=1467900895&id=id&accname=guest&checksum=8E7ACC0A181E3B1E69A0A4223225F83E

Office of Fair Trading (OFT). 2008. *Homebuilding in the UK: A Market Study*. London: OFT.

O'Hara, Phillip Anthony. 1999. *Encyclopedia of Political Economy: L–Z*. Hove: Psychology Press.

ONS (Office for National Statistics). 2013a. '170 Years of Industrial Change across England and Wales'. 5 June. http://webarchive.nationalarchives.gov.uk/20160105160709/http://www.ons.gov.uk/ons/rel/census/2011-census-analysis/170-years-of-industry/170-years-of-industrial-changeponent.html

ONS (Office for National Statistics). 2013b. 'A Century of Home Ownership and Renting in England and Wales'. 19 April. http://webarchive.national archives.gov.uk/20160105160709/http://www.ons.gov.uk/ons/rel/census/2011-census-analysis/a-century-of-home-ownership-and-renting-in-england-and-wales/short-story-on-housing.html

ONS (Office for National Statistics). 2015a. 'Housing Summary Measures Analysis'. 5 August. http://www.ons.gov.uk/peoplepopulationandcommunity/housing/articles/housingsummarymeasuresanalysis/2015-08-05

ONS (Office for National Statistics). 2015b. 'Economic Review, October 2015'. http://www.ons.gov.uk/ons/dcp171766_419024.pdf

ONS (Office for National Statistics). 2015c. 'Main Results from the Wealth and Assets Survey: July 2012 to June 2014'. 18 December. http://webarchive.national archives.gov.uk/20160105160709/http://www.ons.gov.uk/ons/rel/was/wealth-in-great-britain-wave-4/2012-2014/rpt---article-main-results.html

ONS (Office for National Statistics). 2015d. 'Property Wealth, Wealth in Great Britain, 2012 to 2014'. 18 December. http://webarchive.nationalarchives.gov.uk/20160105160709/http://www.ons.gov.uk/ons/rel/was/wealth-in-great-britain-wave-4/2012-2014/rpt-chapter-3.html

ONS (Office for National Statistics). 2016. 'Public Sector Finances: May 2016'. http://www.ons.gov.uk/economy/governmentpublicsectorandtaxes/publicsectorfinance/bulletins/publicsectorfinances/may16.

Orbanes, Philip E. 2007. *Monopoly: The World's Most Famous Game – and How It Got That Way*. Philadelphia, PA: Da Capo Press.

Oswald, Andrew J. 1996. 'A Conjecture on the Explanation for High Unemployment in the Industrialized Nations: Part 1'. *The Warwick Economics Research Paper Series (TWERPS)* no. 475, December.

Oswald, Andrew J. [1999] 2009. 'The Housing Market and Europe's Unemployment: A Non-Technical Paper'. In *Homeownership and the Labour Market in Europe*, ed. Casper van Ewijk and Michiel van Leuvensteijn. Oxford: Oxford University Press.

Overton, Mark. 1996. *Agricultural Revolution in England: The Transformation of the Agrarian Economy 1500–1850*. Cambridge: Cambridge University Press.

Oxley, Michael, Tim J. Brown, A. M. Fernandez-Maldonado, L. Qu, and L. Tummers. 2009. *Review of European Planning Systems*. London: National Housing and Planning Advice Unit. https://www.dora.dmu.ac.uk/xmlui/handle/2086/7536.

Oxley, Michael, and Marietta Haffner. 2010. 'Housing Taxation and Subsidies: International Comparisons and the Options for Reform'. York: Joseph Rowntree Foundation Housing Market Taskforce. https://www.jrf.org.uk/sites/default/files/jrf/migrated/files/housing-taxation-systems-full.pdf.

Paine, Thomas. 1797. *Agrarian Justice*. London: R. Folwell.

Palley, Thomas I. 2007. 'Financialization: What It Is and Why It Matters'. *The Levy Economics Institute Working Paper* no. 525, December.

Parkinson, Sharon, Beverley A. Searle, Susan J. Smith, Alice Stoakes, and Gavin Wood. 2009. 'Mortgage Equity Withdrawal in Australia and Britain: Towards a Wealth-Fare State?' *European Journal of Housing Policy* 9 (4): 365–89.

Patten, Simon N. 1891. 'Another View of the Ethics of Land-Tenure'. *International Journal of Ethics* 1 (3): 354–70.

Payne, Geoffrey. 2004. 'Introduction: Habitat International Special Issue on Land Tenure and Property Rights.' *Habitat International* 28: 167–79.

Pearce, Robert D., and Roger Stearn. 2000. *Government and Reform: Britain 1815–1918*. London: Hodder and Stoughton.

Persaud, Avinash. 2016. 'Breaking the Link between Housing Cycles, Banking Crises, and Recession'. *CIYPERC Working Paper Series* 2016/02, 23 March.

Perugini, Cristiano, Jens Hölscher, and Simon Collie. 2015. 'Inequality, Credit and Financial Crises'. *Cambridge Journal of Economics*. doi:10.1093/cje/beu075.

Pierson, Christopher. 2013. *Just Property: A History in the Latin West. Volume One: Wealth, Virtue, and the Law*. Oxford: Oxford University Press.

Piketty, Thomas. 2014. *Capital in the Twenty-First Century*. Cambridge, MA: Harvard University Press.

Piketty, Thomas, and Gabriel Zucman. 2013. 'Capital Is Back: Wealth-Income Ratios in Rich Countries, 1700–2010'. http://www.piketty.pse.ens.fr/files/PikettyZucman2013BookRevQJE.pdf

Pollock, Frederick, and Frederic William Maitland. 1899. *The History of English Law before the Time of Edward I*. Vol. 2. Cambridge: Cambridge University Press.

Porter, Michael E., and Gordon L. Clark. 2000. 'Locations, Clusters, and Company Strategy'. *The Oxford Handbook of Economic Geography*. Oxford: Oxford University Press.

Prieg, Lydia, and Tony Greenham. 2015. *Reforming RBS: Local Banking for the Public Good*. London: New Economics Foundation. http://b.3cdn.net/nefoundation/141039750996d1298f_5km6y1sip.pdf.

Proudhon, Pierre-Joseph. 1840. *What Is Property? An Inquiry in to the Principles and Right of Government*. Cosimo.

Proudhon, Pierre-Joseph. 2005. *No Gods No Masters: An Anthology of Anarchism*, ed. Daniel Guérin and Paul Sharkey. San Francisco: AK Press.

Purves, Andrew. 2015. *No Debt, High Growth, Low Tax: Hong Kong's Economic Miracle Explained*. London: Shepheard-Walwyn.

Quesnay, François. 1972. *Quesnay's Tableau Économique*. London: Macmillan.

Ramsay, Maureen. 1997. *What's Wrong with Liberalism a Radical Critique of Liberal Philosophy*. Leicester: Leicester University Press.

Reed, Howard. 2016. 'A Citizen's Income: A Recipe for Change'. *Compass Thinkpiece*no.4.http://www.compassonline.org.uk/publications/a-citizens-income-a-recipe-for-change.

Reed, Howard, and Jacob Mohun Himmelweit. 2012. *Where Have All the Wages Gone? Lost Pay and Profits Outside Financial Services*, Touchstone Extras. London: Trades Union Congress.

Reid, Margaret. 1982. *Secondary Banking Crisis in the UK*. Macmillan.

Ricardo, David. 1817. *Principles of Political Economy and Taxation*. Batoche Books.

Ricardo, David. 1973. *The Works and Correspondence of David Ricardo: Volume 11, General Index*, ed. Piero Sraffa. Vol. 11. Cambridge: Cambridge University Press.

Riley, Don. 2001. *Taken for a Ride: Trains, Taxpayers and the Treasury*. Teddington: Centre for Land Policy Studies.

Robert-Hughes, R., W. Fox, and A. Scott-Marshall. 2011. *The Case for Space: The Size of England's New Homes*. London: Royal Institute of British Architects.

Robinson, Joan. 1973. 'Marginal Productivity'. In *Collected Economic Papers*. Vol. 4. Oxford: Basil Blackwell.

Rognlie, Matthew. 2014. 'A Note on Piketty and Diminishing Returns to Capital'. http://www.mit.edu/~mrognlie/piketty_diminishing_returns.pdf.

Rosen, Sherwin. 1981. 'The Economics of Superstars'. *The American Economic Review* 71 (5): 845–58.

Rousseau, Jean-Jacques. 1775. *Discourse on the Origin of Inequality*. Indianapolis, IN: Hackett Publishing.

Rowlands, Rob. 2009. *Forging Mutual Futures – Co-operative, Mutual and Community Based Housing in Practice: History & Potential. Phase 1 Research Report to the Committee on Co-operative and Mutual Housing.* Birmingham: Centre for Urban and Regional Studies, University of Birmingham.

Rowlingson, Karen. 2011. *Does Income Inequality Cause Health and Social Problems?* York: The Joseph Rowntree Foundation. https://www.jrf.org.uk/report/does-income-inequality-cause-health-and-social-problems

RTPI (Royal Town and Planning Institute). 2015. 'Planning as "Market Maker"'. *RTPI Research Report* no. 11, November. http://www.rtpi.org.uk/knowledge/research/projects/small-project-impact-research-spire-scheme/planning-as-market-maker/

Ryan-Collins, Josh. 2016. 'Why You Can't Afford a Home in the UK'. *Medium.* 16 February. https://medium.com/@neweconomics/why-you-can-t-afford-a-home-in-the-uk-44347750646a#.3xvhkhoi4.

Ryan-Collins, Josh, Tony Greenham, R. A. Werner, and Giovanni Bernardo. 2013. *Strategic Quantitative Easing.* London: New Economics Foundation. http://www.neweconomics.org/publications/entry/strategic-quantitative-easing .

Ryan-Collins, Josh, Tony Greenham, Richard Werner, and Andrew Jackson. 2012. *Where Does Money Come From? A Guide to the UK Monetary and Banking System.* 2nd ed. London: The New Economics Foundation.

Ryan-Collins, Josh, Richard A. Werner, and Jennifer Castle. 2016. 'A Half-Century Diversion of Monetary Policy? An Empirical Horse-Race to Identify the UK Variable Most Likely to Deliver the Desired Nominal GDP Growth Rate'. *Journal of International Financial Markets, Institutions and Money* 43 (July): 158–76. http://dx.doi.org/10.1016/j.intfin.2016.03.009

Ryoo, Soon. 2015. 'Household Debt and Housing Bubble: A Minskian Approach to Boom–Bust Cycles'. *Economics Department Working Paper Series* 2015-08. http://scholarworks.umass.edu/cgi/viewcontent.cgi?article=1188&context=econ_workingpaper

Safire, William. 2009. 'Location, Location, Location'. *The New York Times,* 26 June. http://www.nytimes.com/2009/06/28/magazine/28FOB-onlanguage-t.html.

Samy, Luke. 2015. 'Indices of House Prices and Rent Prices of Residential Property in London, 1895–1939'. *University of Oxford Discussion Papers in Economic and Social History* no. 134, April. http://www.economics.ox.ac.uk/materials/papers/13922/number-134.pdf.

Saunders, Peter. 2011. *Beware False Prophets.* Centre for Independent Studies.

Saunders, Peter. 2016. *Restoring a Nation of Home Owners.* London: Civitas. http://www.civitas.org.uk/content/files/Restoring-a-Nation-of-Home-Owners.pdf

Scanlon, Kathleen, and Ben Kochan, eds. 2011. *Towards a Sustainable Private Rented Sector: The Lessons from Other Countries.* London: The London School of Economics and Political Science. http://www2.lse.ac.uk/geographyAndEnvironment/research/london/Home.aspx.

Scanlon, Kathleen, and Christine Whitehead. 2011. 'The UK Mortgage Market: Responding to Volatility'. *Journal of Housing and the Built Environment* 26 (3): 277–93.

Schularick, M., and A. M. Taylor. 2009. 'Credit Booms Gone Bust: Monetary Policy, Leverage Cycles and Financial Crises, 1870–2008'. *NBER Working Paper Series* no. 15512, November.

Schumpeter, Joseph A. 1954. *History of Economic Analysis.* Oxford: Oxford University Press.

Schumpeter, Joseph A. 1975. *Capitalism, Socialism, and Democracy*. Harper.

Schwartz, Herman, and Leonard Seabrooke. 2008. 'Varieties of Residential Capitalism in the International Political Economy: Old Welfare States and the New Politics of Housing'. *Comparative European Politics* 6 (3): 237–61.

Shaheen, Faiza, Eilis Lawlor, Stephen Spratt, and Daiana Beitler. 2011. *Why the Rich Are Getting Richer: The Determinants of Economic Inequality*. London: New Economics Foundation. https://b.3cdn.net/nefoundation/9f13eb419294bb7cfe_abm6bc76e.pdf.

Sheffield, Hazel. 2016. 'London Property Snapped up by Overseas Investors as Domestic Buyers Pull out after Brexit, 28th June 2016'. *The Independent*, 28 June. Business news. http://www.independent.co.uk/news/business/news/london-property-house-prices-brexit-overseas-buyers-first-time-eu-referendum-housing-market-a7108026.html.

Shleifer, Andrei, and Robert Vishny. 2011. 'Fire Sales in Finance and Macroeconomics'. *The Journal of Economic Perspectives* 25 (1): 29–48.

Sillitoe, Paul. 1999. 'Beating the Boundaries: Land Tenure and Identity in the Papua New Guinea Highlands'. *Journal of Anthropological Research* 55 (3): 331–60.

Simons, Henry Calvert. 1951. *Economic Policy for a Free Society*. Chicago: University of Chicago Press.

Simpson, M., Hardy, D., Ward, S. 1992. *British Planning History 1900–1952*. British Planning History Group.

Skidelsky, Robert, Felix Martin, and Christian Westerlind Wigstrom. 2011. *Blueprint for a British Investment Bank*. London: Centre for Global Studies.

Slack, Enid, and Richard M. Bird. 2014. 'The Political Economy of Property Tax Reform'. *OECD Working Papers on Fiscal Federalism* no. 18, 9 April.

Sloman, J., and A. Wride. 2009. *Economics*. 7th ed. Harlow: Prentice Hall.

Smith, Adam. 1776. *An Inquiry into the Nature and Causes of the Wealth of Nations*. W. Strahan and T. Cadell.

Snowdon, Christopher. 2010. *The Spirit Level Delusion: Fact-Checking the Left's New Theory of Everything*. Ripon: Little Dice.

Solow, Robert M. 1956. 'A Contribution to the Theory of Economic Growth'. *The Quarterly Journal of Economics* 70 (1): 65–94.

Stephens, Mark. 1993. 'Housing Finance Deregulation: Britain's Experience'. *Journal of Housing and the Built Environment* 8 (2): 159–75.

Stephens, Mark. 2007. 'Mortgage Market Deregulation and Its Consequences'. *Housing Studies* 22 (2): 201–20.

Stephens, Mark, C. Whitehead, and M. Munro. 2005. *Lessons from the Past, Challenges for the Future for Housing Policy*. London: Department of Communities and Local Government.

Stiglitz, Joseph E. 2012. *The Price of Inequality*. London: Penguin.

Stiglitz, Joseph E., and Linda J. Bilmes. 2012. 'The 1 Percent's Problem'. *Vanity Fair*, 31 May. http://www.vanityfair.com/news/2012/05/joseph-stiglitz-the-price-on-inequality

Stiglitz, Joseph E. 2015a. 'New Theoretical Perspectives on the Distribution of Income and Wealth among Individuals: Part IV: Land and Credit'. *NBER Working Paper Series* no. 21192, May.

Stiglitz, Joseph E. 2015b. 'The Origins of Inequality and Policies to Contain It'. *National Tax Journal* 68 (2): 425–48.

Stiglitz, Joseph E. 2015c. 'The Measurement of Wealth: Recessions, Sustainability and Inequality'. *NBER Working Paper Series* no. 21327, July.

Stiglitz, Joseph E. and Alan Weiss. 1981. 'Credit Rationing in Markets with Imperfect Information'. *The American Economic Review* 71 (3): 393–410.

Stockhammer, Engelbert. 2004. 'Financialisation and the Slowdown of Accumulation'. *Cambridge Journal of Economics* 28 (5): 719–41.

Stockhammer, Engelbert, and Rafael Wildauer. 2016. 'Demand Effects of Financialisation and Changes in Functional Income Distribution in the EU'. *FEPS Policy Report*, April.

Summers, Lawrence H. 2015. 'Demand Side Secular Stagnation'. *The American Economic Review* 105 (5): 60–65.

The Economist. 2007. 'Back from the Grave'. *The Economist*, 11 October.

This is Money. 2015. 'Buy-to-Let Landlords Face Cuts in Mortgage Interest Tax Relief'. *This Is Money*. 8 July. http://www.thisismoney.co.uk/money/buytolet/article-3153541/Profits-slashed-wealthy-buy-let-landlords-Budget-crackdown-mortgage-tax-relief.html.

TCPA (Town and Country Planning Association). 2014. New Towns and Garden Cities – Lessons for Tomorrow. Stage 1: An Introduction to the UK's New Towns and Garden Cities. Town and Country Planning Association.

Thrift, Nigel. 1996. *Spatial Formations*. Vol. 42. London: Sage.

Tobin, James. 1967. 'Life Cycle Saving and Balanced Growth'. In *Ten Economic Studies in the Tradition of Irving Fisher*, 231–56. New York: Wiley.

Tobin, James. 1985. 'Neoclassical Theory in America: JB Clark and Fisher'. *The American Economic Review* 75 (6): 28–38.

Tobin, James. 1986. *Financial Innovation and Deregulation in Perspective*. New Haven, CT: Cowles Foundation for Research in Economics.

Torrance, David. 2010. *Noel Skelton and the Property-Owning Democracy*. London: Biteback.

Turnbull, Shann. 2007. 'Affordable Housing Policy: Not Identifiable with Orthodox Economic Analysis'. SSRN 1027864.

Turner, Adair. 2015a. *Between Debt and the Devil: Money, Credit, and Fixing Global Finance*. Princeton, NJ: Princeton University Press.

Turner, Adair. 2015b. 'The Debt Dilemma'. *Project Syndicate*, 17 April. https://www.project-syndicate.org/commentary/global-debt-dilemma-by-adair-turner-and-susan-lund-2015-04?barrier=true.

Turner, Clive. 2015. *Homes Through the Decades: The Making of Modern Housing*. Milton Keynes: NHBC Foundation.

University of Reading and Three Dragons in association with Hives Planning, David Lock Associates and DLA Piper LLP. 2014. *Section 106 Planning Obligations in England, 2011–12: Report of Study*. London: Department for Communities and Local Government. https://www.gov.uk/government/uploads/system/uploads/attachment_data/file/314066/Section_106_Planning_Obligations_in_England_2011-12_-_Report_of_study.pdf.

Uthwatt, A. 1942. Expert Committee on Compensation and Betterment: Final Report, Cmnd. 6386. London: HMSO.

Van Parijs, Philippe. 1992. *Arguing for Basic Income. Ethical Foundations for a Radical Reform*. London: Verso.

Veblen, Thorstein. 1899. *The Theory of the Leisure Class: An Economic Study in the Evolution of Institutions*. Macmillan.

Ward, Colin. 2002. *Cotters and Squatters: Housing's Hidden History*. Nottingham: Five Leaves Publications.

Ward, Colin. 2004. 'The Hidden History of Housing'. *History and Policy*, 1 September.

Ward, Victoria. 2014. 'Vast Basements Outlawed for Wealthy Property Owners'. *The Telegraph*, 12 March. http://www.telegraph.co.uk/finance/newsbysector/constructionandproperty/11269740/Vast-basements-outlawed-for-wealthy-property-owners.html.

Watson, Matthew. 2009. 'Planning for a Future of Asset-Based Welfare? New Labour, Financialized Economic Agency and the Housing Market'. *Planning, Practice and Research* 24 (1): 41–56.

Webb, K. 2012. *Bricks or Benefits? Rebalancing Housing Investment*. London: Shelter. http://england.shelter.org.uk/professional_resources/policy_and_research/policy_library/policy_library_folder/bricks_or_benefits_rebalancing_housing_investment.

Werner, Richard. A. 1997. 'Towards a New Monetary Paradigm: A Quantity Theorem of Disaggregated Credit, with Evidence from Japan'. *Kredit und Kapital* 30 (2): 276–309.

Werner, Richard A. 2002. 'Monetary Policy Implementation in Japan: What They Say versus What They Do'. *Asian Economic Journal* 16 (2): 111–51. doi:10.1111/1467-8381.00145.

Werner, Richard. A. 2003. *Princes of the Yen: Japan's Central Bankers and the Transformation of the Economy*. Armonk, NY: M. E. Sharpe.

Werner, Richard. A. 2005. *New Paradigm in Macroeconomics: Solving the Riddle of Japanese Macroeconomic Performance*. Basingstoke: Palgrave Macmillan.

West, Edwin G. 2002. 'Property Rights in the History of Economic Thought: From Locke to J. S. Mill'. *Carleton Economic Papers* 01-01. http://econpapers.repec.org/paper/carcarecp/01-01.htm

Westwood, Andy. 2006. *Are We Being Served? Career Mobility and Skills in the UK Workforce*. London: The Work Foundation.

Wicksteed, Philip H. 1914. 'The Scope and Method of Political Economy in the Light of the "Marginal" Theory of Value and of Distribution'. *The Economic Journal* 24 (93): 1–23.

Wilcox, S. 2006. *The Geography of Affordable and Unaffordable Housing: And the Ability of Younger Working Households to Become Home Owners*. York: Joseph Rowntree Foundation.

Wilkinson, Richard, and Kate Pickett. 2010. *The Spirit Level: Why Equality Is Better for Everyone*. London: Penguin.

Wilson, W., and L. Blow, L. 2013. *Extending Home Ownership – Government Initiatives*. London: House of Commons Library.

Wise, Sarah. 2013. *The Blackest Streets: The Life and Death of a Victorian Slum*. London: Random House.

Woetzel, Jonathan, Sangeeth Ram, Jan Mischke, Nicklas Garemo, and Shirish Sankhe. 2014. *A Blueprint for Addressing the Global Affordable Housing Challenge*. McKinsey Global Institute.

Wolf, Martin. 2008. 'US Housing Solution Is Not a Good One to Follow'. *Financial Times*, 9 September.

World Bank. 1993. *The East Asian Miracle, Economic Growth and Public Policy*. Oxford: Oxford University Press.

INDEX

· · · · · · · · · · · · · · · ·

Note: Page numbers followed by
n indicate a footnote with relevant
number; page numbers in italic refer to
figures and those in bold to tables.